"Finally: Harry Heft is getting the recognition he deserves. His careful work has quietly inspired generations of researchers interested in the history and philosophy of psychology, especially pragmatism and the ecological approach. Many of us, myself included, found reading Heft's 2001 masterpiece *Ecological Psychology in Context* to be a transformative experience. That work made the ideas of James Gibson and Roger Barker seem less strange and foreign by providing historical precedent in the late work of William James. This book collects brand new essays by some of those who were inspired by Heft's philosophical and historical analyses, along with a delightful interview with Heft and his response to the collected essays. The interview alone is worth the price of admission and the rest of the collection is a crucial record of the mark Heft has left. Highly recommended."

Prof. Anthony Chemero, *University of Cincinnati, USA*

PLACES, SOCIALITY, AND ECOLOGICAL PSYCHOLOGY

This book presents a collection of essays honoring Professor Harry Heft, a leading figure in the field of ecological psychology, engaging critically with his work, thought, and influence.

Containing 12 chapters written by leading experts from philosophy and psychology, this text critically examines, questions, and expands on crucial ideas from Heft concerning the nature of cognition, its relationship to the body and the environment (including the social and cultural environment), and the main philosophical assumptions underlying the scientific study of psychological functions. It elaborates on the notion of affordance, and its connection to social, cultural, and developmental psychology, as well as on the application of Roger Barker's eco-behavioral program for current psychology and cognitive science. This book includes an extensive interview with Heft, where he reflects about the history, challenges, and future of ecological psychology. Finally, it presents a chapter written by Heft, which offers a systematic response to the critical feedback.

Given the increasing popularity of ecological psychology and the highly influential work of Harry Heft in related areas such as developmental, social, and cultural psychology, and philosophy, this book will appeal to all those interested in the cognitive sciences from a scientific and philosophical perspective. It is also a must read for students of psychology, philosophy, and cognitive science departments.

Miguel Segundo-Ortin is Ramón y Cajal Research Fellow at University of Murcia, Spain. His research interests include philosophy of mind and cognitive science, philosophy of action, comparative cognition, embodied cognition, and ecological psychology.

Manuel Heras-Escribano is Juan de la Cierva-Incorporación Postdoctoral Research Fellow at the University of Granada, Spain. His research interests include philosophy of cognitive science, philosophy of biology, philosophy of mind, and affordances.

Vicente Raja is a Research Fellow at the University of Murcia, Spain, and External Faculty Member of the Rotman Institute of Philosophy at Western University, Canada. His interests include the analysis of behavior and brain activity, along with their relationship, using the different tools provided by dynamic systems theory and complexity science.

Resources for Ecological Psychology

A Series of Volumes Edited By Jeffrey B. Wagman & Julia J. C. Blau

[Robert E. Shaw, William M. Mace, and Michael Turvey, Series Editors Emeriti]

Perception as Information Detection
Reflections on Gibson's Ecological Approach to Visual Perception
Jeffrey B. Wagman and Julia J. C. Blau

A Meaning Processing Approach to Cognition
What Matters?
John Flach and Fred Voorhorst

Behavior and Culture in One Dimension
Sequences, Affordances, and the Evolution of Complexity
Dennis P. Waters

Affective Gibsonian Psychology
Rob Withagen

Introduction to Ecological Psychology
A Lawful Approach to Perceiving, Acting, and Cognizing
Julia J. C. Blau and Jeffrey B. Wagman

Intellectual Journeys in Ecological Psychology
Interviews and Reflections from Pioneers in the Field
Edited by Agnes Szokolszky, Catherine Read and Zsolt Palatinus

Places, Sociality, and Ecological Psychology
Essays in Honor of Harry Heft
Edited by Miguel Segundo-Ortin, Manuel Heras-Escribano and Vicente Raja

PLACES, SOCIALITY, AND ECOLOGICAL PSYCHOLOGY

Essays in Honor of Harry Heft

Edited by Miguel Segundo-Ortin,
Manuel Heras-Escribano, and Vicente Raja

Routledge
Taylor & Francis Group

NEW YORK AND LONDON

Cover image: Getty

First published 2023
by Routledge
605 Third Avenue, New York, NY 10158

and by Routledge
4 Park Square, Milton Park, Abingdon, Oxon, OX14 4RN

Routledge is an imprint of the Taylor & Francis Group, an informa business

© 2023 selection and editorial matter, Miguel Segundo-Ortin, Manuel Heras-Escribano and Vicente Raja; individual chapters, the contributors

The right of Miguel Segundo-Ortin, Manuel Heras-Escribano and Vicente Raja to be identified as the authors of the editorial material, and of the authors for their individual chapters, has been asserted in accordance with sections 77 and 78 of the Copyright, Designs and Patents Act 1988.

All rights reserved. No part of this book may be reprinted or reproduced or utilised in any form or by any electronic, mechanical, or other means, now known or hereafter invented, including photocopying and recording, or in any information storage or retrieval system, without permission in writing from the publishers.

Trademark notice: Product or corporate names may be trademarks or registered trademarks, and are used only for identification and explanation without intent to infringe.

ISBN: 978-1-032-19452-3 (hbk)
ISBN: 978-1-032-19451-6 (pbk)
ISBN: 978-1-003-25924-4 (ebk)

DOI: 10.4324/9781003259244

Typeset in Bembo
by MPS Limited, Dehradun

CONTENTS

Acknowledgments ix
Contributors x

Introduction 1
Vicente Raja, Miguel Segundo-Ortin, and Manuel Heras-Escribano

1 Reflections on ecological psychology: An interview with Harry Heft 10
Erik Rietveld and Julian Kiverstein

2 The social constitution of ecological psychology in the Netherlands 23
Rob Withagen and Ludger van Dijk

3 Contrary imaginations: Radical empiricism or pragmatism? 37
Alan Costall

4 Perception and problem solving 45
Edward Baggs and Sune Vork Steffensen

5 Conceiving the environment from a developmental perspective: Revisiting Roger G. Barker's comparison of Bobby Bryant and Raymond Birch 59
Jytte Bang and Sofie Pedersen

6 Agency in behavior settings: A mindshaping perspective on
   ecological psychology   72
   Miguel Segundo-Ortin and Annemarie Kalis

7 Behavior settings, enabling constraints, and the
   naturalization of social norms   86
   Vicente Raja and Manuel Heras-Escribano

8 Values, affordances, and agency: Giving heft to ecological
   accounts   99
   Bert H. Hodges

9 Young people's responses to the Earth's affordances of
   regeneration   112
   Louise Chawla

10 Humanizing ecological psychology: Heft's incorporation of
   the sociohistorical into perceiving and acting   125
   Kerry L. Marsh and Benjamin R. Meagher

11 Understanding the child's environment   138
   Justine Hoch

12 Toward a psychological ecology   149
   Harry Heft

Index   *179*

ACKNOWLEDGMENTS

We would like to thank the contributors for accepting the invitation to be part of the volume. We are also thankful to Jeffrey Wagman and Julia Blau for accepting our proposal to write this volume in honor of Harry, and to our editors at Routledge, who patiently helped us in this process. Also, we want to thank our partners Ana, Lorena, and Robyn for their love and support. And last, but of course not least, we want to show our gratitude to Harry Heft, whose work, guidance, and personality are an inspiration, both personally and professionally. We hope he will keep inspiring the younger generations of researchers interested in ecological psychology and philosophy. May this volume be a token of admiration and gratitude.

Funding

Manuel Heras-Escribano and Vicente Raja want to express their gratitude to the Juan de la Cierva Incorporación Research Program of the Spanish Ministry of Science.

Miguel Segundo-Ortin's contribution was funded by the Nederlandse Organisatie voor Wetenschappelijk Onderzoek VIDI Research Project "Shaping our action space: A situated perspective on self-control" (VI.VIDI.195.116).

Manuel Heras-Escribano's work was funded by the project PID2019-109764-I00 of the Spanish Ministry of Science. Vicente Raja's work was funded by the project PID2021-127294NA-I00 of the Spanish Ministry of Science.

CONTRIBUTORS

Edward Baggs is an Assistant Professor at the University of Southern Denmark (Denmark).

Jytte Bang is an Associate Professor at Roskilde University (Denmark).

Louise Chawla is a Professor Emerita at the University of Colorado Boulder (United States).

Alan Costall is a Professor of Psychology at the University of Portsmouth (United Kingdom).

Harry Heft is a Professor Emeritus at Denison University (United States).

Manuel Heras-Escribano is Juan de la Cierva-Incorporación Postdoctoral Research Fellow at the University of Granada (Spain).

Justine Hoch is an Assistant Professor at Vanderbilt Peabody College (United States).

Bert H. Hodges is a Professor Emeritus at Gordon College and a Senior Research Scientist at the University of Connecticut (United States).

Annemarie Kalis is an Associate Professor at Utrecht University (The Netherlands).

Julian Kiverstein is a Senior Researcher at the University of Amsterdam (The Netherlands).

Kerry L. Marsh is a Professor of Psychological Sciences at the University of Connecticut (United States).

Benjamin R. Meagher is an Assistant Professor at Hope College (United States).

Sofie Pedersen is an Associate Professor at Roskilde University (Denmark).

Vicente Raja is a Research Fellow at the University of Murcia (Spain) and External Faculty Member of the Rotman Institute of Philosophy at Western University (Canada).

Erik Rietveld is Socrates Professor, Senior Researcher at the University of Amsterdam (The Netherlands).

Miguel Segundo-Ortin is Ramón y Cajal Postdoctoral Research Fellow at University of Murcia (Spain).

Sune Vork Steffensen is a Professor at the University of Southern Denmark (Denmark).

Ludger Van Dijk is a Postdoctoral Researcher at the Eindhoven University of Technology (The Netherlands) and at the University of Antwerp (Belgium).

Rob Withagen is an Assistant Professor at the University of Groningen (The Netherlands).

INTRODUCTION

Vicente Raja, Miguel Segundo-Ortin, and Manuel Heras-Escribano

Harry Heft is one of the key figures of ecological psychology from its very early days. When taken historically, the ecological approach may be already identified by the late 1960s, as its general form was shaped by the works of James and Eleanor Gibson since the 1950s. However, it is not until the number of their students and postdoctoral mentees grew enough during the late 1970s and early 1980s that we can really talk about something like a psychological school in a broad sense. And maybe, even then the idea of "school" can be a little bit misleading. It is not like there was an institution pushing for establishing an ecological psychology. It was not even the case that all students and postdoctoral mentees of James and Eleanor Gibson agreed about all and every aspect of the theoretical and methodological postulates of the ecological approach to psychology. The "school" was more like a few dozens of researchers who were inspired by the key works and ideas of the two founders of the approach (Gibson, 1950a, 1950b, 1966, 1969, 1979, 2000; Gibson & Gibson, 1955; Gibson & Pick, 2000) and who were willing to pursue and expand an ecological psychology. In the following chapters, we will learn more about the way Harry Heft became part of the ecological school and contributed to shape it as we know it now.

Harry Heft was a student of Jack Wohlwill, a developmental psychologist. Then, he moved to Cornell as a postdoctoral researcher to work with the Gibsons. There are a number of quite interesting anecdotes of Harry's time at Cornell, like him becoming the driver of James Gibson. However, there is one small regret he makes clear in the interview that follows this Introduction:

> I was just learning about ecological psychology at the time, and I got to ask him [James Gibson] basic questions. Thinking back, I wish I had a deeper understanding at the time so that I could have asked more incisive questions.

Although we understand that Harry Heft wanted to ask James Gibson more incisive questions, we think he should have no regrets. Why? Because Harry has been asking those questions, maybe not to Gibson himself, but to all of us during the last four decades.

Following his first mentor, Harry Heft defines himself as a developmental psychologist, but we would add that he is a developmental psychologist that has always had an eye for the ecology, both natural and social, surrounding the developing psychological system. He also had an eye for philosophical and theoretical issues that allowed him to analyze key conceptual themes with surgical precision, something that allowed him to be extremely well regarded among ecologically oriented and embodied-situated philosophers. The questions he never got to ask James Gibson about but he has asked ever since are better understood within these coordinates. As an ecological psychologist, Harry Heft has always been interested both in the ecological theory itself and in its historical roots. In fact, at least a couple of generations of psychologists and philosophers have been educated on the Jamesian and Holtian roots of ecological psychology with his monumental *Ecological Psychology in Context* (2001). He has complemented this work with other publications on the scope and reach of E. B. Holt's and William James' psychologies (Heft, 2012, 2017b). Heft has also thoroughly explored different relationships and tensions between ecological psychology and other paradigms or approaches within the sciences of the mind, such as constructivist theories, cognitive psychology, environmental psychology, phenomenology, or enactivism (Glotzbach & Heft, 1982; Heft, 1990, 1981, 1989, 1998, 2014a, 2020a). And, of course, he has provided analyses of key concepts of ecological psychology, such as the notion of affordance or the occluding edge, as well as general analyses of the ecological framework (Heft, 2013a, 2014a, 2014b, 2019).

More generally, Harry Heft has provided ecological psychology with a wide corpus of works on the socio-cultural aspects of psychological life. In his own words, he has studied the social constitution of the perceiver-environment reciprocity (Heft, 2007). And he has done so by thoroughly analyzing the social components of affordances (Heft, 1990, 2003) and the broader relationship of ecological psychology and socio-cultural psychology (Heft, 2017a, 2020b). But if one concept of the socio-cultural environment is associated with the works of Harry Heft within the Gibsonian tradition, it is the concept of behavior setting. The notion of behavior setting was first proposed by psychologist Roger Baker to account for emergent situations in which the activities of people in a particular place give rise to some particular dynamics – e.g., a soccer game, a company meeting, or a university lecture are behavior settings. They already feature in Heft's *Ecological Psychology in Context* (2001), where the works of Baker are studied along with the works of the Gibsons as two different flavors or ecological psychologies. But Harry Heft has expanded his work on Baker's psychology and behavior settings in other places (Heft et al., 2014). And, most importantly, he has expanded the notion of behavior settings to the notion of place in one of the most important advances of ecological psychology toward integrating the socio-cultural environment in its framework (Heft, 2018).

Other aspects of the environment of psychological systems Harry Heft has devoted particular attention are ways and paths. Ways and paths are very interesting features of the environment because they exist out there while, in a very deep way, they only exist for the organism that walks them. Different environmental layouts may or may not be a path depending on whether the organism is a human being or a goat, for instance. Moreover, paths are always part of the social environment. Sometimes they are just found, while other times they are built up by walking or just explicitly constructed by an organism or a community. No matter what, they are always a place for crossing and encountering others. In addition to this, paths prominently feature in navigation studies that, since the discovery of place cells in the 1970s, constitute one of the spearheads of psychology and neuroscience. Harry Heft has worked on all these different facets of ways and paths, from route learning (Heft, 1979) to cognitive maps (Heft, 2013c), including a Gibsonian perspective on navigation (Heft, 1996), and different studies on wayfinding (Heft, 1983, 2013b).

Finally, all these different lines of research converge in developmental psychology while also reflecting it. Heft has studied the environment of children in many different ways throughout the last few decades. For instance, he has studied the affordances present in children's environments (Heft, 1988) and, with Louis Chawla, he has studied the ways children participate and are competent in different communities and ecologies (Chawla & Heft, 2002; Heft & Chawla, 2006). In all these cases, it is easy to see the way other interests and concerns – e.g., ecological psychology or the socio-cultural environment – permeate Heft's works on development. As we mentioned before, when reading his work we must have in mind that Harry Heft is not only a developmental psychologist, but he is a psychologist with an unique, ecological and social perspective on development. And the chapters of this book aim to reflect, to discuss, and to enrich such a unique perspective.

The first chapter of this volume is an interview with Harry Heft, conducted by Erik Rietveld and Julian Kiverstein. The interview begins with a series of personal notes that, as already suggested, help us know how Harry met James and Eleanor Gibson and became an ecological psychologist. We can also learn what ideas of James and Eleanor were most influential in the development of his thought. After this, the interview offers a nice panoramic view of Harry's own interests in psychology and what he takes to be his main contributions to the field. One important topic in the interview is the possible scope and limitations of ecological psychology, and the prospects of building a general ecological theory of cognition, following the suggestions once made by Reed (1996). Harry Heft urges caution on this score, and although recognizes the potential impact ecological psychology may have for how we conceptualize cognition, he calls attention to some crucial challenges that ecological theorists need to address. The interview also focuses on the importance that sociality and culture have in conforming human psychology. According to Harry, socio-cultural aspects of the mind have remained somewhat underappreciated within the ecological tradition, with few exceptions, until now.

One crucial reflection Harry leaves us is that, paradoxically, Gibsonian psychologists might have not paid enough attention to the environment.

In chapter 2, Rob Withagen and Ludger Van Dijk offer a historical reconstruction of the impact and influence of Heft's ideas in the Netherlands. With delicacy and rigurosity, they show how Heft's work, and most prominently his emphasis on the sociocultural dimension of cognition and his way of understanding the methodology of the psychological sciences, has permeated the current generation of philosophers of embodied cognition and ecologically oriented cognitive scientists. In a more personal view, the authors also show how, beyond a mere interest in particular issues, topics, or fields of study, Heft's ideas played a significant role in the decisions they made in their academic careers and their intellectual lives as thinkers and experimentalists. As such, this contribution offers a genuine entrance for anyone who aims to discover how the thought of Heft helped shape the intellectual life of more than one generation of psychologists and philosophers in a single country.

A similar historical vein, although with a completely different angle, may be found in Alan Costall's contribution to this volume. In chapter 3, Costall focuses on one key idea regarding the history of ecological psychology and first advanced by Harry Heft: that Gibson's ecological approach is largely based on James' radical empiricism. Costall disagrees with Heft in this point and argues that Gibson's work was more influenced by James' pragmatism than by its radical empiricism. To support his claim, he provides some evidence that helps understand the influences that helped Gibson form and shape his own ideas on affordances and ecological psychology in a detailed way.

The rest of the chapters do not completely abandon history. All of them are sensitive to important historical aspects of Harry Heft's thought, but they focus on some other favorite topics of him. In chapter 4, Edward Baggs and Sune Vork Steffensen analyze Heft's *Ecological Psychology in Context* (2001). As they rightly note, the book covers two main projects. One is fundamentally historical: placing Gibson's ecological psychology in the context of American pragmatism. The second one is programmatic: expanding Gibsonian psychology and exploring potential connections with Barker's eco-behavioral science (Barker, 1975, 1978) and Hutchins' distributed cognition (Hutchins, 1995). Baggs and Steffensen target this second project and, more particularly, the connection between ecological psychology and distributed cognition. Their main claim is that an analysis of the perceptual basis of problem-solving offers us a productive way to combine these approaches, showing that a Gibsonian theory of perception can deal with cognitive problems involving the use of symbols.

After this, we get three chapters that explore the notion of behavior setting in one way or another. Chapter 5 by Jytte Bang and Sofie Pedersen is inspired by Heft's "Affordances of children's environments: A functional approach to environmental description" (1998). In this paper, Heft offers a functional analysis of the affordances that a seven-year-old boy, Raymond Birch, encounters in his daily life. He does so using the records published by Barker and Wright (1951). Motivated by Barker's concerns regarding the possibility that the psychological world of children living with physical disabilities could differ from those of "typical" children, Bang and Pedersen propose a comparison between Raymond's life and the life of Bobby Bryant, a child living with a congenital heart disease that caused him fatigue and lower levels of physical activity. Their conclusion is that an analysis of the psychological world of people should include a functional dimension in terms of affordances, a social dimension in terms of behavior settings, and a historical-developmental dimension inspired by Vygotsky. Crucially, they argue that only the last one will allow us to gain insight into child-environment variability, recognizing the difficulties that environments designed for "typical" children impose on the psychological development of children with disabilities.

In chapter 6, Miguel Segundo-Ortin and Annemarie Kalis elaborate on a critical idea explored by Harry Heft in multiple papers: that a theory based on behavior settings can be used to understand agency in a situated manner. To flesh out this proposal, Segundo-Ortin and Kalis propose an outline for a situated theory of agency that combines Gibson's ecological psychology, Barker's eco-behavioral science, and McGeer's mindshaping approach (McGeer, 2015, 2021). They divert from Heft's original characterization of agency as the selective control of affordances and propose that human agency involves other abilities (e.g., planning, reflection, and so on) that together enable individuals to perceive and act in goal-directed ways. Following this view, they argue that what makes human agency situated is the fact that these abilities are shaped by the socio-normative practices (including the folk-psychological regulative practices) that are constitutive of behavior settings.

The last paper of the behavior settings tryad is chapter 7 by Vicente Raja and Manuel Heras-Escribano. According to them, Harry Heft proposed Roger Baker's notion of behavior setting as worth exploring and including within the theoretical framework of ecological psychology. Concretely, behavior settings are especially relevant for developing social psychology from the ecological standpoint. The authors are generally sympathetic with Heft's proposal but they claim that it remains unclear how to characterize the role that behavior settings play in the concrete control of action: are behavior settings perceived? If so, how? Is there ecological information specifying them? Should behavior settings be regarded as landscapes of affordances? By combining the notions of ecological and enabling constraints (Raja & Anderson, 2021), Raja and Heras-Escribano offer an initial step to address these and similar questions, and update the notion of behavior settings for current discussions in ecological psychology and adjacent fields. The authors claim that this proposal offers great promise both for operationalizing behavior settings within the ecological approach, and for contributing to the old philosophical problem of how to naturalize normativity.

After the focus on behavior settings, this volume hosts another four chapters each of them addressing important aspects of Harry Heft's works. According to Bert H. Hodges in chapter 8, Harry Heft asked the question "Do you think a person can directly perceive righteousness?" to several ecological psychologists, often receiving an answer in the form of silence. For Hodges, this question is an invitation to think about the role that values could play in an ecological theory of perception. Using classical examples involving the affordances of artifacts (e.g., a postbox), Hodges proposes that values cannot be localized in single objects. Instead, he argues that values are boundary conditions that define what is appropriate to do in a particular ecosystem, providing the necessary criteria by which acts (including psychological acts) can be judged. Thus, values constrain affordances, and agents contribute to realizing values by engaging with these affordances. This idea is coined as the "ecological values-realizing theory" (Hodges, 2007; Hodges & Rączaszek-Leonardi, 2022). In the final part of the chapter, the "ecological values-realizing theory" is used to explore cultural differences and disagreements in an ecological way.

On a different note, Louise Chawla's contribution in chapter 9 expands the idea of affordance to explore the notion of "slow-motion affordances" when people farm, garden, or restore abandoned or degraded land. By reviewing different research studies with young people who participate in ecological restoration projects in their communities, Chawla takes the concept of affordance in a new direction and examines evidence concerning the possibility that nature's dynamics of growth and regeneration afford hope in the natural world's potential to recover from environmental threats such as climate change and biodiversity loss. In this sense, Chawla's approach to slow-motion affordances in the restoration of different areas and habitats allows us to understand the mutuality of affordances in spans of time that are not the traditional ones, pointing to a new research line in which the multidimensionality of experience is understood as rooted in perception and action, reaching to ethical and political implications. Without a doubt, this analysis of the political dimension of experience opens a new way of understanding ecological psychology.

Also related to intervening and taking care of the environment, in chapter 10, Kerry L. Marsh and Benjamin R. Meagher highlight the way Harry Heft humanizes ecological psychology by exploring its social and developmental facets. According to them, this is Heft's main contribution to science: Harry Heft brings a socio-historical perspective to ecological psychology's understanding of affordances and environments that allows him to embed these notions within the notion of culture. More concretely, this chapter examines Heft's use of affordances within a wider environmental description in order to offer critical perspectives within environmentalism, such as restorative environments. A key concept in this project is Heft's theoretical elaboration of places as socially constituted parts of the environment. Throughout this chapter, Marsh and Meagher discuss research they have done in the area of social affordances, affordances of indoor spaces, and restorative environments, much of this inspired by Heft's ideas.

Finally, in chapter 11, Justine Hoch, a student of Harry Heft, somehow brings us back to the beginning of Harry's academic development. More concretely, she brings us back to developmental psychology. Hoch first examines different methods of describing the environment. In this context, she is interested in the diverse ways researchers think and characterize it relates to behavior and development. Harry Heft's (1988) arguments for a functional description of children's environments, as opposed to a description in terms of form and layout, are provided to frame the discussion. Then, Hoch analyzes the benefits Heft's proposal provides for behavioral analysis. Finally, she expands the scope of Heft's argument and evaluates the degree to which new technologies, as novel aspects of the functional environment, influence the advance of theories of learning and development. New technologies, Hoch claims, can capture meaningful features of the environment and even reflect the individual's immediate experience, while closely relating to overt behavior and development.

This book finishes with chapter 12, written by Harry Heft, where he elaborates on the ideas presented in previous chapters and sometimes offers critical assessments. The goal of this chapter is two-fold. On the one hand, it provides cohesion to the whole volume, showing how the different topics connect and relate to each other. But, most importantly, this chapter offers a beautiful example of a philosophical dialogue between an author and those who have received his influence during decades.

In sum, the 12 chapters of this book aim to celebrate Harry Heft's works. The editors of this volume and all the contributors just want to show how beautiful and enriching Heft's works are for anyone with an interest in psychology. But the book goes beyond that. Harry Heft has achieved a very rare status in academia: people from all over the world take him to be a mentor even when he never was officially so. Harry Heft spent most of his life teaching at Denison University, an undergraduate college in the Midwestern United States. This means he did not have cohorts of PhD students to train. However, many students and researchers interested in the ecological approach to psychology take him to be an unofficial professor and advisor. This is the case of the three editors of this volume and, we are sure, of many of the contributors. This is so because of the deep ways in which Harry Heft's ideas and works have shaped our own views on ecological psychology, the socio-cultural environment, and development. But this shaping is not just something happened in the past. On the contrary, it keeps happening, and it will continue so. In the first half of the 21st century, we face challenges that require new and better ways to characterize our relationship with our environments both as individuals and communities. We are convinced that further exploring and expanding Harry Heft's work on an ecological and socio-cultural psychology will help us achieve novel and more humane solutions to these challenges. Let this volume be a little contribution to that aim.

References

Barker, R. G. (1975). *Ecological psychology: Concepts and methods for studying the environment of human behavior*. Stanford University Press.

Barker, R. G. (Ed.). (1978). *Habitats, environments, and human behavior: Studies in ecological psychology and eco-behavioral science from the Midwest Psychological Field Station, 1947–1972*. Jossey-Bass.

Barker, R. G. & Wright, H. F. (1951). *One boy's day; a specimen record of behavior*. New York: Harper.

Chawla, L., & Heft, H. (2002). Children's competence and the ecology of communities: A functional approach to the evaluation of participation. *Journal of Environmental Psychology*, 22(1), 201–216. doi:10.1006/jevp.2002.0244

Gibson, E. J. (1969). *Principles of perceptual learning and development*. Prentice-Hall.

Gibson, E. J. (2000). Perceptual learning in development: Some basic concepts. *Ecological Psychology*, 12(4), 295–302. doi:10.1207/S15326969ECO1204_04

Gibson, E. J., & Pick, A. D. (2000). *An ecological approach to perceptual learning and development*. Oxford University Press.

Gibson, J. J. (1950a). The implications of learning theory for social psychology. In *Experiments in social process: A symposium on social psychology* (pp. 149–167). McGraw-Hill.

Gibson, J. J. (1950b). *The perception of the visual world*. Houghton Mifflin.

Gibson, J. J. (1966). *The senses considered as perceptual systems*. Greenwood Press.

Gibson, J. J. (1979). *The ecological approach to visual perception*. New York, NY: Psychology Press.

Gibson, J. J. & Gibson, E. (1955). Perceptual Learning: Differentiation or Enrichment?. *Psychological Review*, 62(1), 32–41.

Glotzbach, P. A., & Heft, H. (1982). Ecological and phenomenological contributions to the psychology of perception. *Noûs*, 16(1), 108–121. doi:10.2307/2215421

Heft, H. (1979). The role of environmental features in route-learning: Two exploratory studies of way-finding. *Environmental Psychology and Nonverbal Behavior*, 3(3), 172–185. doi:10.1007/BF01142591

Heft, H. (1981). An examination of constructivist and Gibsonian approaches to environmental psychology. *Population and Environment*, 4(4), 227–245.

Heft, H. (1983). Way -finding as the perception of information over time. *Population and Environment*, 6(3), 133–150. doi:10.1007/BF01258956

Heft, H. (1988). Affordances of children's environments: A functional approach to environmental description. *Children's Environments Quarterly*, 5(3), 29–37.

Heft, H. (1989). Affordances and the body: An intentional analysis of Gibson's ecological approach to visual perception. *Journal for the Theory of Social Behaviour*, 19(1), 1–30. doi:10.1111/j.1468-5914.1989.tb00133.x

Heft, H. (1990). Perceiving affordances in context: A reply to chow. *Journal for the Theory of Social Behaviour*, 20(3), 277–284. doi:10.1111/j.1468-5914.1990.tb00187.x

Heft, H. (1996). The ecological approach to navigation: A Gibsonian perspective. In J. Portugali (Ed.), *The construction of cognitive maps* (pp. 105–132). Springer Netherlands. doi:10.1007/978-0-585-33485-1_6

Heft, H. (1998). Essay review: The elusive environment in environmental psychology. *British Journal of Psychology*, 89(3), 519–523. doi:10.1111/j.2044-8295.1998.tb02700.x

Heft, H. (2001). *Ecological psychology in context: James Gibson, Roger Barker, and the legacy of William James's radical empiricism*. Psychology Press.

Heft, H. (2003). Affordances, dynamic experience, and the challenge of reification. *Ecological Psychology*, 15(2), 149–180. doi:10.1207/S15326969ECO1502_4

Heft, H. (2007). The social constitution of perceiver-environment reciprocity. *Ecological Psychology*, 19(2), 85–105. doi:10.1080/10407410701331934

Heft, H. (2012). Holt's "recession of the stimulus" and the emergence of the "situation" in psychology. In E. P. Charles (Ed.), *A new look at new realism*. Routledge.

Heft, H. (2013a). An ecological approach to psychology. *Review of General Psychology*, 17(2), 162–167.

Heft, H. (2013b). Wayfinding, navigation, and environmental cognition from a naturalist's stance. In *Handbook of spatial cognition* (pp. 265–294). American Psychological Association. doi: 10.1037/13936-015

Heft, H. (2013c). Environment, cognition, and culture: Reconsidering the cognitive map. *Journal of Environmental Psychology, 33*, 14–25. doi: 10.1016/j.jenvp.2012.09.002

Heft, H. (2014a). The tension between the psychological and ecological sciences: Making psychology more ecological. In *Entangled life* (pp. 51–77). Springer.

Heft, H. (2014b). What makes an ecological psychology ecological? *MERA Journal, 16*(2), 11–16.

Heft, H. (2017a). Perceptual information of "an entirely different order": The "cultural environment" in *The senses considered as perceptual systems*. *Ecological Psychology, 29*(2), 122–145. doi: 10.1080/10407413.2017.1297187

Heft, H. (2017b). William James' psychology, radical empiricism, and field theory: Recent developments. *Philosophical Inquiries, 5*(2). doi: 10.4454/philinq.v5i2.195

Heft, H. (2018). Places: Widening the scope of an ecological approach to perception–Action with an emphasis on child development. *Ecological Psychology, 30*(1), 99–123. doi: 10.1080/10407413.2018.1410045

Heft, H. (2019). Revisiting "The discovery of the occluding edge and its implications for perception" 40 years on. In *Perception as information detection* (pp. 188–204). Routledge.

Heft, H. (2020a). Ecological psychology and enaction theory: Divergent groundings. *Frontiers in Psychology, 11*, 991.

Heft, H. (2020b). Ecological psychology as social psychology? *Theory & Psychology, 30*(6), 813–826. doi: 10.1177/0959354320934545

Heft, H., & Chawla, L. (2006). Children as agents in sustainable development: The ecology of competence. In C. Spencer & M. Blades (Eds.), *Children and their environments: Learning, using and designing spaces* (pp. 199–216). Cambridge University Press. doi: 10.1017/CBO9780511521232.013

Heft, H., Hoch, J., Edmunds, T., & Weeks, J. (2014). Can the identity of a behavior setting be perceived through patterns of joint action? An investigation of place perception. *Behavioral Sciences, 4*(4), 371–393. doi: 10.3390/bs4040371

Hodges, B. H. (2007). Values define fields: The intentional dynamics of driving, carrying, leading, negotiating, and conversing. *Ecological Psychology, 19*(2), 153–178. doi: 10.1080/10407410701332080

Hodges, B. H., & Rączaszek-Leonardi, J. (2022). Ecological values theory: Beyond conformity, goal-seeking, and rule-following in action and interaction. *Review of General Psychology, 26*(1), 86–103. doi: 10.1177/10892680211048174

Hutchins, E. (1995). *Cognition in the wild* (8. Pr). MIT Press.

McGeer, V. (2015). Mind-making practices: The social infrastructure of self-knowing agency and responsibility. *Philosophical Explorations, 18*(2), 259–281. doi: 10.1080/13869795.2015.1032331

McGeer, V. (2021). Enculturating folk psychologists. *Synthese, 199*(1), 1039–1063. doi: 10.1007/s11229-020-02760-7

Raja, V., & Anderson, M. L. (2021). Behavior considered as an enabling constraint. In F. Calzavarini & M. Viola (Eds.), *Neural mechanisms: New challenges in the philosophy of neuroscience* (pp. 209–232). Springer International Publishing. doi: 10.1007/978-3-030-54092-0_10

Reed, E. (1996). *Encountering the world: Toward an ecological psychology*. Oxford University Press.

1
REFLECTIONS ON ECOLOGICAL PSYCHOLOGY

An interview with Harry Heft

Erik Rietveld and Julian Kiverstein

ER: Erik Rietveld
JK: Julian Kiverstein
HH: Harry Heft

ER: *How did you come to know James Gibson personally?*
HH: While doing my dissertation, and I was searching for ways to conceptualize the environment from a psychological standpoint, my graduate school adviser suggested that I read Gibson's *The Senses Considered as Perceptual Systems* (Gibson, 1966). Doing so made it clear to me what I wanted to do after graduate school. I wanted to learn more Gibsonian psychology. Soon after I met Herb Pick at a conference – Herb was a student of Gibson in the fifties. I asked Herb if I could visit him in Minnesota after I finished my PhD to learn more about ecological psychology. Herb, who is really a wonderful person, said to me, "why do you want to do that when you could go to Cornell instead?" He encouraged me to do so. So I wrote to Gibson and asked if I could visit for a year. Gibson replied to say I would be welcome. When I got there, I found there were several people who hung around Gibson. I was one of the three or four that year. Cornell kindly gave me a room to serve as my office, and I was sitting there one day – I hadn't met Gibson yet – when there was a knock on the door and Gibson walks in and introduces himself. Then he says to me: "so I don't know much about you, what kind of psychologist are you?" I don't recall now how I replied, but he said to me, and this is important, he said: "I'm a behaviourist." At the time this really took me back, however obviously, over time I came to understand exactly what he meant.

ER: *At some point you became Gibson's driver. How did that happen?*
HH: There was a party in the psychology department at Gibsons' house, I'm not sure why, it must have been for a speaker. I was there, being my shy self, and

not talking to many people. Jackie Gibson came up to me and asked if I would do her a favor? She told me Jimmy was going to be teaching a seminar in Binghamton, New York which was about 40 minutes away, and she was uncomfortable with him making the drive on his own in the winter evenings. She asked if I would go with him. As a result, once a week I did. He drove on the way there, and I drove back. However, we usually stopped at a bar on the way back to Ithaca. I was just learning about ecological psychology at the time, and I got to ask him basic questions. Thinking back, I wish I had a deeper understanding at the time so that I could have asked more incisive questions.

ER: *What impact did your visit to the Gibsons' have on you?*

HH: Well, it intensified my interest in the subject matter. The seminar in Binghamton was co-taught by Gibson and David Hamlyn, long-time editor of *Mind*. Hamlyn, who was sympathetic but not completely sold on the Gibsonian approach, would constantly challenge Gibson in the seminar. Seeing how Gibson responded to challenges to his position was really a great learning experience.

ER: *I can imagine, yes. It's very tempting to ask more about this time, but I'll just jump to the next question. What is the main thing that you have learned from James Gibson that is currently underappreciated in the field of ecological psychology?*

HH: That's a good question. I think the most important one, and this is actually one of the last conversations I had with him when I was leaving, was being very attentive to language. Being very careful with words and concepts, and being clear just what it is that we mean by particular terms. This is a lesson I have carried with me ever since.

ER: *We have the same question actually about what you've learned from Eleanor Gibson that is under appreciated in ecological psychology today?*

HH: That's an easy one and the answer is development. Much of the research in ecological psychology has focused mostly on Jimmy Gibson's writings. And yet while he was certainly sensitive to development, it isn't at the forefront of what he writes. I consider myself to really be a development psychologist with an ecological focus, something I learned from Eleanor Gibson, and brought with me from graduate school. My graduate school advisor, Jack Wohlwill, was a developmental psychologist.

ER: *What do you see as the main contributions that you have made to ecological psychology?*

HH: First, the work I did a while ago, trying to look at the affordances of children's' everyday environments, which was sort of a refinement of what my dissertation was about. My work on the affordances of play environments for children has been a stimulus for a lot of my subsequent research by others. There are two other things, one is certainly the historical roots of Gibson's thinking. As I explained to you, Erik when we first met, what was puzzling to me, even when I was with Gibson at Cornell, was that I didn't really know where his ideas came from. He was not good in providing that information.

I knew that Jimmy was really interested in William James. I had been reading James' work from the 1890s, *The Principles of Psychology* (James, 1890). It was only when I turned to the later work on radical empiricism that a sort of a light bulb went off. The third thing is really what my focus has been for the past decade or so, which is trying to push ecological psychology more in the sociocultural direction. That's what I've been concentrating on in my reading and in my writing over the past ten years or so, and it is what I'm currently engaged in now.

JK: *My question connects nicely to what you were just saying. It concerns the contribution you've made to uncovering the historical and intellectual foundations of ecological psychology. You've done a lot of historical work on pragmatist thinkers like Holt, Dewey, and James. What do you think we can learn from the history of psychology about how to practice psychology today?*

HH: Well, first we can uncover the assumptions that have been driving a lot of psychological enquiry, especially since the Enlightenment to the present time, so that we have a better sense of what assumptions contemporary psychology is making. But also I think, these thinkers can help us to develop a better understanding of the relational and socially constituted nature of human functioning. One of the people I've been reading lately is Charles Taylor (2016). He has described a perspective on language in thinkers like Herder and others that seems very compatible with ecological psychology, looking at how humans are constituted as participants in a language community. We can develop a better appreciation of a sociocultural view of human functioning by looking at some history in the philosophy of mind.

JK: *Totally agree. Going to James specifically, you've written about his later writings in his radical empiricist phase, how those writings are crucial for providing alternative conceptual foundations for what you describe as a "non-dualist psychology." One of the key concepts that you pick up on is the field of experience. Could you explain that concept to us and why you think it's so important for psychology?*

HH: Psychologists tend to begin with a subject-object dichotomy, there is the world out there, the object out there, the other person out there and then there's me, the thinker. James' field of experience is not differentiated in that way from the start, but only becomes differentiated over time or at least with further reflection. The immediate field of experience is relational, it's also dynamic. I've got bits and pieces of another book, and in this book I write about how James was working within the early stages of field theoretic thinking. He was very much aware of field theory in physics. Faraday is credited with developing field-theoretic thinking in physics, and Faraday and James' father were friends. Even in the first chapter of *The Principles*, James gives you an example of field theoretic thinking when he talks about what happens if you have iron filings and a magnet and you put a card between them. If you start with his writings on radical empiricism and then go back to read *The Principles*, you'll find that James' early writings are already shot through with field theoretic thinking.

ER: *In Merleau-Ponty's phenomenology, the concept of a field of experience is also important (Merleau-Ponty, 1945/2012). In our own work, we've introduced the concept of the field of relevant affordances to describe how an individual experiences an entire field of multiple inviting affordances rather than just one inviting affordance at a time. You've been writing about the concept of the field of experiences as it was used in James and also in the work of the gestalt psychologist Kurt Lewin. Do you see any connections between our use of the concept of responsiveness to the field of relevant affordances and this historic notion of the field of experience?*

HH: I guess what comes to mind first is that amazing paper by Kurt Lewin on the war landscape (Lewin, 1917/2009). Lewin was a soldier in the First World War, and he wrote about the phenomenology of being on the front. Of his writing, that's the one I think comes closest to what you guys have been writing about in terms of the field of relevant affordances. He is really taking in the whole immediate field, it's not just a particular affordance but it's much broader. That broader view has really been lost with the exception of what you two have written and a few others recently. The affordance literature has been mostly about particular objects, not the field of possibilities, although this seems to be changing. We also need a much richer account of affordance of the kind that you two have been developing, which is not only in terms of use meanings if you will, but also their invitational qualities.

A quick historical aside, the person who recruited Gibson to come to Cornell was Robert MacLeod. Robert MacLeod is not as well-known as he should be because he spent a lot of his time as an administrator. But he ran the psychology department at Cornell, and he was among the foremost phenomenological psychologists in America. MacLeod had a big influence on Jimmy and certainly saw the phenomenology in Gibson's earlier work. I'm also sure they had a lot of conversations together. When I was at Cornell, I worked every day in the library of the psychology department filled with Robert MacLeod's books who had died before I got there. I had around me all of the works on phenomenology that MacLeod had collected. Of course, I didn't merely sit at a table and work, I also browsed his collection and that was really helpful to me. By the way, Jimmy never mentioned to me when I was at Cornell that he read Merleau-Ponty. Later on after I learned a bit about Merleau-Ponty's work through a philosopher friend, I wrote to Jimmy and asked if knew anything about him? He said, I read some of that and then in the letter he wrote back to me, he quoted passages from Merleau-Ponty, probably off the top of his head. During a recent visit to the Gibson archives at Cornell, I came across some notes on Merleau-Ponty.

JK: *That's a perfect lead into our next question which is kind of about Merleau-Ponty. We're going to turn to your paper from 1989 in which you use the phenomenological concept of intentionality to provide an analysis of the relation of affordances to the body (Heft, 1989). Can you explain how this phenomenological concept of intentionality is important for understanding both affordances and the body?*

HH: When I wrote that paper, I was very uneasy writing about intentionality. I was bothered by the possible taint of mentalism in the notion of intentionality. Still it seemed to me that the notion of intentionality was unavoidable, especially the more that I read Merleau-Ponty. Gibson was forthright in talking about the organism as being purposive and engaging the world, perceptual systems are about sort of engaging the world. The only other word that came close to capturing this is Merleau-Ponty talking about "projects." In some ways in retrospect, I like the word "projects" better than intentionality because "projects" seems to me to capture more of the whole organism. It's more about what an individual is doing in the world. If I was writing that '89 paper again would I use "projects" rather than "intentionality"? I'd think hard about it.

ER: *I think the next question is actually related to what you were saying on projects because you propose an understanding of affordances in relation to goal directed action. However, that raises the question of what makes it the case that the agent has this goal rather than another goal in the particular situation?*

HH: That's a really great question and I'm glad you asked it. It goes back to something I said earlier: I would take more of a developmental approach, that is to say, organisms are historical beings. Certainly, we have goals, but they don't come out the blue, ex nihilo. Our goals are part of our ongoing history. We'd be well served to emphasize development much more, and the historicity of the developmental process. If you embed that kind of issue in a historical framework, you're not in the organism anymore, you're in a dynamical system which has hysteresis. This is a really important concept which I first learned about through the Kerry Marsh's experiments on moving planks, which I think is a greatly underappreciated experiment (Richardson et al., 2007). Hysteresis provides a way of talking about the tendency for organisms considered as systems to go in one direction as opposed to another.

JK: *In your 1989 paper, you discussed how affordances offer an alternative to a mechanistic understanding of the relation of an animal to its environment. Rather than thinking of affordances as causing our behavior, you suggest that affordances can be thought of as constraints. You complement this suggestion by adding that affordances also create possibilities. There's a sense in which affordances are both constraining and enabling. Could you elaborate on how thinking of affordances as constraints on action provides an alternative to mechanistic explanations of behavior?*

HH: I want to refer back to my previous answer. Part of the answer to how affordances constrain action has to do with the ways in which you've been engaged objects previously. We're historical creatures as we see from the classical experiment on functional fixedness (Duncker, 1945). In these experiments, people are given the task of solving a problem that requires the use of familiar objects in novel ways. It's really hard for us to do that because we are not used to using those objects in those ways. Another factor is what Alan Costall has so importantly highlighted, and that is normativity. Affordances have constraints not only because of their material properties but also because of the history of the organism and also because of socially normative influences (Costall, 1995).

JK: *Our next question is exactly on this point, so in the same paper you talk about how behavior and behavior settings, using the example of a child Maude acting in the behavior setting of a drugstore (Heft, 1989). You describe how Maude appears to be coerced by the collective social forces that give rise to the behavior setting. How do social forces constrain the behavior of individuals?*

HH: Well there's two ways I'd like to come at this. If I were to start my career over again, I would study children learning about behavior settings in their community, learning place-appropriate actions. Barker, who developed the concept, claimed that behavior settings are perceivable; they have a physiognomy. We have some data on this point (Heft et al., 2014). What I would like to understand is how children come to perceive the meaning of behavior settings. Certainly Maude, as a child, learned about behavior settings through modeling, seeing what's the proper way to behave by looking mainly probably at what her mother does It would have been great to study these social dynamics. In the recent work, we propose that perceiving the meaning of a behavior setting principally involves detecting structure from motion among the setting's participants.

The way I conceptualize behavior settings is that they are emergent collective structures. In order for the drug store to operate, everybody there needs to be doing their job, carrying out their role, at least working within the right parameters of what their responsibilities are. The behavior setting is a higher-order, emergent structure arising from their collective actions. In turn, each individual's actions are constrained for the implicit purpose of generating this higher order structure. Collectively, activities generate a higher order structure and by virtue of doing that, individual actions are constrained. In other words, there's this top-down, bottom-up process that's going on all the time.

Initially, a child learns what the proper behaviors are, largely through modeling, but over time at a later point, after those behaviors have become habitual, when the child goes into a store in the neighborhood, their actions are constrained in two ways – as they carry out immediate goals by engaging the affordances of the setting – and as they operate within the normative behavioral contexts of the setting as previously learned. By doing so in the latter regard, they contribute, as a matter of course, to the continuing overall functioning of that setting. Their actions are constrained within the context of the overall setting as they engage particular affordances (what Barker called milieu) in the setting. That's why I would approach constraints with regards to affordances a little differently than behavior settings.

JK: *Can you elaborate on that last point?*

HH: Yes, I mean the constraints in the behavior settings – but I don't like this next phrase – are top-down in a way. As a participant in a behavior setting, you are limiting your actions – operating within particular degrees of freedom – based on prior experience as you carry out your immediate goals in the setting; and in doing so – if you will, as an unintended consequence perhaps – your actions sustain the behavior setting. It is the activities normatively appropriate to the setting that contribute to sustaining the behavior setting overall. Thus, a person's developmental history enters in at two points: a history of appropriate ways to engage affordances, and a history of normative actions with regard to the setting overall within which affordances are nested.

JK: *Turning now to a more general question, Ed Reed wrote about how ecological psychology could be a replacement for cognitive psychology as a whole (Reed, 1991). I was wondering what you think about the scope of ecological psychology. Could ecological psychology explain cognition as a whole?*

HH: My inclination, on the one hand, is that we should push ecological psychology as far as we can. But I do think that it's going to hit a limit. And I'm wondering if the limit isn't somewhere in the domain of non-perceptual processes.

ER: *But wouldn't that imply that we would need to ask cognitivism to help us out there?*

HH: Perhaps, but still the way we conceptualize perceiving is going to affect how we conceptualize non-perceptual cognitive processes. I firmly believe that. Whether it's going to be a continuous line or whether there's going to be some kind of discontinuity, I don't know. I worry about symbols and certainly ecological psychologists have not contributed very much to that discussion. Symbols are really a big challenge.

ER: *Perhaps we can approach this issue from a slightly different angle. Do you see ecological psychology as being able to deal with the environment that is not local but distal such as the blackboard behind you or the plants that need watering in your garden?*

HH: I'd like to separate a couple of different things here, and raise the issue of perceiving over time. This is related to the problem I brought to Gibson when I was in Cornell. I was interested in wayfinding, how we find our way across some expanse of the landscape. I was rebelling against the idea of a cognitive map because it's not temporal. I have since written about this further (Heft, 2013). Following Gibson, I wrote about navigation and wayfinding from the point of view of terrestrial organisms. Spatial navigation is the quintessential phenomena of perceiving over time. In perceiving a route over time, I can look quite far ahead. So that's one case. The other case is imagining that I'm going to do something at a future time. It seems to me these are not quite the same issue. I'd have to figure out how to put those two together or whether they need to be treated separately.

Let me get back, if I may to symbols for just a minute. Merlin Donald's book *The Origins of the Modern Mind* has had a profound influence on me (Donald, 1991). Donald wants to know, in his words, how do you go from an episodic mind, which he considers primates to have, to a symbolic mind. The link that he draws and I think he's totally right is mimesis. I think if we're going to draw the link between perceiving and language, it's going to run through mimesis. That's where it would go.

JK: *This does connect quite nicely to your social constitution EP paper (Heft, 2007). You raised a question in that paper, what's the place of the social in ecological psychology? You describe how there's been a lot of attention paid to topics in social perception. But you're after something different which you describe as the social understood as a "background condition" for ecological psychology. Can you explain what you meant by thinking of the social as a background condition for everything that ecological psychology is concerned with investigating?*

HH: I was too conservative in that paper, I pulled my punches, if you will. Erik might remember this, when we were both down in Cincinnati and I gave a little talk there. I basically said everything is social. I believe that's the case because we are sociocultural creatures from the get go. Our species evolutionary history regarding collective action and especially how unformed we are at birth shows this. Again, I point to Donald's (1991) work. Bruner is quite good on this as well. There's this background of the social which has to play a role in everything we do. Often we think about affordances in a very abstract way. Take as an example stair affordances. We can ask not only can I step on this surface but also "is this a stair that I should go up?"; "Where does this stair lead?" You can make all kinds of caveats here. I've been reading a lot of Bourdieu and I think Pierre Bourdieu's work on habitus fits really nicely with this. It just fits hand and glove for me with an ecological approach. I was really being much too cautious in the earlier paper.

ER: *Actually, Harry, the next question is related to this, because Gibson suggested that the notion of affordances is relevant for what he called the entire spectrum of social significance for humans. Why is there so little attention to this in ecological psychology, or at least in the experimental mainstream of ecological psychology?*

HH: I'm going to answer your question in a roundabout way. There's a book, that's being put together now, of interviews that were conducted in the nineties with people involved in ecological psychology at that time (Szokolszky et al., forthcoming). The interviews were done just when Ed Reed died, so unfortunately he's not in the book. Most of the Connecticut people were interviewed, but also Alan Costall and David Lee. I was asked to write the historical introduction. What I tried to do, without stepping on anyone's toes, is to trace out these different streams within ecological psychology after Gibson. Obviously, the major force in this era has been the Connecticut school (CESPA). What they're up to, and I think it's a noble task, is trying to clarify first principles, that's their phrase, that apply to all living things. They've done really great work in bringing dynamical systems into ecological psychology. However, if you're looking at first principles that are shared across organisms, you're not going to be talking about sociocultural issues. That's just not going to be part of the framework. You have to look elsewhere in the ecological psychology literature for that, to Costall, Reed,

Hodges, for example. In my opinion, Ed Reed's *Encountering the World* (1996) remains underappreciated.

    Here's a recent example of these two streams. Julia Blau and Jeff Wagman have just written a great introduction to ecological psychology for the beginning student to be published by Routledge in July (Blau & Wagman, 2022). It's really wonderful, but it follows the Connecticut line, chapter, and verse. There's a chapter on the social but not in the background sense that we've just been talking about. In other words, it's social more in line with first principles argument, such that all organisms have a social side. But humans are different. We are cultural beings, and I don't think there's been much interest in that among the Connecticut school. Now what's really pleasing to me is that in the past ten years there's a bunch of folks, certainly Alan, he's been doing this since the nineties, but also Rob and Ludger, you and Julian, Vicente, Manuel, and Miguel are focusing on those sociocultural dimensions – returning to much of Reed's work – and that really pleases me a lot. So I think we're finding some balance.

ER: *There's this gap between recent theoretical developments and experimental research. Might there be other methods that are empirical but perhaps not experimental. We have been using ethnography. Do you know of other methods that are perhaps suited to give empirical substance to the theoretical importance of the social?*

HH: Yes, my first answer would be ethnography. I think that's a really good tool. The other is observational work, and this goes back to William Whyte who influenced me quite a bit and I know, Erik, that his ideas have influenced you as well. So for example, here's a study, maybe you can find some students to do. In William Whyte's (1980) book, he makes the claim that public spaces are self-leveling, that is, individuals have a "feel" for the optimal or a maximum number of persons a place can accommodate, and this results in some stability limiting overuse. One could observe a lot of public spaces to see whether that, in fact, plays out. There's a lot that we could do in terms of observational work. We need to broaden our methods in the ways that environmental psychologists, to be distinguished from ecological psychologists, were talking about way back in the sixties and seventies. The late Bob Sommer's methods book is a good resource.

JK: *In your "places" paper, you talk about natural history (Heft, 2018), so this kind of observational work has been going on in biological sciences since Darwin?*

HH: Absolutely, I'm glad you said that, I think that's so important and again, it gets back to this notion of the history of an organism, development, and time. We need to be more developmental. Working in laboratories makes having a developmental perspective incredibly difficult. Some people like Karen Adolph have figured out how to do it, but not many people are as clever as Karen. Also note that Karen who studies the development of crawling and walking in the laboratory has also carried observational studies of how much young children locomote in their homes on a daily basis. This is in the tradition of natural history research.

JK: *Changing gear slightly, what do you see as your main contributions to the field of environmental psychology?*

HH: I laugh because I don't think I've made much of a mark on environmental psychology, even though this is where I started my career, because it has remained very cognitivist over the decades. In the textbooks of environmental psychology if they wanted to nod to Gibson, they'd write a paragraph and cite me but that was about it. Even my navigation work was not picked up within environmental psychology.

ER: *And related to that, the environmental design community you've been engaging with?*

HH: I've had some involvement with some landscape designers in the Open Space Programme in Edinburgh … . Also, there's Robin Moore's program at North Carolina State University, where they focus on affordances and behavior settings in outdoor play environments for children. Finally, Louise Chawla on the importance of early environmental experience for developing a sensitivity to the biosphere.

ER: *Actually the next question is related to that because you care a lot about where society is heading: We're living in a times of ecological crisis. Is there a role for ecological psychology to play there?*

HH: I guess I want to take the Gibsonian admonition, and urge everyone to "look for yourself." The more that we can present visual images of environments in the midst of change that people don't necessarily have contact with, I'd like to think that the data themselves will be overwhelming.

ER: *But do you mean visual images to touch them affectively about the impact of climate change?*

HH: Right, looking at photos from different time periods I think you can't help but be struck by the fact that the environment has drastically changed. Obviously, the rate of change has picked up.

ER: *If James Gibson would have address the next ICPA conference do you think climate crisis would be his topic, if he were still alive? Or would he also just carry on with students in a lab?*

HH: That's a great question. Attention to climate change is going on within environmental psychology, but not yet within ecological psychology. I can't think of anyone who has done anything relating to climate change. That is understandable given its focus on laboratory research to date.

ER: *Do you see your collaboration with Louise Chawla as relevant for the current climate crisis?*

HH: What's important about Louise's work, and I give her the credit for this, is showing the importance of children's experience of places that are not built, that are not constructed, but are dominated by organic features, features that change, that grow (Chawla, 2021). I am intentionally avoiding invoking a nature-culture dichotomy here. There's wonderful work by Nancy Wells at Cornell where she has kids with low economic means working in gardens

(Wells, 2021). When I first heard about work along these lines by others long ago, I thought, this is pretty frivolous, but it isn't really because the kids are seeing things grow and directly contributing to that. They're seeing how their actions can make a difference. The important theme that came out of my work with Louise, and it's continued to be important to me is the notion of self-efficacy – the experience stemming from actions where one can make a change in the immediate surround. Reed rightly said this can be a source of hope. Louise and I have worked with Inger Lerstrup in Denmark. We just published a paper on children engaging with small animals like snails and worms and small things that require a certain delicacy but that are animate (Lerstrup et al., 2020). These kinds of experiences can be really valuable for children for learning about the complexities of organic life and about caring for the world.

JK: *We've reached the last question.*

ER: *It's a difficult one. What do you see as the main challenge or challenges for the coming ten years for the field of ecological psychology?*

HH: Well, oddly I would say that with its past emphasis on action and coordination, ecological psychology has not given sufficient attention to the environment. For example, how are affordances and behavior settings integrated in the flow of everyday activity, and how do they structure action? In some strange way, I think collectively we've taken our eye off the ball. We really need to look at the environments of everyday life, which is a strange thing to say to an ecological psychology audience.

JK: *I guess playing devil's advocate I can imagine researchers in ecological psychology saying no, that's exactly what we've doing. So what are they missing?*

HH: Are we out there, looking at people and children in everyday environments, and trying to understand the place of affordances in those contexts? To take but one example, Rob Withagen has looked at optimal distances between stepping stones in the design of children's playgrounds (Jongeneel et al., 2015). That's a really good setting for research. Those are the kinds of questions and the sites for research that I think we ought to be pursuing. During these pandemic times I guess an interesting question for the future would be, what's been the impact of the pandemic on people's use of outdoor environments in the long run? What happens when things settle, how will the environments that we live in have changed? What a great thing to look at in Amsterdam, where you two live – the use of the city post-pandemic.

ER: *Actually, we are collaborating with the mayor of Amsterdam on a project that is about how lessons from the pandemic and also from the years before the pandemic, where things were also not perfect, could contribute to better public space for the future. There's of course a lot of open questions there.*

HH: I remember something you showed me Erik, a number of years ago, and I've not seen it in later writings that was like a park area that's new?

ER: *The floating Trusted Strangers park. We proposed it for the 750th birthday for the city of Amsterdam which will happen in 2025, and we were waiting to hear if they will embrace it.* We have been presenting it to the mayor and to other people at the municipality. But there's of course more people who have ideas on what should be the focus point.

HH: It would be wonderful, even apart from the post-pandemic, to have ongoing data collection at that site to see how people use the area. How its use, and even the area itself, changes over time. The history of a public space. That would be a really wonderful affordance-inspired study.

ER: *Thanks a lot Harry, it was really great to talk with you. I think we shouldn't end without asking if there's anything that you would want to add because we couldn't of course cover everything.*

HH: Something that I spent a lot of time on in recent years is the impact of theories of perception on developments in the visual arts; the parallels between the development of art history and the development of theories of visual perception. I've become quite interested in how much developments in the physical and biological sciences in the 19th century changed the visual arts, while 20th-century psychology for the most part was untouched by them, still clinging to mechanistic models.

ER & JK: *Thanks again for super-interesting conversation.*

References

Blau, J. J. C. & Wagman, J. B. (2022) (forthcoming). *Introduction to ecological psychology: A lawful approach to perceiving, acting and cognizing*. New York: Routledge, Taylor & Francis Group.

Chawla, L. T. (2021). Knowing nature in childhood: Learning and well-being through engagement with the natural world. In A. Schutte, J. Torquati, & J. Stevens (Eds.), *Nature and psychology: Biological, cognitive, developmental, and social pathways to well-being* (pp. 153–194). Nebraska Symposium on Motivation, Vol. 67, Springer. doi:10.1007/978-3-030-69020-5_8

Costall, A. (1995). Socializing affordances. *Theory & Psychology, 5*(4), 467–481.

Donald, M. (1991). *Origins of modern mind: Three stages in the evolution of culture and cognition*. Cambridge, MA: Harvard University Press.

Duncker, K. (1945). On problem solving. *Psychological Monographs, 58*(5), i–113.

Gibson, J. J. (1966). *The senses considered as perceptual systems*. Boston, MA: Houghton & Mifflin.

Heft, H. (1989). Affordances and the body: An intentional analysis of Gibson's ecological approach to visual perception. *Journal for the Theory of Social Behaviour, 19*(1), 1–30.

Heft, H. (2007). The social constitution of perceiver-environment reciprocity. *Ecological Psychology, 19*(2), 85–105.

Heft, H. (2013). Environment, cognition, and culture: Reconsidering the cognitive map. *Journal of Environmental Psychology, 33*, 14–25.

Heft, H. (2018). Places: Widening the scope of an ecological approach to perception-action with an emphasis on child development. *Ecological Psychology, 30*(1), 99–123.

Heft, H., Hoch, J. E., Edmunds, T., & Weeks, J. (2014). Can the identity of a behavior setting be perceived through patterns of joint action? An investigation of place perception. *Behavioral Sciences, 4*, 371–393. doi:10.3390/bs4040371

James, W. (1890). *The principles of psychology*. New York: Henry Holt & Company.

Jongeneel, D., Withagen, R., & Zaal, F. T. J. M. (2015). Do children create standardised playgrounds? A study on the gap-crossing affordances of jumping stones. *Journal of Environmental Psychology, 44,* 45–52.

Lerstrup, I., Chawla, L., & Heft, H. (2020). Affordances of small animals for young children: A path to environmental values of care. *International Journal of Early Childhood Environmental Education, 9*(1), 58–77.

Lewin, K. (1917/2009). The landscape of war (Translated by J. Blower). *Art in Translation, 1*(2), 199–209.

Merleau-Ponty, M. (1945/2012). *The Phenomenology of Perception* (Translated by C. Smith). London: Routledge.

Reed, E. (1991). James Gibson's ecological approach to cognition. In A. Still & A. Costall (Eds.), *Against cognitivism: Alternative foundations for cognitive psychology.* London: Harvester Wheatsheaf.

Reed, E. S. (1996). *Encountering the world: Toward an ecological psychology.* New York: Oxford University Press.

Richardson, M. J., Marsh, K. L., & Baron, R. M. (2007). Judging and actualising intrapersonal and interpersonal affordances. *Journal of Experimental Psychology: Human Perception and Performance, 33,* 845–859.

Szokolszky, A. Read, C., & Palatinus, Z. (2022) (forthcoming). *Pioneers of ecological psychology: Interviews then and now.* New York: Routledge, Taylor & Francis Group.

Taylor, C. (2016). *The language animal: The full shape of the human linguistic capacity.* Cambridge, MA: Harvard University Press.

Wells, N. M. (2021). The natural environment as a resilience factor: Nature's role as a buffer of the effects of risk and adversity. In A. Schutte, J. Torquati, & J. Stevens (Eds.), *Nature and psychology: Biological, cognitive, developmental, and social pathways to well-being* (pp. 195–234). Nebraska Symposium on Motivation, Vol. 67, Springer. doi:10.1007/978-3-030-69020-5_8

Whyte, W. (1980). *The social life of small urban spaces.* Ann Arbor, MI: Edwards Brothers Inc.

2
THE SOCIAL CONSTITUTION OF ECOLOGICAL PSYCHOLOGY IN THE NETHERLANDS

Rob Withagen and Ludger van Dijk

2.1 Introduction

Over the last two decades, the eminent historical, theoretical, and empirical work of Harry Heft has influenced ecologically inspired scholars in the Netherlands. Recently it has for instance begun making its way to such diverse fields of research as phenomenology (Dings, 2018, 2021), technology studies (De Boer, 2021), and medical anthropology (Van der Niet, 2017). Before that, Rietveld and Kiverstein (2014) drew heavily on the sociocultural approach to affordances that was initiated and developed by Heft (1989, 2001, 2007) and others (Costall, 1995, 1997; Hodges & Baron, 1992). Likewise, in our own work, over the years the influence of Heft's thinking is clearly visible (Prieske et al., 2015; Van Der Schaaf et al., 2020; Van Dijk, 2016, 2021; Van Dijk & Withagen, 2014; Van Dijk & Rietveld, 2018; Withagen, 2004; Withagen & Van Wermerskerken, 2010).

Ecological psychology has a relatively long history in the Netherlands, starting in the early 1980s. Heft wrote some pivotal papers in the 1980s and 1990s (Heft, 1988, 1989, 1993), yet it took some years before Heft's work rose to prominence in the Dutch ecological community. In this chapter, we will sketch in broad strokes the history of ecological psychology in our country. How did the Gibsonian approach take root in the Netherlands? When did Dutch ecologically inclined authors find inspiration in Heft's work? After this historical background, we will discuss some of Heft's ideas in more detail and consider the impact they had on the ecological movement in the Netherlands.

2.2 The ecological movement in the Netherlands

James Gibson saw himself as an "American thinker" (Reed, 1988, p. 205), but he was clearly also following and inspired by developments in European psychology. He organized several conferences and workshops in which European scholars were invited to present their ideas. In addition, he visited Europe on several occasions to meet, among others, Michotte in Belgium and Johansson in Sweden. However, to our knowledge, Gibson never made it to the Netherlands. Yet, a few years after Gibson completed his final book, a diverse group of human movement scientists, working at the Vrije Universiteit Amsterdam (VU for short), found inspiration in his ideas.

John Whiting was a key figure in this respect. Although this British sport psychologist was trained within the information processing approach that prevailed in his days, he was keen on studying natural tasks, in particular the acquisition of ball skills such as catching and hitting (Whiting, 1969). More importantly, he was receptive to new ideas – when he met some ecological psychologists (including Ed Reed and Peter Kugler) at conferences, he was inspired by their new way of thinking (Whiting, 1984). Together with a group of young scientists working at his department (including Peter Beek, Reinoud Bootsma, and Geert Savelsbergh), and more senior theorists (including Piet van Wieringen, Onno Meijer, and Jan Tamboer) Whiting studied and discussed this new branch on psychology's tree in what they called "the Action Club." The Gibsonian ideas fell on fertile ground at the department. Ever since its founding years, phenomenology (e.g., Buytendijk, Merleau-Ponty) and the relational ontology it entailed were central to the members' thinking about human movement (Tamboer, 1985). After studying Reed's (1982) paper on action systems, the Amsterdam group invited him over to give a seminar. Reed was housed in the Toro hotel, where the Talking Heads had also settled down for the recording of a video clip, resulting in a lively discussion about the inimitable movement idiom of David Byrne (Peter Beek, personal communication, 12 November 2021).

From an entirely different angle, the neuropsychologist Theo Mulder from Radboud University Nijmegen, who was inspired by the Russian action theorists (e.g., Luria, Leontiev, Anokhin) and by German neurology and biology in the early 20th century (e.g., Von Uexküll, Mittelstaedt, Goldstein), was impressed by Reed's (1982) action paper as well, and he traveled to Philadelphia to meet the author. In the paper, Reed made a sharp distinction between motor approaches and action approaches. In his view, goal-directed movements are not specific to the mechanism that cause them, but to the function they perform. As Reed (1985, pp. 262–263 emphasis in original) would put it:

> Far from being indifferent to changes in function, movements and postures (and their underlying mechanisms) are often precisely attuned to the animal's 'motor problem.' Thus I proposed the hypothesis that behaviors are *functionally* specific (i.e., supported by resources specific to behavior, by affordances) as a counter to the traditional hypothesis that behaviors are functionally indifferent (or mechanically specific, which comes to the same thing).

In 1985, together with the group of psychologists working at the University of Bielefeld, the Amsterdam group organized a conference with presentations and debates centered on this distinction. Ed Reed delivered a keynote (and was actively involved in the lively discussion) and so did another promising and young ecological psychologist, William Warren. A few years later, an influential volume appeared at Elsevier with contributions of the keynote speakers, and with one of the lively discussions at the conference completely written out (Meijer & Roth, 1988).

However, after the 1985 conference in Bielefeld, the influence of Reed on the ecological movement in the Netherlands faded. Although Reed's work still figured prominently in Meijer's (1988) dissertation on the "hierarchy debate", there is no reference to his work in the dissertations of Beek (1989) and Bootsma (1988). The latter two found more inspiration for their experimental work in Turvey and Kugler's physical ecological approach (Kugler & Turvey, 1987) than in Reed's evolutionarily inspired perspective. Indeed, at the University of Connecticut, Turvey, Kugler, Kelso, and others were developing new ideas on how to approach Bernstein's degrees of freedom problem. Rather than viewing this problem from an "engineering perspective" in which the body (with its many degrees of freedom) must be controlled by a controller (the brain, or more generally, a nervous system), the Connecticut group developed a natural-physical perspective, and one that was embraced by Beek and Bootsma. Bootsma, who examined information-movement couplings in rapid interceptive actions, was attracted to Turvey and Kugler's ecological perspective, primarily because it "offers the possibility of ... a *lawful* account of behaviour" (Bootsma, 1988, p. 11, emphasis added). In his dissertation on juggling dynamics, Beek (1989) was equally attracted to a lawful, physical account: "[human movement coordination is] a problem continuous with the problem of pattern formation in open systems" (p. 4). And, accordingly, the principles of non-linear dynamics can be applied to come to grips with how coordinative structures in human and nonhuman behavior come about.

In 1991, Beek, Bootsma, and Van Wieringen managed to bring the world conference of the International Society of Ecological Society (now known as ICPA) to Amsterdam. And in the very same year, Claire Michaels, an ecological psychologist from the Connecticut group, was appointed as full professor of "psychology with regard to human movement" at the VU, replacing the retiring John Whiting. Students were trained in the ecological approach as developed by Gibson and furthered by Turvey and colleagues. The Amsterdam group delivered a whole series of dissertations in which ecological principles were applied to the study of perception and action.[1]

In the 1980s and 1990s, ecological psychology was flourishing at the VU and had inspired some Dutch scientists working at other universities. This includes Ad Smitsman at Radboud University, and Gerda Smets, Pieter Jan Stappers, and others at Delft University of Technology (two members from Delft, Kees Overbeeke and Caroline Hummels, would later bring ecologically inspired research to Eindhoven University of Technology). Meanwhile, Heft had written some important papers. He emphasized the social structuring of the human econiche in which perception and action unfolds. Heft understood that Gibson's approach should and could extend far beyond visual perception. As a young scientist, he had been interested in accounting for "cognitive" behavior by studying the ecological context of such skills (Heft, 1979, 1983). He extended Gibson's (1958) work on the laws of locomotion in order to understand wayfinding as "the perception of information over time" (Heft, 1983, p. 133). In addition, Heft saw the need to bring out the experiential aspects of human behavior (Glotzbach & Heft, 1982). Considering the sociocultural origin of meaning and Merleau-Ponty's conception of the body, for instance, Heft (1989) developed an intentional analysis of affordances in which the environment might be experienced not only relative to one's bodily dimensions but relative to an organism's abilities or skills. Despite the initial phenomenological inclinations at the VU, the first wave of Dutch ecological psychologists was, generally, not very responsive to these considerations.

However, at the turn of the 21st century, things started to change. The original Amsterdam group was falling apart as their members went in different ways. Claire Michaels had moved back to the University of Connecticut in 2001, although she kept supervising some of her students at the VU in the years that followed. Moreover, the interests of the original members of this group evolved. Beek's primary interest has always been in coordination dynamics, and over the years he found more inspiration in Haken's work. And Savelsbergh, arguably the first scientist who put Lee's tau hypothesis to an empirical test (Savelsbergh et al., 1991), now followed an ecologized version of Milner and Goodale's neuropsychological model in his study of interceptive actions, an approach that was carefully articulated in Van Der Kamp et al. (2008). Of the original group, only Bootsma was still working from the Gibsonian framework that was advocated and furthered by Turvey and colleagues. However, while Bootsma kept close ties with some of the Gibsonians in the Netherlands (in particular with Frank Zaal and Raoul Bongers), he had moved to Marseille in 1992.

On top of that, in 2001, Heft published his seminal book *Ecological Psychology in Context*, fortifying his influence as a theoretical psychologist. The book rekindled Gibsonian psychology's historical ties to the work of pragmatist philosopher and radical empiricist William James and his student Edwin Holt (in turn Gibson's supervisor). It moreover introduced the Gibsonian community to the ecological psychology of Roger Barker. Shortly after the publication of this book, Rob met Harry at the ICPA conference in Storrs, Connecticut, and they stayed in touch ever since. Rob had studied psychology in Leiden but became enamored with the ecological approach and was conducting his PhD research under Michaels at that time. A couple of months after the conference, the remaining Gibsonians at the VU (Frank Zaal, Raoul Bongers, and Rob) started a reading group discussing Harry's book. This was Rob's first encounter with the work of both Holt and Barker which immediately affected his theorizing. Indeed, Rob drew heavily on Holt's and Heft's ideas to develop new ways of understanding the use of nonspecifying variables in perceiving (Withagen, 2004).

In the meantime, Theo Mulder was appointed as professor and head of the Center for Human Movement Sciences at the University Medical Center

Groningen and the University of Groningen. And within three years of time, Frank Zaal, Raoul Bongers, and Rob were successively hired in Groningen, shifting the center of gravity of ecological psychology in the Netherlands to the north of the country. This shift was further reinforced by the arrival of Ralf Cox, a former student of the ecological psychologist Ad Smitsman, who was going to strengthen the Psychology Department at the University of Groningen. At the Center for Human Movement Sciences, Harjo De Poel, Gert-Jan Pepping, and Joanne Smith, three other ecological psychologists by training, also joined the group (although Pepping moved to Australian Catholic University in 2014). Consequently, the University of Groningen came to boost a strong line of research, training graduate students in different aspects of ecological psychology, including the approaches that were developed by Turvey, Kugler, Reed, Costall, and Heft. Among the students at that time was Ludger who studied human movement sciences in addition to philosophy. In 2006, when the human movement scientists in Groningen organized the European Workshop on Ecological Psychology, Harry visited the Netherlands for the first time (at least for professional purposes). He presented his work on the social constitution of ecological psychology, which was published a year later (Heft, 2007).

At that very conference, the philosopher Erik Rietveld was in the audience. He came to Gibsonian theory from an entirely different angle than the scholars trained at the VU. Rietveld had just started his PhD project and was inspired by the affordance concept, mainly through the writings of Hubert Dreyfus (2004, 2007). He came to the conference expecting to learn more about the ins and outs of affordances, and he was surprised by the great number of presentations on tau and other sources of information (Rietveld, personal communication, 25 January 2022). Yet, Harry's presentation and his meeting with Rietveld certainly made up for that. Rietveld and Heft shared an interest in the work of Merleau-Ponty, the body in psychological theorizing, and the sociocultural take on affordances. Rietveld was eager to learn as much as possible from the established specialist in Gibsonian theory (ibid.).

Harry and Erik Rietveld would keep in contact and in the 15 years that followed, Rietveld would play a significant role in bringing ecological considerations to philosophy in the Netherlands and beyond. He received several grants, allowing him to train several PhD students (including Jelle Bruineberg) and hire senior researchers and post-docs (including Julian Kiverstein and Ludger), who were inspired by Heft's work. Through the work of Rietveld and his colleagues, Heftian considerations about the social constitution of the human environment made their way to a large audience of philosophers and theorists of mind. Moreover, Rietveld and his brother Ronald founded RAAAF, an experimental, multidisciplinary architecture studio, through which they brought a socialized affordance concept to people working not only in philosophy but also in the arts, design, architecture, and sociology.

Over the past 20 years ties have grown between Harry and the ecological community in the Netherlands. After his initial visit in 2006, Harry traveled to the

Netherlands on multiple occasions. In 2014, when RAAAF launched the *End of Sitting*, an office landscape of the future consisting of slanted surfaces that afford working in several non-sitting postures, Harry was invited for a talk. A year later, Harry presented at the SMART Cognitive Science conference in Amsterdam. When the time came for Ludger to defend his philosophical dissertation in 2016, his supervisors Erik Myin and Rob invited Harry as one of the key opponents at the University of Antwerp (Belgium). Two years later, Harry visited the Annual Meeting of the Jean Piaget Society in Amsterdam. And in 2019, Harry again made his way to the Netherlands, but now for the ICPA conference that was hosted in Groningen.

In a sense, this conference illustrated the changed ecological landscape in the Netherlands. A new wave of scholars was drawn to ecological theorizing, sparking a productive exchange with other disciplines. At the ICPA in Groningen, the physical perspective was still well represented (with Michael Turvey notably in the audience). In a pluralist spirit however, the organizers (Raoul Bongers and Frank Zaal) included talks from neighboring fields from philosophy and biology to enactivism and modern Gestalt psychology. Moreover, the ICPA boosted a host of other ecological approaches; talks inspired by Reed's work as well as multiple talks developing ecological ideas along Heftian lines. So what are the major themes in Harry's work and in what way did they influence the thinking of ecologists in the Netherlands?

2.3 The nature of the environment and psychology's job

One of the central concerns throughout Harry's work is the need for psychology to have a proper conception of the environment. This was recently emphasized, for example, in his critique of enactivism (Heft, 2020). It was also central to his book *Ecological Psychology in Context* (Heft, 2001), and formed the motivation for his early paper on how to describe the environments of children (Heft, 1988). In this paper, one of his most cited works, Harry made a strong plea for a functional approach to children's environments. Indeed, describing those environments in terms of affordances gives rise to a description that is "more psychologically meaningful than the standard form-based classification of environmental features" (Heft, 1988, p. 29). To understand what, for example, a certain park *means* to a child, it should be described not in terms of trees, benches, and lawns, but in terms of the possibilities for action (the climb-on-ability, sit-on-ability, walk-on-ability, and so on) that are available at that spot.

To develop a taxonomy of affordances of the children's environments, Harry scrutinized, among other things, Barker and Wright's book *One Boy's Day*. In this exceptional book, all the actions a seven-year-old boy performed on a single day are detailed. Here is a small excerpt (Barker & Wright, 1951, p. 49) that gives an impression of the book's unique nature:

> 8:24. He jumped up with a stone in his hand, threw it into the air, and fanned at it with a bat.

He hit the stone and yelled in a very surprised tone, "Hit it!"
As he swung the bat around, it accidentally hit the metal flagpole.
This made a wonderful, hollow, ringing noise, so he preceeded to hit the flagpole again.

8:25. He went around and around and around the pole, hitting it with the bat as he did so, until he became so dizzy that he fell down, bat and all. ...
As soon as he got his bearings, he leaped up.
He hit the flagpole harder and harder, rhythmically, and, as he hit it harder, he went faster and faster around the pole.
He fanned the air with the bat, missing a beat or two.
He hit the flagpole again and again.

While the description of all these activities may seem trivial at first, the power of *One Boy's Day* becomes apparent if you allow yourself to carefully absorb its contents. Indeed, the long list of activities suggests that much of psychology is on the wrong track. Obsessed with laboratory studies in which all the "confounding" factors can be controlled, a significant group of psychologists has lost sight of what it is supposed to explain: the natural behavior of people in their environments. And building upon Barker's writings, Heft's theoretical and empirical work does a tremendous job in showing this. Among other things, the taxonomy of affordances that he drafted in his 1988 paper proved useful to understand the natural playing behavior of children. Scientists from Scandinavia (Kyttä, 2002, 2004; Sandseter, 2009), the Netherlands (Van Dijk-Wesselius et al., 2022), and other parts of the world (Dobson et al., 2021) found inspiration in Harry's taxonomy to come to grips with both the nature of different settings and the behavior children and adults can and do perform in it.

For Rob, the reading of Heft's writings and the work that preceded (Barker & Wright, 1951) and followed it (Kyttä, 2002, 2004) was the reason for leaving the lab in his empirical studies. Rob was warned before by Reed about the horrible state psychology is in – "it is scandalous ... that psychologists know nothing about ... activities [as] pounding, chopping, cutting, tying, molding, dyeing, shaping, hearing, poking, etching, smearing, and roasting ..." (Reed, 1996, p. 122). But it took some time for Rob to leave behind the experimental tradition in ecological psychology that he had been trained in during his PhD. Yet, in 2014, he decided to change course and started to study, together with colleagues and students (Prieske et al., 2015; Van Der Schaaf et al., 2020; Withagen & Caljouw, 2017), the effects of architectural interventions on the daily behavior of people. How do the environment's affordances shape and constrain our everyday behavior and experience?

2.4 The primacy of the social in a changing world

Heft's theorizing about the human environment also affected the philosophical work of Rietveld, Kiverstein, Bruineberg, and Ludger, albeit in slightly different ways. Heft emphasized that it is chiefly through the "social constitution of the agent-environment system" that a wider world opens up to human organisms (Heft, 2007). Across generations the human way of living has become constitutionally social, affecting the evolution of human and nonhuman animals alike. The social aspects of human life, Heft asserted, are thus emphatically not separate additions to non-social processes of perception and action. Rather, the ongoing social constitution of our niche means that perceiving and acting has been shaped by normative demands and needs to conform to ways of doing things (Costall, 1995, 1997; Hodges & Baron, 1992). It is in that sense an environment "of an entirely different order" as Heft approvingly quotes Gibson (Heft, 2017, p. 128). Indeed, much of the possibilities for action we perceive are co-created with other people. In Heft's (2007, p. 90, emphasis in original) words:

> [o]ne would be hard-pressed to find a place on Earth that does not bear the mark of human actions of both an intentional and an unintentional nature .... Even our so-called natural areas in cities (urban parks) are in fact designed and require constant maintenance to preserve their "natural" qualities. In more remote locations in the United States, places such as national parks are *products* of conservation efforts that go back to the early 20th century.

Such considerations led Heft to rethink ecological psychology's central notion of "affordance." If affordances are to account seamlessly for social life, it needed to be a developmental concept — affordances, in short, became sociohistorical over time. This would prove of crucial importance to several ecological theories developing in the Netherlands. Rietveld and Kiverstein's (2014) paper "A rich landscape of affordances" notably elaborates on this very idea. In this paper, a strong plea is made for understanding affordances in relation to "abilities available in a form of life" (Rietveld & Kiverstein, 2014, p. 330). And "in the human case, this form of life is sociocultural, hence the abilities that are acquired by participating in skilled practices are abilities to act adequately according to the norms of the practice" (ibid.).

An important implication of tying affordances to skills and social practices is that ecological psychology can "scale up." As already anticipated by Gibson (1979/1986, p. 255 ff.), and demonstrated by, among others, Heft (1989, 2001, 2007), the ecological approach is not confined to explaining motor behaviors as the catching of balls or the diving of gannets, but has the potential to be developed into a whole new psychology (Costall, 1995; Reed, 1996).

Of particular interest here is Heft's discussion of Roger Barker's discovery of the "behavior setting," which had a significant impact on current ecological thinking in the Netherlands. After compiling several close studies of single subjects, as in *One Boy's Day*, Barker noticed something profound: the behavior of a single child across different social situations showed more variability than the behavior of different children within a particular situation. Such situations or "behavior settings" are crucial to the everyday structuring of one's activities. A behavior setting, Heft taught us, is a sociocultural situation produced by the collective activity of multiple participants with definite temporal and geographical boundaries (Heft, 2007, p. 98).

Heft has contributed significantly to reviving some of Barker's ideas and moreover connected them in a fruitful way to Gibsonian theorizing. This has reverberated globally throughout the ecological community (Araujo & Davids, 2009; Kiverstein & Rietveld, 2012; Marsh et al., 2009; McGann, 2014). In the Netherlands, it was for instance taken up by Bruineberg and Rietveld (2014, pp. 3–4) in the development of their ideas on the selective openness to relevant affordances:

> [P]lace-affordances (the affordances of say, university libraries, railway stations, supermarkets, swimming pools or restaurants) are the contexts in which many of our activities unfold … . Which affordances are relevant depends on the "behavior setting" (Barker, 1968; Heft, 2001): the possibility of calling a waiter is relevant in a restaurant but not when we are in a supermarket. Being in a restaurant constrains or pre-structures which affordances are relevant to me. In order to be responsive to the appropriate affordances of a situation (e.g., calling out a waiter in a restaurant), one needs to be well attuned to the current context (one needs to have the ability to deal and be ready to deal with restaurants and waiters).

People have learned to be responsive to a rich variety of behavior settings, from drugstores, and baseball games to restaurants and classrooms. A student, say, entering a classroom will be immediately drawn to do the right thing, to sit facing the blackboard, to make notes, listen or ask questions. They typically learned not to talk too loud, burst into song, stand on the tables or take the teacher's seat. The normative demands of a behavior setting can in fact be thought of as directly experienced by its participants, as we shall see later. Moreover, one's responsivity to the appropriate affordances reciprocally sustains that very normativity for all others involved.

2.5 Taking experience seriously

The final important theme which Heft brought to the ecological community in general and to developing theories in the Netherlands in particular is his emphasis on the experiential aspect of human perception and action. Consider the opening remarks to Heft's (1989, p. 2) paper on the intentional analysis of affordances:

> At the simplest level, environmental features are often experienced as attractive, positive, and alluring, or inversely as unattractive, negative, and repelling. Moreover, environmental features are often experienced with respect to their functional significance: we perceive features in terms of the ways we can interact with them. In short, the features of our world are not value-free.

Inspired by Merleau-Ponty's phenomenology of the living body, Heft found a place for the intentional character of perception and action in ecological theorizing. Within an ongoing sociohistorical process, affordances have an experiential pull, they "invite" us to do something. And as the organism-environment relation that defines affordances for humans is continuously developing within a social environment, so too could our experience of said environment grow. This view resonated strongly with Dutch theorists who were following Dreyfus' phenomenology of the invitational nature of our surrounding world. Indeed, ever since his reading of Dreyfus' work, Rob examines the soliciting character of the environment in both his empirical and his theoretical work. For instance, his recent attempt to develop an affective Gibsonian psychology is rooted in the phenomenological insight that the world does something to us, that it moves us (Withagen, 2022). Also Dings, Bruineberg, Kiverstein, Rietveld, De Haan, and Ludger examined this experiential pull in their (philosophical) work. For example, in an insightful series of studies, De Haan et al. demonstrated that the lived environment (i.e., "the field of soliciting affordances") of people suffering from obsessive compulsive disorder can change drastically after a deep brain stimulation (De Haan et al., 2013).

In order to broaden the scope of ecological psychology to include an endless variety of human involvement, Heft's view however requires a conception of experience that, for instance, enables the normativity of behavior settings to be perceived along with the affordances that come to stand out in light of that context. In his book, Heft notably explores the relation between ecological psychology and James' radical empiricism. On James' account of experience, "the relations that connect experiences must themselves be experienced relations, and any kind of relation experienced must be accounted as 'real' as anything else in the system" (James, 1904, p. 534, emphasis suppressed). Such considerations, as well as those from Gestalt psychology and elsewhere, lead Heft to consider experience in terms of a "relational field of person and environment" (Heft, 2001, p. 362; Heft, 2017). Experiences, from normativity to knowing, reflecting to caring, can and should be understood in terms of a widening field of practical relations one maintains with the environment across a lifetime.

Heft's reorientation of psychology, to look for the wider environment to understand its subject, was not only an inspiration to Rob. It would in turn be an important source of inspiration for Ludger. Heft's approach resonated with Ludger's "horizontal" attitude of looking closer at the wider context of action to understand human experience (Van Dijk, 2016; Van Dijk & Withagen, 2014). Moreover, on a radical empiricist's view, ambiguity, fragility and indeterminacy are everyday experiences and, as such, should be considered perfectly real aspects of our environmental engagement (Van Dijk, 2020). Heft's work in this radical empiricist spirit as well as the pragmatist ideas in works by, for example, Shotter (1983) and Costall (2004) would inspire Ludger to consider the reality of "transitional" experiences as on par with more determinate aspects of our environment.

2.6 Concluding remarks

Ecological psychology in the Netherlands goes way back. In the early 1980s, a group of human movement scientists in Amsterdam found inspiration in the physical approach that was developed by Turvey, Kugler, and colleagues. Although the center of gravity of the ecological movement in our country shifted to Groningen in the last decades, this principled physical approach continues to have an impact on the thinking of a substantial group of Dutch ecologists. Meanwhile, Harry has worked tirelessly to open the field up to other ways of thinking. Another group of ecologically inclined thinkers in our country, some coming out of the old tradition, some from philosophical quarters, found inspiration in such an approach. In their view physical law is not always a good starting point for understanding the human ecology. We are first and foremost social beings who exist in relation to one another, who collectively search for meaning in the environment, and create new meaning in never ending social practices.

We saw how Harry combines seminal theoretical contributions with a keen historical awareness. Perhaps because of the latter, Harry tends to develop his own views by letting his historical subjects speak: Gibson, Barker, Holt, James and others. We too could not discussing Harry's work, in part, through discussing these scholars. Harry himself emphasizes time and again that his views on ecological psychology are already present in Gibson's writings (Heft, 2007, p. 88 ff.). Yet in our view, Harry's work goes beyond the work of any of his subjects in isolation – including that of Gibson. Harry steadily but forcefully brought a rich sociohistorical perspective on human life to ecological psychology. His efforts to strengthen forgotten historical lines and search for a productive exchange with other disciplines, old and new, makes for an enriched and enduring ecological psychology for the decades to come.

Acknowledgments

We gratefully acknowledge Peter Beek, Reinoud Bootsma, Caroline Hummels, Claire Michaels, Theo Mulder, Erik Rietveld, Audrey Van Der Meer, John Van Der Kamp, Ruud Van Der Weel, and the Groningen group for sharing all the wonderful stories about the ecological movement in the Netherlands and for providing us with feedback on an earlier draft of this chapter. Thanks also to an anonymous reviewer for useful comments on an earlier version of this chapter.

Note

1 At this point, it is interesting to note that some ecologists who have been trained at the VU have also gone abroad for their PhD and/or have now established their lab outside The Netherlands (including Reinoud Bootsma in France, David Jacobs in Spain, Beatrix Vereijken, Audrey Van der Meer and Ruud Van Weel in Norway, and Gert-Jan Pepping in Australia). In this chapter, however, we outline some movements that have taken place *within* our

country, focusing on the impact of Heft's work. Moreover, as with any attempt to present a history, especially an attempt as brief as ours, the presentation is necessarily selective. We apologize to those we left out.

References

Araujo, D., & Davids, K. (2009). Ecological approaches to cognition and action in sport and exercise: Ask not only what you do, but where you do it. *International Journal of Sport Psychology, 40*(1), 5.

Barker, R. G. (1968). *Ecological psychology: Concepts and methods for studying the environment of human behavior*. Stanford, CA: Stanford University Press.

Barker, R. G., & Wright, H. F. (1951). *One boy's day*. New York: Harper & Row.

Beek, P. J. (1989). *Juggling dynamics*. Amsterdam: Free University Press.

Bootsma, R. J. (1988). *The timing of rapid interceptive actions: Perception-action coupling in the control and acquisition of skill*. Amsterdam: Free University Press.

Bruineberg, J., & Rietveld, E. (2014). Self-organization, free energy minimization, and optimal grip on a field of affordances. *Frontiers in Human Neuroscience, 8*, 599.

Costall, A. (1995). Socializing affordances. *Theory & Psychology, 5*, 467–481.

Costall, A. (1997). The meaning of things. *Social Analysis, 41*, 76–85.

Costall, A. (2004). From Darwin to Watson (and cognitivism) and back again: The principle of animal-environment mutuality. *Behavior and Philosophy, 32*, 179–195.

De Boer, B. (2021). Explaining multistability: Postphenomenology and affordances of technologies. *AI & Society*, 1–11.

De Haan, S., Rietveld, E., Stokhof, M., & Denys, D. (2013). The phenomenology of deep brain stimulation-induced changes in OCD: An enactive affordance-based model. *Frontiers in Human Neuroscience, 7*, 653.

Dings, R. (2018). Understanding phenomenological differences in how affordances solicit action: An exploration. *Phenomenology and the Cognitive Sciences, 17*, 681–699.

Dings, R. (2021). Meaningful affordances. *Synthese, 199*, 1855–1875.

Dobson, J., Birch, J., Brindley, P., Henneberry, J., McEwan, K., Mears, M., Richardson, M., & Jorgensen, A. (2021). The magic of the mundane: The vulnerable web of connections between urban nature and wellbeing. *Cities*, 102989.

Dreyfus, H. L. (2004). Merleau-Ponty and recent cognitive science. In T. Carmen & M. B. Hansen (Eds.), *The Cambridge companion to Merleau-Ponty* (pp. 129–150). Cambridge: Cambridge University Press.

Dreyfus, H. L. (2007). The return of the myth of the mental. *Inquiry, 50*, 371–377.

Gibson, James J. (1979/1986). *The ecological approach to visual perception: Classic edition*. Boston: Houghton Mifflin.

Glotzbach, P., & Heft, H. (1982). Ecological and phenomenological contributions of the psychology of perception. *Nous, 16*, 108–121.

Heft, H. (1979). The role of environmental features in route-learning: Two exploratory studies of way-finding. *Environmental Psychology and Nonverbal Behavior, 3*(3), 172–185.

Heft, H. (1983). Way-finding as the perception of information over time. *Population and Environment, 6*, 133–150.

Heft, H. (1988). Affordances of children's environments: A functional approach to environmental description. *Children's Environments Quarterly, 5*, 29–37.

Heft, H. (1989). Affordances and the body: An intentional analysis of Gibson's ecological approach to visual perception. *Journal for the Theory of Social Behaviour, 19*, 1–30.

Heft, H. (1993). A methodological note on overestimates of reaching distance: Distinguishing between perceptual and analytical judgments. *Ecological Psychology*, *5*, 255–271.

Heft, H. (2001). *Ecological psychology in context: James Gibson, Roger Barker, and the legacy of William James's radical empiricism*. Mahwah: Lawrence Erlbaum Associates.

Heft, H. (2007). The social constitution of perceiver-environment reciprocity. *Ecological Psychology*, *19*, 85–105.

Heft, H. (2017). William James' psychology, radical empiricism, and field theory: Recent developments. *Philosophical Inquiries*, *5*(2), 111–130.

Heft, H. (2020). Ecological psychology and enaction theory: Divergent groundings. *Frontiers in Psychology*, *11*, 991.

Hodges, B. H., & Baron, R. M. (1992). Values as constraints on affordances: Perceiving and acting properly. *Journal for the Theory of Social Behaviour*, *22*, 263–294.

James, W. (1904). A world of pure experience. *The Journal of Philosophy, Psychology and Scientific Methods*, *1*(20), 533–543.

Kiverstein, J., & Rietveld, E. (2012). Dealing with context through action-oriented predictive processing. *Frontiers in Psychology*, *3*, 421.

Kugler, P., & Turvey, M. T. (1987). *Information, natural law, and the self-assembly of rhythmic movement*. Hillsdale: Lawrence Erlbaum Associates.

Kyttä, M. (2002). Affordance of children's environments in the context of cities, small towns, suburbs and rural villages in Finland and Belarus. *Journal of Environmental Psychology*, *22*, 109–123.

Kyttä, M. (2004). The extent of children's independent mobility and the number of actualized affordances as criteria for child-friendly environments. *Journal of Environmental Psychology*, *24*, 179–198.

Marsh, K. L., Johnston, L., Richardson, M. J., & Schmidt, R. C. (2009). Toward a radically embodied, embedded social psychology. *European Journal of Social Psychology*, *39*(7), 1217–1225.

McGann, M. (2014). Enacting a social ecology: Radically embodied intersubjectivity. *Frontiers in Psychology*, *5*, 1321.

Meijer, O. G. (1988). *The hierarchy debate: Perspectives for a theory and history of movement science*. Amsterdam: Free University Press.

Meijer, O. G., & Roth, K. (Eds.) (1988). *Complex movement behavior: 'The' motor-action controversy*. Amsterdam: Elsevier.

Prieske, B., Withagen, R., Smith, J., & Zaal, F. T. J. M. (2015). Affordances in a simple playscape: Are children attracted to challenging affordances? *Journal of Environmental Psychology*, *41*, 101–111.

Reed, E. S. (1982). An outline of a theory of action systems. *Journal of Motor Behavior*, *14*, 98–134.

Reed, E. S. (1985). An ecological approach to the evolution of behavior. In T. Johnston & A. Pietrewicz (Eds.), *Issues in the ecological study of learning* (pp. 357–383). Hillsdale: Lawrence Erlbaum Associates.

Reed, E. S. (1988). *James J. Gibson and the psychology of perception*. New Haven: Yale University Press.

Reed, E. S. (1996). *Encountering the world: Toward an ecological psychology*. New York: Oxford University Press.

Rietveld, E., & Kiverstein, J. (2014). A rich landscape of affordances. *Ecological Psychology*, *26*, 252–325.

Sandseter, E. B. H. (2009). Affordances for risky play in preschool: The importance of features in the play environment. *Early Childhood Education Journal, 36*, 439–446.
Savelsbergh, G. J. P., Whiting, H. T. A., & Bootsma, R. J. (1991). Grasping tau. *Journal of Experimental Psychology: Human Perception and Performance, 19*, 315–322.
Shotter, J. (1983). "Duality of structure" and "intentionality" in an ecological psychology. *Journal for the Theory of Social Behaviour, 13*, 19–44.
Tamboer, J. W. I. (1985). *Mensbeelden achter bewegingsbeelden*. Haarlem: De Vrieseboch.
Van Der Kamp, J., Rivas, F., Van Doorn, H., Savelsbergh, G. (2008). Ventral and dorsal system contributions to visual anticipation in fast ball sports. *International Journal of Sport Psychology, 39*, 100–130.
Van Der Niet, A. G. (2017). When I say ... affordance perception. *Medical Education, 52*(4), 362–363.
Van Der Schaaf, A. L., Caljouw, S. R., & Withagen, R. (2020). Are children attracted to play elements with an open function? *Ecological Psychology, 32*, 79–94.
Van Dijk, L. (2016). Laying down a path in talking. *Philosophical Psychology, 29*(7), 993–1003.
Van Dijk, L. (2020). Temporalizing ontology: A case for pragmatic emergence. *Synthese, 198*, 1–14.
Van Dijk, L. (2021). Psychology in an indeterminate world. *Perspectives on Psychological Science, 16*, 577–589.
Van Dijk, L., & Rietveld, E. (2018). Situated anticipation. *Synthese*, 1–23.
Van Dijk, L., & Withagen, R. (2014). The horizontal worldview: A Wittgensteinian attitude towards scientific psychology. *Theory & Psychology, 24*, 3–18.
Van Dijk-Wesselius, J., Maas, J., Van Vugt, M., & Van den Berg, A. E. (2022). A comparison of children's play and non-play behavior before and after schoolyard greening monitored by video observations. *Journal of Environmental Psychology, 80*, 101760.
Whiting, H. T. A. (1969). *Acquiring ball skills: A psychological interpretation*. London: Bells and Sons.
Whiting, H. T. A. (Ed.) (1984). *Human motor actions: Bernstein reassessed*. Amsterdam: Elsevier.
Withagen, R. (2004). The pickup of nonspecifying variables does not entail indirect perception. *Ecological Psychology, 16*, 237–253.
Withagen, R. (2022). *Affective Gibsonian psychology*. New York: Routledge.
Withagen, R., & Caljouw, S. R. (2017). Aldo van Eyck's playgrounds: Aesthetics, affordances, and creativity. *Frontiers in Psychology, 8*, 1130.
Withagen, R., & Van Wermeskerken, M. (2010). The role of affordances in the evolutionary process reconsidered: A niche construction perspective. *Theory & Psychology, 20*, 489–510.

3
CONTRARY IMAGINATIONS
Radical empiricism or pragmatism?[1]

Alan Costall

3.1 Introduction

In 1929, Arthur Lovejoy published a book critically reviewing what he termed "the revolt against dualism."

> The supposition, so long accepted as unchallengeable, that all apprehension of objective reality is mediated through subjective existents, that "ideas" forever interpose themselves between the knower and the objects which he would know, has become repellent and incredible to many of our contemporaries; and the cleavage of the universe into two realms having almost no attributes in common, the divorce between experience and nature, the isolation of the mental from the physical order, has seemed … to be unendurable in itself and the source of numerous artificial problems and gratuitous difficulties … . (Lovejoy, 1929, pp. 3–4)

The contemporaries he identified as being repelled by this kind of dualism were quite a mixed bunch, including Samuel Alexander, Edwin E. Burtt, John Dewey, George Herbert Mead, Arthur E. Murphy, Bertrand Russell, the wonderful but side-lined Susan Stebbing,[2] Alfred North Whitehead, and the person in this bunch most relevant for this commentary, Edwin B. Holt.

Gibson's work could be regarded as a later contribution to this revolt against dualism. However, in order to place the rest of this chapter in context, it is important to bear in mind that Gibson regarded his work as providing reasons for *realism* (Gibson, 1967a; Reed & Jones, 1982).

3.2 Radical empiricism and/or pragmatism?

Harry Heft (2001/2016) in his very fine book, *Ecological Psychology in Context*, identified important influences and connections with Gibson, such as Gestalt psychology and Roger Barker's ecological psychology. The important point is that the book is structured around Harry's primary argument that Gibson's approach was largely based on William James's *radical empiricism* – not *realism* – thanks in large part to the mediating role of Edwin B. Holt. Holt was a devoted student of William James, and Gibson, in turn, was, at least for a time, a devoted follower of Holt. Harry certainly makes a very good case for this intellectual lineage.

I have read Holt in some detail and his attack on representationalism is outstanding. It is witty and about the best critique I have seen (Costall, 2011). But I have never managed to get my head around *radical empiricism*. The problem is that I had already become set in my ways long before I read Harry's book. I had seen a different kind of historical context for Gibson, one which runs from John Dewey, then to William James, and on to figures such as George Herbert Mead. This is the tradition of *pragmatism*, with its emphasis on the primacy of action, the rejection of what Dewey called the spectator theory of knowing, and, with Dewey and Mead, the reminder that we are essentially – biologically – social animals.[3] Most importantly, there is pragmatism's recognition of the pivotal role of Charles Darwin in setting psychology off in the right direction.[4]

My purpose in this chapter is not to insist that my "take" on Gibson is right and Harry's is wrong. There are two main reasons for putting up with our "contrary imaginations."

First, William James was devoted both to pragmatism *and* radical empiricism:

> To avoid misunderstanding at least let me say that there is no logical connection between pragmatism, as I understand it, and a doctrine I have recently set forth as 'radical empiricism'. The latter stands on its own feet. One may entirely reject it, and still be a pragmatist. (James, 1907, Preface, p. ix)

So, thanks to the permission of William James, I think Harry and myself can agree to feel free to disagree.

Second, there is a serious problem Gibson sets anyone of us trying to place him historical context. Gibson was a shocker about failing to acknowledge the specific influences of other people on his own thinking. The following are some examples:

1. The essence of Gibson's early "ground theory" (Gibson, 1950, p. 6) had already been set out perfectly clearly by Harvey Carr on the opening page of his textbook on space perception: "Any two separated objects are seen against an intervening background consisting of a part of some other object or group of objects such as a wall, a forest, a lake, the ground, or the sky" (1935, p. 1). Gibson does not credit Carr at all with this basic idea, even though he did cite him in relation to a different and much more obscure topic: binocular vision

and the "horopter" (for more on Carr's influence upon Gibson, see Reed, 1988, pp. 119–120).
2. Gibson's influential concept of optic flow (Gibson, 1979) was anticipated in an unpublished report by G. C. Grindley at Oxford, and, according to John Mollon (1997), Gibson had actually read it. Gibson never acknowledged Grindley.
3. Gibson had in his possession a "well-marked" copy of a paper by T. A. Ryan which set out the basic idea of affordances, including the claim that affordances can be immediately perceived (Gibson, 1982, pp. 61–62): "'The dollar bill is an object with which I can pay', a book may be 'a weight to hold my papers down' and a hammer 'a thing for pounding'" (Ryan, 1938, p. 642). Gibson does refer to this paper in a chapter on "meaning" in his first book, which anticipates the concept of affordances, but this is a chapter disconnected from his obsession with surfaces in the rest of the book (Gibson, 1950, p. 199). However, Gibson makes no subsequent references to Ryan, not even when he set out the historical background to his "theory of affordances" (Gibson, 1979, pp. 138–140).
4. Gibson was impressed by the work of Merleau-Ponty and recommended his work to his students. There are some distinct echoes of Merleau-Ponty in Gibson's later publications, notably concerning our embodied awareness of our selves. Gibson did make a fleeting reference to him in a contribution to an edited book on the psychology of knowing: "There is nothing special about 'depth' in the environment." As Merleau-Ponty somewhere pointed out, "depth is nothing but breadth seen from the side" (Gibson, 1972, p. 223). I can find no other references in Gibson's writings to this major figure in the philosophy of perception.
5. Although Gibson made general references to Koffka and Holt, both of whom must have surely been among the most influences on his thinking, he never explained in detail their *positive* impact, and, as far as I can see, did his best to distance himself from both of them (Gibson, 1967b, 1971).
6. Finally, I can't believe that Fritz Heider did not also have a significant influence on Gibson, probably the first to set out an ecological approach (along with Brunswik). But I can find no reference to him at all in Gibson's 1979 book (but see Gibson, 1950, p. 63, and Gibson, 1966, p. 187). Gibson and Heider were both based at Northampton for an extended period during Gibson's time at Smith College. You could say the same about Gibson's treatment of Edward Tolman (see later).

In short, we cannot rely on the sacred texts to resolve whether Gibson is best placed within either the tradition of radical empiricism or else pragmatism. For all I know, it might be best to place him in both. The interesting question is in which ways each of these two interpretations of Gibson can help us to decide *where to go next*. That, after all, is the pragmatist approach: "truths should have practical consequences" (James, 1909, p. 31).

3.3 Gibson and the legacy of pragmatism

When we take pragmatism as a basis to the ecological approach, we need to be clear what it is we think we are approaching. The standard line is that the ecological approach is about perception, and more definitively about "*direct* perception." As I realized some time ago, "direct" in this context is a contrastive term, and what Gibson understood by *indirect* perception ended up as by no means coherent (Costall, 1989). It involved a contrast between inferential cue-based rather than information-based perception, the perception of pictures, etc., rather than encountering the world, and, for me the most troublesome, perception that is not *socially* mediated. These contrasts do not line up. After all, Gibson argued that pictures were themselves based on information, such as formless invariants. And surely, infants entering into their home country and also adults visiting a distant country rely on the support of others to make sense of the world around them.

From a pragmatist perspective, the focus shifts from perception to action, and a notion of an environment that implies "supports" for agency. These are what Tolman termed *discriminanda* and *manipulanda*:

> Behavior cannot go off *in vacuo*. It requires a complementary "supporting" or "holding-up." ... A rat cannot "run down an alley" without an actual floor to push his feet against, actual walls to steer between, actual free space ahead to catapult into. And in a discrimination-box, he cannot "choose" the white side from the black without actual whites and blacks continuously to support and verify such a choice. Behavior-acts ... demand and are sustained by later coming *behavior-supports*. (Tolman, 1932, p. 85)[5]

This brings me to my fundamental point: that mind and agency cannot be understood independently of such supports. In short, we are talking about the principle of *mutuality*.

Here is probably one of the earliest pragmatist statements about this business of *being in the world*:

> The idea of environment is a necessity to the idea of organism, and with the conception of environment comes the impossibility of considering psychical life as an individual, isolated thing developing in a vacuum. (Dewey, 1884, p. 285)

And here is William James making the point even more explicitly about mutualism:

> The great fault of the older rational psychology was to set up the soul as an absolute spiritual being with certain faculties of its own ... *Mind and world ... have been evolved together, and in consequence are something of a mutual fit*. (James, 1892, pp. 3–4)

But agents are not just receptive but structure their circumstances:

> The organism does not stand about, Micawber-like, waiting for something to turn up. It does not wait passive and inert for something to impress itself upon it from without. The organism acts ... upon its surroundings. (Dewey, 1920, p. 86)

We *make* our circumstances, if (as Marx once put it) *not* under conditions of our own choosing:

> In spite of inventions which enable men to use the energies of nature for their purposes, we are still far from habitually treating knowledge as the method of active control of nature and experience. We tend to think of it after the model of a spectator viewing a finished picture rather than after that of the artist producing the painting. Thus there arise all the questions of epistemology with which the technical student of philosophy is so familiar, and which have made modern philosophy in especial so remote from the understanding of the everyday person and from the results and processes of science. For these questions all spring from the assumption of a merely beholding mind on one side and a foreign and remote object to be viewed and noted on the other. They ask how a mind and world, subject and object, so separate and independent can by any possibility come into such relationship to each other as to make true knowledge possible. If knowing were habitually conceived as active and operative, after the analogy of experiment guided by hypothesis, or of invention guided by imagination of some possibility, it is not too much to say that the first effect would be to emancipate philosophy from all the epistemological puzzles which now perplex it. For all these arise from a conception of the relation of mind and world, subject and object, in knowing, which assumes that to know is to seize upon what is already in existence. (Dewey 1950, pp. 107–108)

And here is William James making this point (in a way that his elegant, and much too wordy novelist brother Henry could hardly have done):

> I, for my part, cannot escape the consideration, forced upon me at every turn, that the knower is not simply a mirror floating with no foot-hold anywhere, and passively reflecting an order that he comes upon and finds simply existing. The knower is an actor, and co-efficient of the truth on one side, whilst on the other he registers the truth which he helps to create. Mental interests, hypotheses, postulates, so far as they are bases for human action; action which to a great extent transforms the world; help to *make* the truth which they declare. In other words, there belongs to *mind, from its birth upward, a spontaneity, a vote. It is in the game, and not a mere looker-on* ... . (James, 1878, p. 17, final italics added)

Finally, John Dewey made this same point about the mutual – reciprocal – relation between agents and world:

> The increasing control over the environment is not as if the environment were something there fixed and the organism responded at this point and that, adapting itself by fitting itself in, in a plaster-like way … . The psychological or historical fallacy is likely to come in here and we conceive the environment, which is really the outcome of the process of development, which has gone on developing along with the organism, as if it was something which had been there from the start, and the whole problem has been for the organism to accommodate itself to that set of given surroundings. (Dewey, 1898/1976, pp. 283–284)

The reviewer of this chapter raised the following question: "is [pragmatism] not the way we are understanding Gibson already?" I can't say that I have seen the aforementioned radical points made by James and Dewey showing up prominently, if at all, in the ecological literature. Admittedly it is a long time ago, but when Stuart Katz and Bill Noble and I questioned Gibson's case for realism, we were faced with disbelief verging on hostility from the Gibsonian fundamentalists (Costall, 1981; Katz, 1987; Noble, 1981).[6]

3.4 Conclusion

So, what is the point of approaching Gibson from the direction of pragmatism. The problem with perception is that it doesn't, in itself, make *anything* happen. Even now the concept of affordances continues to be framed as involving a relation between the environment and a *perceiver*. This is why, for me, placing Gibson within the tradition of pragmatism could (appropriately) *make a difference*: putting the emphasis on the primacy of action. Whether Gibson placed himself in the tradition of pragmatism is a moot point. Gibson, as I have said, was pretty effective at covering his traces.

Finally, the reviewer of this chapter also suggested I should provide a more definite conclusion. I would like to think I have already made myself implicitly clear, except to stress that Harry Heft and I are agreed (I think!) on one point: Gibson wasn't really a realist.

Notes

1 I had planned to use the subtitle "When Alan met Harry" but on the good advice of a fellow contributor to this volume I have hidden this away in this footnote so that nobody will ever know about it.
2 Susan Stebbing (1937) weaned Gibson away from Eddington's dualistic nonsense about two worlds. See Gibson (1968, p. 22).
3 "The non-social individual is an abstraction arrived at by imagining what man would be if all his human qualities were taken away" (Dewey, 1888, p. 232).

4 That is until John Watson came along and undermined the very good work of the pragmatists and functionalists, and led the way to cognitivism (Costall, 2004).
5 Tolman does not show up in Gibson's last book! Tolman along with Gibson was a student of Holt.
6 In 1992, Ed Reed and I exchanged several emails about whether affordances were independent or relational, Ed adopting the manner of an old testament sage. Eventually, we could see that we were getting nowhere and gave up.

References

Carr, H. A. (1935). *An introduction to space perception*. New York: Longmans, Green.
Costall, A. (1981). On how so much information controls so much behaviour. In G. Butterworth (Ed.), *Infancy and epistemology* (pp. 30–51). New York: St. Martin's Press/Brighton: Harvester Press.
Costall, A. (1989). A closer look at 'direct perception'. In A. Gellatly, D. Rogers & J. A. Sloboda (Eds.), *Cognition and social worlds* (pp. 10–21). Oxford: Clarendon Press.
Costall, A. (2004). From Darwin to Watson (and Cognitivism) and back again: The principle of animal-environment mutuality. *Behavior & Philosophy*, *32*, 179–195.
Costall, A. (2011). Against representationalism: James Gibson's secret debt to E. B. Holt. In E. P. Charles (Ed.), *A new look at new realism: The psychology and philosophy of E. B. Holt* (pp. 243–262). New Brunswick: Transaction Publishers.
Dewey, J. (1884). The new psychology. *Andover Review*, *2*, 278–289. http://psychclassics.yorku.ca/Dewey/newpsych.htm
Dewey, J. (1888/1967). The ethics of democracy (1888). In J. A. Boydston (Ed.), *The early works, 1882–1898* (Vol. 1). Carbondale: South Illinois University Press.
Dewey, J. (1898/1976). *Lectures on psychological and political ethics: 1898* (Edited with an introduction by D. L. Koch). New York: Haffner Press.
Dewey, J. (1920). *Reconstruction in Philosophy*. New York: Holt and Co.
Dewey, J. (1950). *Reconstruction in philosophy* (With a new introduction by the author). New York: The New American library.
Gibson, J. J. (1950). *The perception of the visual world*. Boston: Houghton Mifflin.
Gibson, J. J. (1966). *The senses considered as perceptual systems*. Houghton Mifflin Company.
Gibson, J. J. (1967a). New reasons for realism. *Synthese*, *17*, 167–172.
Gibson, J. J. (1967b). Autobiography. In E. G. Boring & G. Lindzey (Eds.), *A history of psychology in autobiography*, Vol. 5 (pp. 127–143). New York: Appleton-Century-Crofts.
Gibson, J. J. (1968). *The senses considered as perceptual systems*. London, UK: Allen & Unwin. (Original work published 1966.)
Gibson, J. J. (1971). On the legacies of Koffka's principles. *Journal of the History of the Behavioral Sciences*, *7*, 3–9.
Gibson, J. J. (1972). A theory of direct visual perception. In J. R. Royce & W. W. Rozeboom (Eds.), *The psychology of knowing* (215–240). New York: Gordon & Breach.
Gibson, J. J. (1979). *The ecological approach to visual perception: Classic edition*. Houghton Mifflin.
Gibson, E. J. (1982). The concept of affordance in development: The renascence of functionalism. In W. Andrew Collins (Eds.), *The concept of development* (pp. 55–82). Hillsdale, NJ: Lawrence Erlbaum.
Heft, H. (2001/2016). *Ecological psychology in context: James Gibson, Roger Barker, and the legacy of William James's radical empiricism*. London: Routledge. (First published in 2001.)
James, W. (1878) Remarks on Spencer's definition of mind as correspondence. *The Journal of Speculative Philosophy*, *12*(1), 1–18.

James, W. (1892). *Psychology: The briefer course*. New York: Henry Holt.
James, W. (1907). *Pragmatism: A new name for some old ways of thinking*. New York: Longmans, Green and Co.
James, W. (1909). *The meaning of truth: A sequel to "pragmatism."* New York: Holt.
Katz, S. (1987). Is Gibson a relativist? In A. Costall & A. Still (Eds.) *Cognitive psychology in question* (pp. 115–127). Brighton, UK: Harvester Press.
Lovejoy, A. O. (1929). *The revolt against dualism: An inquiry concerning the existence of ideas.* LaSalle, ILL: Open Court.
Menand, L. (2001). *The Metaphysical Club: A story of ideas in America*. New York: Farrar, Straus & Giroux.
Mollon, J. (1997). ... On the Basis of Velocity Clues Alone": Some Perceptual Themes 1946–1996. *The Quarterly Journal of Experimental Psychology Section A, 50*, 859–882.
Noble, W. (1981). Gibsonian theory and the pragmatist perspective. *Journal for the Theory of Social Behaviour, 11*, 65–85.
Reed, E. S. (1988). *James J. Gibson and the psychology of perception*. New Haven & London: Yale University Press.
Reed, E., & Jones, R. (1982). *Reason for realism: Selected essays of James J. Gibson*). Hillsdale, NJ: Lawrence Erlbaum.
Ryan, T. A. (1938). Dynamic, physiognomic, and other neglected properties of perceived objects: A new approach to comprehending. *American Journal of Psychology, 51*, 629–650.
Stebbing, L. S. (1937). *Philosophy and the physicists*. London: Methuen.
Tolman, E. C. (1932). *Purposive behavior in animals and men*. New York: The Century Co.

4
PERCEPTION AND PROBLEM SOLVING

Edward Baggs and Sune Vork Steffensen

4.1 Introduction

Gibsonian psychology sometimes comes in for criticism along the following lines (Clark, 1998, 149 ff.). First, the critic grants that, yes, Gibson's ecological approach may provide a useful description of how perception works, at least for some limited set of animals and situations. But the critic then asserts that Gibson's approach simply cannot scale up to provide an account of how humans perform genuinely cognitively demanding tasks. Gibsonian psychology, we are told, is a non-starter when it comes to explaining, say, how we are able to remember the recipe for a lemon drizzle cake, or how we can plan what we will be doing at this time next Tuesday.

Harry Heft has done more than most to defend Gibson's approach from such criticisms. Much of Heft's work has been focused on situating Gibson's perceptual program within the broader theoretical landscape of psychology.

Heft's 2001 book, *Ecological Psychology in Context*, encompasses two projects. The first project is historical. In the first half of the book, Heft situates Gibson's ecological approach to perception within a particular historical tradition that begins with the phenomenologically rich psychology of William James and continues through the work of James's student, E. B. Holt. Heft's second project is more programmatic. In the second part of the book, Heft aims to expand ecological psychologists' understanding of what the environment is. Gibson's work was often narrowly focused on the psychology of perception, and this led him to emphasize animals' interactions with the inanimate furniture of the world around them: the substances, surfaces, and objects. Heft wants to draw ecological psychologists' attention to the fact that the perceiving animal exists not only in a physical environment but also in a social environment, and moreover that learning to negotiate this social environment involves, at least in humans, a long history of development.

For Heft, the question of whether Gibson's perceptual program can be scaled up to encompass higher cognition is ill-posed. It is ill-posed because Gibson's program was not intended to provide a new account of cognition, only a new account of perception. To demand that Gibson's program be scaled up to encompass higher cognition is to imply that Gibsonians can only ever think of higher cognition as an outgrowth of the kinds of perceptual processes that Gibson himself was interested in. Cognition, on this framing, would be a kind of perception-plus. This is a framing that Gibsonians should reject. It would be overly restrictive to assert that all problems in psychology are problems of perception.

Gibson's account of perception does, however, provide a potentially useful starting point for rethinking psychology more broadly. The approach that Heft has advocated is to take Gibson's account of perception as the starting point, and then to situate the perceiver within the context of the rich, temporally extended structure of the social environment (Baggs, 2021; Heft, 2001, 2007, 2020a).

In this chapter, we focus on an important but overlooked suggestion that Heft has made. Heft has suggested that Gibson's perceptual program, developed principally in the four decades from the start of the Second World War to Gibson's death in 1979 (Gibson, 1950, 1966, 1979), is deeply compatible with the distributed cognition program developed primarily by cognitive scientists working in southern California in the 1980s and 1990s. Distributed cognition theory views cognition as a process that happens not only inside individuals but also extends into the social and material environment (Hollan et al., 2000). We here aim to draw out the connection between perception as a direct process (as described by Gibson) and the kinds of socially distributed problem-solving processes described by the distributed cognition theorists. We want to demonstrate that human problem solving often constitutively involves a perceptual component.

4.2 The problem solver as perceiver

The cognitive scientist Herbert Simon once noted that the format in which a problem is posed can affect how straightforward it is to find a solution. He wrote, "We all believe that arithmetic has become easier since Arabic numerals and place notation replaced Roman numerals, although I know of no theoretic treatment that explains why" (Simon, 1996, 132). On the same page, Simon offers a definition of problem solving. He writes, "Solving a problem simply means representing it so as to make the solution transparent" (Simon, 1996, 132).

This is an interesting definition of problem solving because the definition immediately raises a further question. What does Simon mean when he says that the solution to a problem can become "transparent"? What he seems to be saying is that the aim of problem solving is take some difficult-to-interpret symbolic input in the form of a question (i.e., the "problem") and to manipulate this input until it is in a format that can be dealt with by the perceptual system. In other words,

Simon is suggesting that to solve a problem is to manipulate the environment so that the problem's solution goes from being difficult to perceive to being easy to perceive.

The principal text within the field of distributed cognition is Edwin Hutchins's *Cognition in the Wild* (Hutchins, 1995). In the book, Hutchins makes use of Simon's definition of problem solving. Hutchins's text is based on observations of a navigation team on board a naval vessel. One of the main tasks that this team performs is to continuously plot the current position of the ship onto a paper navigation chart. This is achieved through the coordinated use of a series of instruments, procedures, and communication techniques, the result of which is a set of three pencil marks drawn on the paper navigation chart, forming a triangle that indicates where the ship currently is. Echoing Simon, Hutchins writes,

> The basic procedures of navigation are accomplished by a cycle of activity, called the fix cycle, in which representations of the spatial relationship of the ship to known landmarks are created, transformed, and combined in such a way that the solution to the problem of position fixing is transparent. (Hutchins, 1995, 117)

To assert that a problem's solution can be "transparent" would seem to be similar to asserting that the solution can be perceived directly. If this is correct, then we have prima facie reason for thinking that Gibson's program is compatible with the distributed cognition program. There are other reasons to think that the two programs are compatible. In more recent work, Hutchins explicitly appeals to Gibson's perceptual program to support a distributed conception of the social environment (Hutchins, 2010, 2014). Meanwhile, according to Heft (2001), Hutchins's 1995 book is itself already an example of ecological psychology in the Gibsonian tradition: "Hutchins's work is an important contribution to [Gibsonian] ecological psychology, taking the analysis of meaningful environmental structures to a level of complexity rarely considered" (Heft, 2001, 367). The key to unifying the two programs will be to formulate a version of distributed cognition theory that is grounded in direct perception. It will here be necessary to briefly outline what Gibson meant by his claim that perception can be direct.

4.3 Direct perception is based on structure in energy

Visual perception seems to operate at a distance from the worldly objects toward which it is directed. When you look at the objects situated at the other side of a room, it seems as though the only evidence that you could possibly draw upon for detecting the structure of the world "over there" is the energy that you are able to detect at your receptor surfaces. The question that follows is: how do organisms overcome the seeming epistemic gulf between distal environmental structure and local receptor surfaces?

The classical theory of perception has it that animals are able to overcome this epistemic gap because they add something to the incoming sensory data (Vicente & Burns, 1996). For many classical theorists, including such influential figures as Kant and Helmholtz, sensory data enter into the perceptual process as an unorganized manifold, a patchwork of momentary impressions. According to this classical theory, perceiving a world is only possible if the perceiver imposes an organization on the manifold. Most fundamentally, the perceiver is said to impose a spatial organization on the incoming signals. The perceiver is said to construct a world extending in three dimensions from a jumble of sensory impressions received at a receptor surface, the retina, that extends in only two spatial dimensions.

Gibson's theory of direct perception solves the problem of the epistemic gap in a very different way. Gibson solves the problem by denying that there is a gap in the first place. For Gibson, there is no need for the nervous system of the perceiver to organize the input because the input is already organized. The stimulus information available in the energy surrounding an observer is in fact infinitely rich in structure. This rich structure is a result of interactions between energy media (e.g., light, sound) and the substances and surfaces of the environment. The problem that the perceiver is faced with is one of selection. The perceiver must learn to attend specifically to the useful dimensions of the richly structured ambient energy.

An example of a structural element in stimulus information that we make use of in visual perception is the occluding edge (Gibson, 1979; Heft, 2020b). The occluding edge is informative about the spatial configuration of surfaces in the environmental layout. When we move from one room to another in a building, the first room is occluded from our sight, while the second room opens up as a new vista. We can reverse this transition by retracing our steps backward. Another example of a useful structural element of the optic array is the center of optic expansion. Pilots make use of this structure when guiding their plane toward a runway for landing (Gibson, 1950). The occluding edge and the center of optic expansion are invariant structures in the optic array. Such structures are what make direct perception possible.

4.4 Examples of perception in problem solving

To perceive the environment, then, the perceiver must have access to structures in ambient energy (differences in the structure of light, sound, heat, and so on) that are informative about the structure of the environment. This is what Gibson means by direct perception. We now want to suggest that this description of direct perception is immediately applicable to the domain of human problem solving. Problem solving requires perception. And for at least some subclass of human problems, a solution is found when the problem solver comes to perceive the solution via structure in ambient energy.

We will not here attempt to provide a definition of human problem solving, or a taxonomy of the different types of problems that might exist. We simply provide some examples of problem-solving behaviors, collected both from the laboratory and from the real world. Our aim is to demonstrate that problem solving is often bound up with perception. And to the extent that it is true that problem solving involves perception, Gibson's theory is relevant for theorizing about how humans solve problems.

4.4.1 The 17 animals problem

Our first example is the *17 animals problem*. The 17 animals problem presents participants with the following puzzle: "Describe how to put 17 animals in 4 enclosures in such a way that there is an odd number of animals in each enclosure." While the numerals mislead participants to look for an arithmetic solution, the solution is set theoretical. It requires that two (or more) enclosures overlap so that one animal (or another odd number of animals) can be placed in the overlap of at least two enclosures.

Frédéric Vallée-Tourangeau and colleagues have made use of the 17 animals problem in a series of experiments. One question that these authors have investigated is whether participants are more likely to find a solution to the problem if they are given physical objects that they can use to represent the animals and the enclosures, compared to if they are only given paper and a pencil. In one study, participants in one of the groups were given 17 plastic zebra figurines to represent the animals, along with a stack of pipe cleaners that could be used to construct the enclosures. Participants in the other group in the study were given an electronic tablet and a stylus that could be used much like a piece of paper and a pencil. The results were clear. Of the participants in the pipe cleaners condition, 41% found a full or a partial solution to the problem, while none of the participants in the tablet condition solved the problem (Vallée-Tourangeau et al., 2016). The authors trace this difference to the materiality of the problem presentation. Using the blank tablet and stylus, participants can try to represent the problem arithmetically, or they can try to draw shapes representing enclosures. But drawings of enclosures are immovable structures that remain where drawn. In contrast, an "enclosure" that is constructed out of pipe cleaners can easily be picked up and moved around. By physically moving the zebra figurines and the pipe cleaner enclosures, participants are more likely to serendipitously stumble upon a non-arithmetic solution (Ross & Vallée-Tourangeau, 2020).

Here we want to draw attention to the fact that this pipe cleaner assisted mode of problem solving involves an important perceptual component. We will draw on a case study provided by Steffensen et al. (2016). Here, a single participant in the pipe cleaner condition has made a non-overlapping layout and has spent the last four minutes struggling to find a solution. She realizes that she is stuck. At this point, she tries a different approach to the problem. She performs what the Gestalt psychologists called a figure-ground inversion. First, she empties the enclosures by piling all the animals in the middle of the work surface (Figure 4.1(a)). This changes the enclosures from being a stable backdrop for the movable animals into

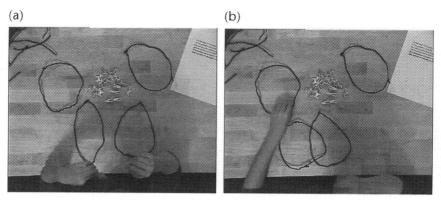

FIGURE 4.1 The layout of the four circles representing enclosures for animals, (a) before and (b) after the participant's manipulation of the bottom left enclosure

being objects of attention. The participant then turns her attention to one enclosure whose shape deviates from that of the others. She manipulates it and reshapes it. But while she is manipulating this pipe cleaner enclosure, it accidentally gets caught up with another enclosure. As she lays it back down, a visible overlap with the other enclosure is established (Figure 4.1(b)).

This overlap, as we know, is the prerequisite for a solution. However, at the moment that the overlap is created, the participant has not yet noticed this. A compelling moment in the video recording occurs 400 ms later, where we can literally observe the participant noticing that the overlap is the key to solving the problem. As illustrated in Figure 4.2, she initiates a movement of her right hand, with her thumb extended downward, and with the apparent intention of separating the two pipe cleaner enclosures from one another. But this hand movement is not concluded. Immediately prior to contact with the enclosure, the participant interrupts the movement and retracts her hand. She has perceived the solution-to-be, and

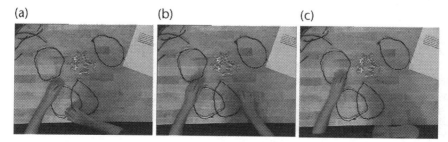

FIGURE 4.2 The participant noticing the overlap: (a) she has just placed the left enclosure down and begins a rightward movement of her right hand with her thumb extended downward; (b) immediately before touching the right enclosure and pushing it right to remove the overlap, (c) she interrupts her movement and lifts her hand to her head. There are 400 ms between the frame shown in (a) and the frame shown in (b); frame (c) is 240 ms after frame (b)

within 90 seconds, she has formed another two overlaps and distributed the animals to form a successful solution.

Both the overall series of experiments and the case study illustrate the importance of perception in solving this form of puzzle. The key difference between the two conditions in the experiment seems to be that participants in the pipe cleaner condition are more likely to create the circumstances in which the problem's solution becomes available for visual selection.

4.4.2 Visual proof of the Pythagorean theorem

A classic domain of problem solving that cognitive scientists have been interested in is mathematical theorem proving. Theorem proving is a domain of problem solving that is richly symbolic. Indeed, it is a problem domain that is deeply cognitive in the modern sense that it constitutively involves the manipulation of symbols. One is tempted to say that mathematical theorem proving has little to do with perception at all. Interestingly, however, this is not the case. Many classical problems in mathematics arise from the manipulation of geometric shapes.

A good example is the Pythagorean theorem. The theorem states that for a right triangle (Figure 4.3(a)), the square of the hypotenuse, c, is equal to the sum of the squares of the remaining sides, a and b. The theorem as just stated is quite familiar. Probably most adults remember it from school. But we are perhaps less familiar with the various proofs that can be given for the theorem. Several compelling proofs of the theorem involve visual manipulation of geometric figures.

A good first step that allows us to see what the theorem is saying is to construct three different squares that each share one of their sides with one of the three sides of the triangle. This is shown in Figure 4.3(b). We now see that what the theorem is saying is that the area of the big square, c^2, is equal to the area of the two other squares, a^2 and b^2. We can verify this by plotting the figure on paper and using scissors to cut up the two smaller squares into pieces that can be placed on top of the larger square. If we do this correctly, we will find that the pieces of paper from the two smaller squares perfectly cover the bigger square.

Still better, however, is the rearrangement proof shown in Figure 4.3(c). Here, a larger square is constructed using four identical copies of the original triangle. The side of this larger square is the same as the sum of the two smaller sides of the triangle, $a + b$. The triangles are arranged in such a way as to again create the square c^2 in the center (left panel of Figure 4.3(c)). The triangles can then be rearranged in order to create the configuration shown in the right panel in Figure 4.3(c). This second arrangement contains the same four triangles as before, and also contains the two smaller squares, a^2 and b^2. Crucially, both arrangements take up exactly the same area. In both cases, the larger square of side $a + b$ is entirely filled. Since the four triangles are the same four triangles in both arrangements, we can conclude that the remaining area, occupied by c^2 in the arrangement on the left, is the same as the remaining area occupied by $a^2 + b^2$ in the arrangement on the right.

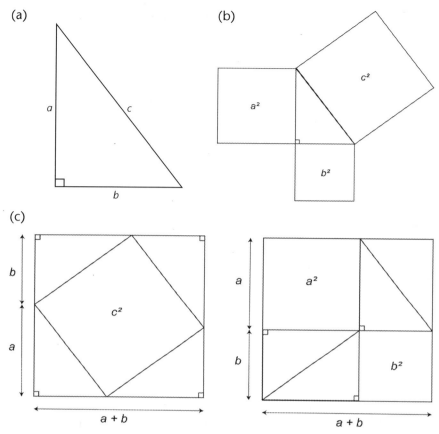

FIGURE 4.3 (a) a right triangle; (b) a visual illustration of the Pythagorean theorem: area c^2 is equal to the sum of areas of a^2 and b^2; (c) a rearrangement proof of the Pythagorean theorem demonstrating that area c^2 genuinely is equal to the sum of areas of a^2 and b^2

The rearrangement proof is an elegant proof of the Pythagorean theorem. It is true, of course, that in order to understand the proof one needs to have an appreciation of the symbols involved. What makes the proof compelling, however, is that we can see it. We can see that the larger square is perfectly filled by the four triangles and the smaller squares. We can see that there are no gaps between the pieces, no overlaps, no occluding edges to indicate that one shape is partly covering another (Gibson, 1979; Heft, 2020b). The elegance of the proof is to be found in the facts of visual perception.

4.4.3 Stove knobs

We now turn to some more everyday examples of perception's role in problem solving. A particularly rich source of examples here is to be found in the world of

Perception and problem solving

mass-produced consumer products. Consider the layout of burners on the stove in your kitchen. One problem that the designers of the stove had to address was to decide where to position the knobs or buttons that control the individual burners (Norman, 2013, 114). One option that the designers could have chosen would have been to place each knob immediately adjacent to the burner that it controls. This kind of design can work well on a simple two-burner stove of the type that is designed to be taken on camping trips. But domestic kitchen stove tops typically have more than one row of burners. For the kitchen stove top, the each-knob-immediately-adjacent-to-its-burner solution does not work so well. The problem is with the burners in the back row. Placing the knobs immediately adjacent to the back burners would require the user to reach over a potentially hot stove surface, and perhaps over steaming pots that are resting on the front burners. This would be an unsafe design.

A common solution that designers have used to avoid this problem is to place all of the knobs in a line on the front edge of the stove top. An instance of this kind of design is shown in Figure 4.4(a). This kind of design is certainly safer than the hypothetical design we just considered. But a new problem arises. The problem with the knobs-in-a-line design is that it is not immediately clear which knob controls which burner. The problem here arises from the fact that the burners are laid out in a two-dimensional spatial configuration while the knobs are laid out using only a one-dimensional spatial configuration. The relationship between the knobs and the burners is unclear because information has been lost in the compression from two-dimensionality to one-dimensionality. The designers are forced to address this by adding a small diagram next to each knob to indicate which burner the knob is connected to. This adds an additional layer of visual search. The user is now forced to visually examine each diagram in turn. The visual search terminates only after the user has discovered the knob they were looking for.

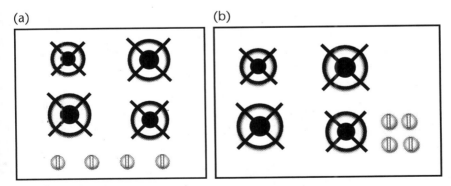

FIGURE 4.4 Two configurations for knobs on a stovetop with four burners: (a) the two-dimensional burner configuration is mapped to a one-dimensional knob configuration; (b) a more user-friendly design preserves the two-dimensional configuration of burners in the configuration of the knobs (images from Wikimedia Commons)

A more user-friendly layout of the knobs is one that maintains the spatial configuration of the burners. If the burners are laid out in a square, then the knobs should also be laid out in a square. This kind of configuration is shown in Figure 4.4(b). This kind of configuration is referred to by interface design theorists as one that maintains a "natural mapping" between controlled elements and interface elements (Norman, 2013).

It is obvious that the design in Figure 4.4(b) is easier to understand, is more user-friendly, than the one in Figure 4.4(a). But why is this, exactly? And what does it mean to say that knob configuration in Figure 4.4(b) presents a natural mapping?

One way to formalize the relationship between the layout of the burners and the layout of the knobs in Figure 4.4(b) would be to say that the knob layout is a geometric transformation of the burner layout. The absolute location of the knobs is not the same as the absolute location of the burners in space, and yet an invariant spatial configuration is maintained across the geometric translation connecting the two. Our suggestion is that the design in Figure 4.4(b) is effective because it exploits a property of our visual perceptual system. The knobs-to-burners transformation in Figure 4.4(b) is perceivable because it is similar in form to the kinds of optical transformation that we deal with all the time as we move around in the environment while looking at objects (Michaels & Carello, 1981, 30 ff.).

We can say that a natural mapping, in product design, is one where the relation of mapping elements to mapped elements is presented to the user in a format such that the invariant relation between the two sets of elements is available to the user in ambient energy.

4.4.4 Campus navigation maps

Our final example involves actual maps. Here, we are thinking of the kind of maps that are placed around the built environment as navigation aids for visitors who are unfamiliar with the local layout. An important design decision that has to be made here is over what orientation the map should have.

There are two obvious options. First, the map could be oriented so that north on the map is pointing vertically up. This is a reasonable option. We are all familiar with the convention that on maps north equals up. Maps that are printed on paper are likely to have north at the top. However, in the case of the kind of maps we are considering here, namely, maps as in-place navigation aids, there is something odd about placing the map so that north points directly up. The difficulty arises from the fact that the map is not only a representation of the local environment around the map, but it is also a part of that local environment. In order to make sense of the map, the viewer needs to be able to see, firstly, their own current position on the map. This is usually indicated by an arrow or dot marked "you are here." And secondly, the viewer must also be able to discern the relationship between the configuration represented on the map and the configuration of the environment around them. Orienting the map so that north is at the top is not

Perception and problem solving **55**

necessarily the best option, from the viewer's point of view. In fact, putting north at the top usually presents the viewer with a new problem: the viewer is now required to "mentally rotate" the map in some way so that it corresponds to the environment. (There is an exception to this rule. In the special case where the map is placed on a south-facing surface, the north-up orientation requires no rotation, for reasons that will become clear later.)

The second option is to orient the map so that what is at the top of the map represents the part of the environment that lies in front of the viewer, and what is at the bottom of the map represents the part of the environment that lies behind the viewer. This orientation is much easier to understand than the north-up map. The reason for this is that the map is already oriented in a way that makes sense relative to the front-back orientation of the viewer's own body. Conceptually, the "you are here" dot divides the map in two. The dot divides the map into a front-facing upper part and a back-facing lower part.

An example of this kind of forward-up map orientation is shown in Figure 4.5. The two photographs depict two maps that are situated on opposite sides of the same window. Notice that the map in Figure 4.5(a) is a 180°-rotated version of the map in Figure 4.5(b) (the running track shown at the bottom right in Figure 4.5(a) is the same as the one at the top left in Figure 4.5(b)). When the two versions of the map are placed alongside one another, as they are in Figure 4.5, we have the impression that something is not quite right. Looking at the two photographs, we are tempted to ask: is one of these maps upside down? In the real world, however, we suspect that few people notice the rotation. When you encounter either of these maps in their real-world context, then whichever map you are looking at, the top part of the map always depicts the world in front of you. When you are using the map as an in-place navigation aid, what you care about is the

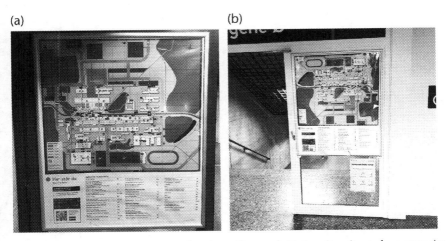

FIGURE 4.5 Two campus maps at Southern Denmark University, situated on opposite sides of the same window. The map in (a) is the same as that in (b) except rotated by 180° (notice the location of the running track in the two images)

correspondence between the map that you are looking at and the world that you are looking at. The north-up convention is irrelevant.

Note, also, that vehicle satellite navigation systems are designed to use a similar principle. When you are entering your destination into the system, the screen often shows you a conventional map with north at the top. But when you switch to driving mode, the system switches to showing you a dynamically updating map where forward is up.

The forward-up orientation of campus navigation maps (and maps in vehicle navigation systems in driving mode) is effective because it is consistent with a structural property of the optic array. In the optic array, structure that is higher up often corresponds to objects that are farther away. Think about looking out over a grassy prairie that stretches off to the horizon. The ground surface is projected into your visual field as a continuous texture gradient. The parts of the ground that are closer to your feet appear lower down in the visual field than do the parts of the ground that are closer to the horizon (Gibson, 1950). Forward-equals-up is a natural mapping here because it corresponds to a structure in the optic array that we already make use of when we perceive the world without the aid of the map.

4.5 The distributed Gibson

The four examples we have considered above demonstrate different ways that the visual perceptual system can enter into the solving of problems. Solving the 17 animals problem requires an act of perceptual selection. It requires a gestalt switch from seeing the enclosures as four individual and separate entities to noticing the spaces created inside the enclosures, and noticing the fact that the enclosures can be overlapped. Something different is at play in our second example, the visual proof of the Pythagorean theorem. The rearrangement proof of the theorem makes the solution perceivable by reformatting the problem in such a way that our visual system can easily apprehend what is going on. The rearrangement proof is effective because it turns the Pythagorean problem from a problem about metric length into a problem of surface perception.

Our other two examples illustrate how good design can prevent cognitive problems from arising in the first place. The more user-friendly design of the stove knob layout uses a configurational invariant to make transparent the relationship between individual knobs and individual burners. Likewise, campus navigation maps that use the forward-up orientation are user-friendly because they exploit an inherent forward-up property of our visual perceptual system.

Our aim here has been to illustrate one way that the Gibsonian perceptual program can be productively combined with the distributed cognition program. By understanding problem solving as a constitutively perceptual phenomenon, we begin to dissolve the scaling-up problem that allegedly prevents Gibsonians from having anything useful to say about symbolic cognition.

The stove example and the map example can both be understood as classic instances of distributed problem solving involving a designer and a user. Hollan et al. (2000) propose that we can think of user interface design as an extended event in which a designer constructs an environment which the user later encounters and interacts with. Well-designed stoves and navigation maps work because they have been designed by a designer who made sensitive "implicit psychological hypotheses" about the needs of the user (Ball & Ormerod, 2000, 148). Good design involves making good hypotheses about human perceptual systems.

We agree with Harry Heft that a unified program combining Gibson's ideas with those of the distributed cognition theorists can potentially be very fruitful (Heft, 2001, 2021). A further attractive feature of the distributed cognition program is that it offers a way to demystify language and symbols. On the distributed view, language is primarily a process of the public creation of meaningful structure. Hutchins summarizes his view of symbol use as follows:

> Humans, more than any other species, spend their time producing symbolic structure for one another. We are very good at coordinating with the regularities in the patterns of symbolic structure that we present to one another … . Ontogenetically speaking, it seems that symbols are in the world first, and only later in the head. (Hutchins, 1995, 370)

Future work in this direction should explore developmental processes (on how the use of symbols comes to enter into perception, see Reed, 1996; Rogoff, 1990), problem solving in social interaction (for the most impressive work that has already been done in this direction, see Hutchins, 1995), and problem solving in non-human animals (Barrett, 2011). The Gibsonian strategy is to assert that all of these questions can best be approached by starting from the solid ground of an accurate theory of how perception works. A distributed ecological psychology is perhaps the most promising avenue for extending Gibson's perceptual program into the social realm.

References

Baggs, E. (2021). All affordances are social: Foundations of a Gibsonian social ontology. *Ecological Psychology*, *33*(3–4), 257–278.

Ball, L. J., & Ormerod, T. C. (2000). Putting ethnography to work: the case for a cognitive ethnography of design. *International Journal of Human-Computer Studies*, *53*(1), 147–168. 10.1006/ijhc.2000.0372

Barrett, L (2011). *Beyond the Brain: How body and environment shape animal and human minds.* Princeton, NJ: Princeton University Press.

Clark, A. (1998). *Being There: Putting brain, body, and world together again.* Cambridge, Massachusetts: MIT Press.

Gibson, J J. (1950). *The Perception of the Visual World.* Boston: Houghton Mifflin.

Gibson, J J. (1966). *The Senses Considered as Perceptual Systems.* Boston: Houghton-Mifflin.

Gibson, J J. (1979). *The Ecological Approach to Visual Perception.* Boston: Houghton-Mifflin.

Heft, H. (2001). *Ecological Psychology in Context: James Gibson, Roger Barker, and the legacy of William James's radical empiricism.* Mahwah, NJ: Lawrence Erlbaum Associates.

Heft, H. (2007). The social constitution of perceiver-environment reciprocity. *Ecological Psychology, 19*(2), 85–105.

Heft, H. (2020a). Ecological psychology as social psychology? *Theory & Psychology, 30*(6):813–826.

Heft, H. (2020b). Revisiting "The discovery of the occluding edge and its implications for perception" 40 years on. In Wagman, J. B. & Blau, J. J. C., editors, *Perception as Information Detection: Reflections on Gibson's Ecological Approach to Visual Perception,* (pp. 188–204). New York: Routledge.

Heft, H. (2021). Grasping what? Ecological anchors for abstract thought. *Human Development, 65*(2), 94–99.

Hollan, J., Hutchins, E., & Kirsh, D. (2000). Distributed Cognition: Toward a New Foundation for Human-Computer Interaction Research. *ACM Transactions on Computer-Human Interaction.* 7, 174–196. 10.1145/353485.353487.

Hutchins, E. (1995). *Cognition in the Wild.* Cambridge, Massachusetts: MIT Press.

Hutchins, E. (2010). Cognitive ecology. *Topics in Cognitive Science, 2*(4), 705–715.

Hutchins, E. (2014). The cultural ecosystem of human cognition. *Philosophical Psychology, 27*(1), 34–49.

Michaels, C. F., & Carello, C. (1981). *Direct Perception.* Englewood Cliffs, NJ: Prentice-Hall.

Norman, D. A. (2013). *The Design of Everyday Things: Revised and expanded edition.* Cambridge, Massachusetts: MIT Press.

Reed, E. S. (1996). *Encountering the World: Toward an ecological psychology.* New York: Oxford University Press.

Rogoff, B. (1990). *Apprenticeship in Thinking: Cognitive Development in Social Context.* Oxford: Oxford University Press.

Ross, W., & Vallée-Tourangeau, F. (2020). Microserendipity in the Creative Process. *The Journal of Creative Behavior,* jocb.478-undefined. 10.1002/jocb.478

Simon, H. A. (1996). *The Sciences of the Artificial.* Cambridge, Massachusetts: MIT Press, 3rd edition.

Steffensen, S. V., Vallée-Tourangeau, F., & Vallée-Tourangeau, G. (2016). Cognitive events in a problem-solving task: a qualitative method for investigating interactivity in the 17 animals problem. *Journal of Cognitive Psychology, 28*(1), 79–105. 10.1080/20445911.2015.1095193

Vallée-Tourangeau, F., Steffensen, S. V., Vallée-Tourangeau, G., & Sirota, M. (2016). Insight with hands and things. *Acta Psychologica, 170,* 195–205. 10.1016/j.actpsy.2016.08.006

Vicente, K. J. & Burns, C. M. (1996). Evidence for direct perception from cognition in the wild. *Ecological Psychology, 8*(3), 269–280.

5
CONCEIVING THE ENVIRONMENT FROM A DEVELOPMENTAL PERSPECTIVE

Revisiting Roger G. Barker's comparison of Bobby Bryant and Raymond Birch

Jytte Bang and Sofie Pedersen

5.1 Introduction

This chapter is inspired by Harry Heft's 1988 paper "Affordances of children's environments: A functional approach to environmental description" in which he carries out a functional analysis of the affordances of a seven-year-old boy, Raymond Birch. We find Heft's analysis intriguing both with regard to its overall theoretical contribution to ecological psychology and with regard to its potentialities for the study of development from an ecological-psychological perspective. Inspired by this, we suggest to expand Heft's functional analysis in two ways: (1) Heft uses the analysis of Raymond Birch to develop a taxonomy of the inanimate objects of his environments. We follow this thread and suggest an expansion in order to include people. (2) Heft's analysis focuses on the child-environment relationships of a "typical" child. We suggest an expansion by including a "less typical" child; namely a child living with a (physical) disability. This child is Bobby Bryant, who is from the same sample of research as Raymond Birch: the everyday child studies carried out at *The Midwest Psychological Field Station* led by Roger G. Barker and his research team in the town of Oskaloosa in the late 1940s and the early 1950s. By proposing this expansion, we want to shed light on the *variability* of the child-environment relationships and the potentials of such variability for developmental opportunities.

Our interest in the children of Oskaloosa does not solely derive from our reading of Heft's functional analysis of Raymond Birch. In fact, in 2016, we visited the Kenneth Spencer Research Library in Lawrence, Kansas, and dug ourselves into the archive material of the Midwest study. The description of Raymond Birch is well known as the record of the day study of him is published in the book *One Boy's Day* in 1966. However, the archive also contained unpublished records from other children, including children living with physical disabilities, such as Bobby Bryant. At the archive, we found outlines indicating that Barker and his

DOI: 10.4324/9781003259244-6

research team had already caught an interest in the comparison of the two boys. These outlines were intriguing to us, as Barker and his co-researchers carried out systematic and numerical child-environment analyses, which served to shed light on the variability of the two boy's everyday lives.

In this chapter, we shall work with ideas from both Heft's functional analysis and from Barker's study of Raymond and Bobby as there are connections between those two contributions. Heft argues for a functional taxonomy of the environment by drawing on the Raymond Birch full-day study carried out by Barker and the Midwest Psychological Field Station. Barker elaborates on his behavior setting theory and uses it in his outline of a comparison of Raymond and Bobby. We are interested in both contributions and intend to take them a step further.

To briefly contextualize, the Field Station, from which both Heft's and our interest derive, ran for 25 years, from 1947 to 1973. In the beginning, the researchers carried out several full-day studies of the children in Oskaloosa (which was the original name of the town they referred to as "Midwest"). These studies were part of the growing interest in child development following the end of World War II. They were carried out by a team of researchers, who followed each child during a full day and created a behavioral record for each of the children. Interestingly, rather than ending up with a study of individual differences between the children, Barker and his research team realized that different patterns of behavior were associated with different places at different times, rather than with different persons. In other words, they discovered the "standing pattern of behavior" and termed this unit of analysis a "behavior setting" (Barker, 2016). Examples of behavior settings could be a classroom, a church, or a grocery store.

5.2 A functional taxonomy of the environment as an important contribution

In his 1988 paper, Harry Heft derives his "functional taxonomy" of the environment from the statement that *psychology is in the need of a concept of the environment from a psychological perspective.*

Heft argues for a *functional taxonomy* of the environment to overcome what he terms the "form-based" classification of environmental features. A functional approach to the interrelationship of the individual and the environment offers opportunities to understand how a person's interrelationship with the environment may change over time, that is, it offers opportunities to analyze *development*, in that *the functional possibilities of an environment change with development.* It may happen that functional possibilities of environmental features, which "exist at one time of life" may not do so later in an individual's life; new affordances may emerge throughout development "as maturation and experience interact to expand the individual's behavioral repertoire" (Heft, 1988, p. 37; see also Heft, 1989). This implies that the functionally significant properties of the environment *are perceived qualities that emerge from person-environment relations.* Heft derives a functional taxonomy as a way of talking about the environment in a psychologically meaningful way. He reaches his conclusions by integrating points from Barker's conceptual work and his analysis of the seven-year-old boy, Raymond Birch (from Barker's data), with the concept of affordance (from Gibson). This double theoretical inspiration offers an opportunity for Heft to describe the psychological resources of children's outdoor activities.

Gibson's concept of affordance (Gibson, 1979/1986) puts a focus on the functional significance (the functional meaning) of an object. Heft emphasizes that Gibson suggested the affordances of the environment to be its functionally significant properties considered in relation to an individual and that this functional meaning is directly perceivable to a perceiver. As Heft analyzes the behavior of Raymond Birch from the perspective of affordance theory, he is able to identify the specific instances of its occurrences from the full-day behavior record. A few examples illustrate the productive character of such a perspective:

Affordance	*Occurrence*
Climb-on-able feature	Railing of a bandstand; garage in backyard; second floor home railing; a bench; a crate; a fence; a tree; doghouse in yard
Run-on-able surface	Courthouse lawn; school yard; slope in school yard
Throw-able objects	Green board; pieces of inner tube; bat; rock; dirt clod; lid of can
Pick-able object	Leaf; bud; twig; flower

Affordances are relationally specified and enable an analysis of how environmental features and features belonging to a person relate. Although form-based descriptions of environmental features (e.g., tree, fence, road, etc.) are more abstract ways of experiencing the environment, the categorical distinction following a functional approach to the environment includes the (changing) perspective of the individual. In other words, there is an *experiential primacy* to the functional approach, which allows for including, e.g., the developmental position of a person.

However, important experiential primacy is that it does not unfold itself in a vacuum. Persons and their experiences and relations, places, things, institutions, habits, behavioral patterns, etc., embed and contextualize experiential primacy. It all exists in terms of *becoming* and of *change*; of reproduced *steadiness*, of habits and routines, etc. That is, as history. In this sense, a functional analysis may gain by including a more explicit historical perspective: the *history* and the *historical becoming* of things, places, people, events, practices, etc. Such processes manifest themselves (are objectified) and become part of the environment. Therefore, such processual objectifications should become an integral *part of the environment from a psychological perspective*. When Raymond Birch moves around outdoor and from moment to moment finds himself relating to objects and places, he does not merely engage in an ongoing stream of behavior from the perspective of a functional taxonomy. He also inscribes himself into the history of materialized action (Bang, 2009; Leontjev 1977, 1981; Pedersen & Bang 2016; Schraube, 2022, in press) also known as the *human(ly created) environment*.

5.3 Revisiting the full-day study of Bobby Bryant and Raymond Birch

From the perspective of a *historized functional concept of the environment*, let us examine its importance for the study of development.

One of the research questions that Barker asked himself repeatedly was that of the differences between children living with and without physical disabilities. And one of the ways, in which he investigated those possible differences, was by looking into the everyday lives of Bobby Bryant and Raymond Birch. He wrote:

> Our problem is this: Do the social-psychological worlds of these boys differ and if they do, is there any evidence that the physical disability of Bobby is crucial factor in determining these differences. (Barker, 1950, p. 4)

To try to answer this question, Barker and his co-researchers carried out a comparative analysis of Bobby and Raymond's stream of behavior in different behavior settings while handling behavior objects and relating to people around them, during the course of one day. Their analysis took departure in Barker's statement that a physical disability may enforce "a way of life upon the disabled person which affects his behavior and over a long period of time his personality" (1950, p. 1).

To investigate more in depth the implications of a historical perspective on the momentary behavioral occurrences for a psychological perspective on the environment, we will revisit the full-day study of Raymond Birch (in which Heft also found inspiration) as well as the full-day study of Bobby Bryant (both seven years old in 1949).

Bobby Bryant: Bobby had, since birth, suffered from a congenital heart disease, a condition that caused fatigue and lower activity levels. His impaired circulation meant that he could not walk a block at a normal pace or run more than half a dozen steps. Because of Bobby's condition, his grandmother moved in with the family (Barker et al., undated).
Raymond Birch: Raymond was an ordinary healthy boy, who could move around his town environments on his own. He lived in a house with his parents and their dog, Honey. Both sets of grandparents lived on farms in the nearby area, which meant that Raymond often visited and spent time with them.

5.3.1 Analyzing variability

As previously stated, Barker was preoccupied with determining whether "the social-psychological worlds of Bobby and Raymond differed, and if so, would there be any evidence that the physical disability of Bobby is crucial factor in determining these differences" (Barker, 1950, p. 4). Vygotsky had a similar interest in the psychology of disability. He was occupied with conceiving the developmental conditions and opportunities of a handicapped child from a cultural-historical perspective. His overall theoretical main point is that all human development should be thought of as culturally embedded and as a process of appropriating cultural tools. For a child with no physical disability, there is a common path of cultural appropriation. In comparison, life is less easy for a child who lives with a disability. One reason is that the human world is usually culturally prepared for "typicality." Those who do not fit into the cultural arrangements often has to undergo the alternative path of development: that of *compensatory* activities. This, we believe, is the case for Bobby in comparison with Raymond, and by analyzing the variability between the two regarding their environmental engagements, we can specify in more detail what the environment for each of them look like (from a psychological perspective), and how such environmental variability offers them different developmental conditions. According to Vygotsky (2004), the child living with a disability faces a contradiction between what are the developmental obstacles for the child (due to the disability) and what are the developmental demands (due to society). He suggests that to develop within the cultural and societal (historical) realities, the child encounters specific challenges to overcome to *compensate* for the disability. In general, the development of a child depends on the availability of culturally developed tools, and we suggest both of these considerations relevant for our revisited analysis of Bobby and Raymond: Barker offers insights into *numerical variations* as for the availability of behavior settings, behavior objects, and social relations; and Vygotsky offers insight into *compensatory* processes. In combination, these insights offer a tool to study developmental *variability* among children.

5.3.1.1 Analysis of behavior settings

When Barker and his team analyzed the settings common to Bobby and Raymond (Barker, 1950, 1951), they found a profound variation regarding the amount of time spent in settings in which the two boys took part in free indoor activities. Although Raymond spent 50 minutes during his day with free indoor activities, Bobby spent 434 minutes. This indicates that Bobby spends a lot more time with freely selected indoor activities, whereas Raymond does this to a remarkable lesser degree. It probably indicates that whereas Raymond gets up and ready in the morning and then does something else (outdoor), Bobby stays indoor for much of his time and can do whatever he enjoys.

	Common behavior setting	No. of minutes spent
Bobby	Indoor, free	434
Raymond	Indoor, free	50

If we compare the behavior settings offered to Bobby and Raymond, the activities in which each of them takes part, and the people with whom they interact, the picture of variation becomes more accurate. For illustration, we have selected some episodes from each of the full-day records for Bobby and Raymond.

5.3.1.1.1 Morning activities after breakfast

After breakfast, Bobby stays indoor where he spends time with his mother, his grandmother, and his younger brother sharing homely activities (making cookies):

> Bobby waited patiently to get started with making the cookies as he first watched what grandmother did with the cookie cutter. He squealed happily with anticipation. He watched his younger brother cut cookies and then grandmother urged Bobby to cut some. Very carefully and after much deliberation he chose the star cutter. With extreme care and in slow-motion he picked it up and placed it on the dough. He pressed down firmly several times. (Barker et al., undated, p. 10)

After breakfast, Raymond goes out of the house where he spends time with his father:

> He followed his father outside and behind the house where his father started to practice casting (fishing) at the barn. His cast was successful and immediately, Raymond ran enthusiastically down to the end of the line, and he ran along as his father reeled in the line. He carried Honey (dog) to the house and raised her up to the kitchen window so that she could be seen by his mother. Then Raymond put her down and jumped a time or two as if for the sheer pleasure of jumping. When his father cried to Raymond that he had lost his plug, Raymond immediately ran down toward the barn looking for the plug. (Barker & Wright, 1966, p. 31)

5.3.1.1.2 Schoolwork activities

Being seven years old, both boys were engaged in learning activities. However, variations were seen here as well both regarding where and under which circumstances each of them engaged with schoolwork activities and regarding how long time they spent with it. This draws the picture of rather significant variance of time, place, and general social conditions regarding schoolwork. Due to his physical condition, which did not allow him to go to school, Bobby was homeschooled by his grandmother, who was a former teacher. He spent 63 minutes of his day doing schoolwork at home. In comparison, Raymond attended school and spent 236 minutes there, doing study lessons at school.

	Settings unique to each boy	No. of minutes spent in each
Bobby	Schoolwork at home	63
Raymond	School, study lessons	236

In addition to the time and place variance, it is interesting to consider variance from a developmental point of view when it comes to how the schoolwork activities are approached by the adults (grandmother and teacher, respectively), and how each of the boys relate to it. To Bobby, doing schoolwork is one of his ways to spend time with his grandmother:

> Bobby and grandmother went upstairs, and Bobby sat down at his study table and began to work immediately. As he wrote, he followed the directions given in a lesson book which lay on the table. He half smiled as he wrote and bent double when concentrating. He wrote the word "hen," murmuring to himself, "hen-n-n-n." Grandmother sat down opposite to him and fingered a scrap book with which she expected to occupy herself as he studied. She told Bobby that him writing 'hen' reminded her of those hens she was always "dreaming" about and the farm she used to have where she would gather eggs every day. Bobby looked up at her and said laughingly, "But you can't gather eggs at night in dreams." She smiled in answer. (Barker et al., undated, pp. 86–87)

To Raymond, doing schoolwork activities means joining the class and taking part in the classroom activities mastered by the teacher:

> The teacher announced that it was time to get quiet now. She said "There isn't much time to tell stories this morning. Sit up straight now! Sit up straight and put your feet under your desk where they belong! Sit up straight!" Raymond did like the teacher told and the story telling began. Susanna Hall was the first to volunteer and Raymond listened attentively and with great interest. He began to slide down his chair so that his feet stretched out under the seat in front of him. Then Jimmy Olson was next to tell a story. Bobby's interest waned almost immediately, probably because of the difficulty in following the main thread of the story. He bent down to take a storybook from his desk. He carefully leafed through the book. He did not notice the other children were laughing when Jimmy's story became quite funny. Raymond was buried in his book and was generally unaware of the change of storytellers. With an inadvertent motion he pushed his plastic gun-shaped pencil box off the desk, scattering its content in all directions. Surprised and embarrassed, he bent over immediately and picked up his pencil box in a quick, furtive way. The teacher looked up and said with some irritation, "What's the matter?" Then she walked down the aisle, looking for the source

of the disturbance. She stopped at Raymond's desk and frowned at him. (Barker & Wright, 1966, pp. 137–139)

5.3.1.2 Analysis of behavior objects

We can further qualify our comparative analysis of Bobby and Raymond by exemplifying what behavior objects are available in their respective behavior settings. Barker emphasized that behavior objects are those things in the person's physical-social environment which the person notices in the course of his/her behavior. For comparison reasons, Barker and his team listed the behavior objects with which Bobby and Raymond interacted as well as the overall number of different behavior objects with which each of the boys interacted. And here they found quite a difference:

	Bobby	*Raymond*
Interaction with behavior objects	263	413

Further, Barker found that Bobby interacted with more *imaginary behavior objects* than Raymond (37 compared to 29), and that Bobby interacted with more behavior objects that were *play-things* than Raymond did (28 in relation to 24) (Barker, undated). Below a few examples to illustrate the difference.

5.3.1.2.1 Relating to behavior objects

> Bobby seemed to enjoy playing with his toy gun. As he was not allowed to play with it indoors, it offered him a chance to go outside and play on the porch. Bobby began to put a cap into his gun and then he shot his gun without aiming at anything. He seemed to shoot merely for the pleasure of shooting. A dog sniffed around in the back yard. Bobby said that he was going to shoot the dog. By the time he shot the next cap, so it exploded, the dog was about a hundred feet away. Methodically he loaded and deliberately shot the gun twice. A little proudly he said, "This gun really smokes." (Barker et al., undated, p. 29–30)

Although Bobby played at home and close to his relatives who could always keep an eye on him, Raymond moved around freely in town without anyone watching what he was doing. This meant that he could explore the qualities of the environment and the behavior objects that he passed without any other purpose than exploring:

> On his way to school, Raymond had to go on his own from the courthouse (where his mother worked) to the school. He went down the steps to the street level. Suddenly, he leaped up to the top of the retaining wall.

> He ambled along the top of the wall until he came to the benches that were grouped together on one corner of the courthouse lawn. He sat down on one of the benches with a pleasant, relaxed expression. He rocked the bench back and forth for a few seconds, then jumped up and began rocking the bench as he stood on the ground at one end of it. Raymond easily jumped from the wall to the sidewalk with a rather high jump without hesitation. He then walked along the sidewalk until he came to the corner. He stepped off the curb and looked to both sides for cars. (Barker & Wright, 1966, pp. 50–51)

5.3.1.3 Analysis of the social world

In line with the fact that Raymond was able to move more around on his own, he also took part in more behavior episodes without associates, he interacted with a greater number of persons, and his associates were to a lesser degree family members – in comparison with Bobby:

	Bobby	Raymond
Percentage of behavior episodes in which the child had an associate	93	76
Number of persons with whom the child interacted	12	38
Percentage of associates who were family members	82	39

In short, Bobby had much more companionship – primarily his family members – and he interacted with much fewer persons than Raymond. Raymond, on his part, moved around and did activities on his own, he interacted with more different persons and more of them were not family members, but different people he met outside his home. A few examples illustrate this variance of their lives.

5.3.1.3.1 Social interactions and play activities

Although Bobby interacts with his close family members also when outside the home setting, Raymond spends time with schoolmates and friends of his own age:

> Bobby, Jack, and his mother walked to the nearby park. When Bobby sighted the playground equipment: swings, climbing poles, teeter-totters, etc., he squealed out, dancing up and down on his toes, "I want that swing first." Jack, however, dashed ahead of him to the swing that Bobby had picked out for himself. Bobby got disappointed and angry, but he did not attempt to catch up with Jack. Not only was he not allowed to run, but he could not run for more than four or five steps before lack of oxygen automatically stopped him. His mother, trying to avoid a fuss, said, "Well, there are two swings there, after all … ." Bobby did not want to go to one of the crooked swings but after a little while, Jack was off to some other

playthings, and Bobby's first choice of swings was free now. Bobby crawled onto it with pleasure rampant all over his face. He was pushed and gleefully his voice rang out: "Oh, oh, I'm Superman!" After having tried the swing, Bobby was excited to try the teeter-totter with Jack, but after a little while, he wanted to get off. Jack purposely slid off his end of the teeter-totter when they were balanced about even. That let Bobby down with a terrific bump. Bobby got furious at Jack but then started to cry quietly. When his mother heard him call out for her, she was very disturbed that she had rested on a bench while the boys were playing and therefore did not watch well nor stayed close to Bobby. Kindly, she made a move to make up for her mistake, asking quietly, "Should I get on with you and play with you for a while?" Bobby's face cleared up again. (Barker et al., undated, pp. 174–181)

As mentioned, Raymond did not always have his close family members nearby him but was able to spend time on his own and in the company with child associates. For example, he played with other children and took part in play-related negotiations with other children, e.g., at recess in school:

Raymond dropped down on his knees in a sandpile. He pushed the piles of sand back and forth and let the sand slip through his fingers. He picked up an eight-inch sliver of a shingle to use as a scraping implement, carefully making designs in the sand. Then another boy, Roy Harkness, came over. He asked: "What are you making?" At the same time, he inadvertently stepped close to the sand designs. Raymond felt his design was threatened, for he looked up, startled, and said in a definitively commanding but pleasant enough voice, "Don't you step on it." Roy stopped in his tracks and asked curiously, "Are you making a road?" Raymond answered calmly and with relief: "Sure." A girl, Susan, came by to play with Raymond. Roy stayed for a while and even asked if he could join them, which Susan did not want and answered him with a "Huh uh." After a short while, Roy walked over close to Raymond. With a foot-long, dried-up twig that represented an airplane, he "buzzed" over the area where Raymond was playing. Teasingly he dipped low just above Raymond's head so that the plane almost brushed Raymond's hair. Then he swooped on down tantalizingly close to Raymond's face. He repeated this, all the while imitating the roar of an airplane motor. Raymond tried hard for a time to ignore Roy, until suddenly he reached out and plucked the plane out of Roy's hands. He moved gently but very purposefully as he did this. His actions were aimed at removing the plane, not Roy. Roy was so surprised that he stood motionless. Raymond then teasingly flew the plane over Roy's head and with a smooth, easy, outflung gesture, flipped the plane away so that it landed in another part of the playground. (Barker & Wright, 1966, pp. 116–121)

5.4 Drawing variability profiles

On the basis of the revisited analysis, we can now draw variability profiles for Bobby and Raymond. Much of his time, Bobby stays indoor where he spends time with his mother and his grandmother, that is, female relatives who take care of all the planning around him and for him. The emotional distress that Bobby experienced, when Jack ran ahead and took the swing that Bobby wanted, illustrates how "fighting" about a toy may keep him on a developmental level below his own age. This total situation (with reference to Lewin, 1935) implies that he is mostly occupied with whatever is available to him around his home, and that much of his time he must relate to the same few people. Bobby is seldomly alone and any initiative from him is immediately evaluated in terms of "is this a problem or not, given his physical condition." Bobby is helped to live in a state of regulated (low) excitement and his close female associates help compensate for his physical disability in terms of organizing his day in order to make it as normal as possible. For example, Bobby "goes to school" at home during ordinary school hours, yet, his school day does not compare to ordinary school. His school activities go on in his own room and right next to his grandmother, and so, his schoolwork implies the full attention of a helping adult who, from time to time, dozes and adjusts her questions to activate him at a proper level of excitement; and she regulates the overall situation by creating an atmosphere of "coziness" by mixing schoolwork with homely activities. Bobby never meets the unpredictable challenges and demands from other children his age nor from a schoolteacher in an unpredictable classroom setting. Hence overall, *protection* and *emotional regulation* co-constitute his psychological environment. However, Bobby does not yet seem to have a meta-perspective on all of this. It may become more difficult in the future to protect him from his experience of his own personal history, which may not have enabled him sufficiently to meet new and more demanding challenges.

In comparison, Raymond lives in a "richer" world, as illustrated by Barker. Raymond finds himself participating in more behavior settings, he relates to more varied behavior objects, and he interacts with more different people. By doing so, he experiences accordingly "richer" developmental potentialities with accordingly more open prospects. For example, the analysis emphasized how Raymond can move around on his own while exploring whatever he meets on his way. He also spends time with his father in outdoor activities that require some physical robustness, and he experiences his body as part of doing new and sometimes physically challenging things. Within the frame of ordinary everyday activities and institutional settings, he can do what he wants – no extraordinary protection keeps him back. For this reason, Raymond does not have to appropriate a protective view of himself, he can freely relate to the open possibilities offered by his environment from time to time. His functional possibilities are greater, and he can learn a lot about physical realism (body things) from the many behavior objects with which he relates (e.g., how to jump down from something and how to rock something) and from the extended territory which he inhabits. Therefore, we imagine how this may influence his self-awareness and self-experience now and for the future. When it comes to Raymond's social interactions, he lives a less protected life as well. For example, in school he must deal with both the social psychology of mass boredom and the critical view of him from his teacher. He balances on the one side the "freedom" given by the many children (to hide in the crowd) and on the other side, the awareness of doing as told. There are restricted possibilities for non-participation (if one learns to do so without gaining the teacher's attention, which Raymond failed to do in the observation). He therefore had negative attention from the teacher, whose motive was to master the classroom, not to serve Raymond's learning in particular. Hence, Raymond has to find his own way in all the school-related complexity. He meets demands, resistance, and even hostility and must learn to master it. He must also learn how to negotiate social relations with children his own age, which is illustrated in the play situation where Raymond negotiates with an "intruding" boy to avoid confrontation and at the same time protect his own play engagements. This kind of social "receiving," "negotiating," and "enduring" is offered Raymond as developmental potentialities only because he masters to live in a less protected and safe world. Raymond therefore meets more people with more (complex) motives, some of which may be close to "hostile" or reprimanding. In other words, Raymond lives a common life for a boy his age.

5.5 Concluding remarks

Heft's functional approach offers a valuable perspective on the specific environmental features, which "invite" Raymond to do things with these features. The analysis puts a focus on the *moment-to-moment* affordances of the environment as Raymond moves around outdoor and encounters a variety of objects at different places. A moment-to-moment perspective on Raymond's behavior as he moves around offers a stream of *nows* of child-environment relationships. Heft convincingly argues how such a functional analysis contributes to overcoming mainstream psychological ideas of the environment and of individual-environment relations. What we have suggested in this chapter is to contextualize this kind of analysis historically and by doing so gain insights into child-environment variability. The variability profile of Bobby and Raymond is the result of a joined Barker- and Vygotsky-based analysis. Such a joined perspective enables new possibilities to evaluate developmental potentialities of the stream of behavior and of the functional relationships with the environment for each of the boys. For example, we can view Bobby's activities at the playground from this perspective. There are standing patterns of behavior at a playground: there are places to run and equipment to play with. Bobby adjusts to all of this, but at the same time, he seems developmentally caught in an "out of timing" situation, as we assume that the kind of behavior settings and, objects, that he is offered here, are most often offered to younger children. It is not just Bobby's functional relationship with the swing or with other equipment at the playground, which informs us about the developmental potentialities of his environmental engagements. We are also informed about those potentialities by taking our analysis *beyond* a momentary functional approach by considering both the environmental affordances for each of the boys and the "typicality" of those affordances from the perspective of society.

Therefore, we propose that a *concept of the environment from a psychological perspective* should include three dimensions: a *functional* dimension (in line with Heft and Gibson), a *setting* dimension (in line with Barker), and a *historical* dimension (in line with Vygotsky and with cultural-historical psychology). Such a combination, we suggest to have great potential for the study and comprehension of variabilities in the child-environment relationships as well as for the comprehension of (different) developmental paths.

References

Bang, J. (2009). An environmental affordance perspective on the study of development - artefacts, social others, and self. In M. Fleer, M. Hedegaard, & J. Tudge (Eds.), *Childhood studies and the impact of globalization: Policies and practices at global and local levels* (pp. 161–181). World Yearbook of Education 2009. New York and London: Routledge.

Barker, J. S. (2016). Why 25 years? Notes on the long trajectory of Roger Barker's research in Oskaloosa. *Ecological Psychology*, 28(1), 39–55.

Barker, R. G. (undated). The psychological situations and behavior of Raymond Birch and Bobby Bryant – some sample results. Archive manuscript.

Barker, R. G. (1950). *A preliminary comparison of the psychological situations and behavior of Raymond Birch and Bobby Bryant*. Archive manuscript, September 28, 1950.

Barker, R. G. (1951). Behavior settings and behavior objects. Archive manuscript (sheet), January 1951.

Barker, R. G., & Wright, H. F. (1966). *One boy's day*. Archon Books.

Barker, Wright, & Remple (undated). Bobby Bryant – A full day record. Archive manuscript.

Gibson, J. J. (1979/1986). *The ecological approach to visual perception*. New York and London: Psychology Press.

Heft, H. (1988). Affordances of children's environments: A functional approach to environmental description. *Children's Environments Quarterly*, 5(3), 29–37.

Heft, H. (1989). Affordances and the body: An intentional analysis of Gibson's ecological approach to visual perception. *Journal for the Theory of Social Behaviour*, 19(1), 1–30.

Leontjev, A. N. (1977). Activity and consciousness. In *Philosophy in the USSR: Problems of dialectical materialism* (pp. 180–202). Moscow: Progress Publishers.

Leontjev, A. N. (1981). Psychologie des Abbilds. In B. Grüter, F. Haug, K. Holzkamp, Ute H.-Osterkamp, W. Maiers, M. Markard, & C. Ohm (Eds.), *Handlungstheorie, anthropologie, theorie-praxis, faschismus* (pp. 5–19). Forum Kritischer Psychologie.

Lewin, K. (1935). *A dynamic theory of personality – Selected papers*. New York and London: McGraw-Hill Book Company.

Pedersen, S., & Bang, J. (2016). Historicizing affordance theory: A rendezvous between ecological psychology and cultural-historical activity theory. *Theory & Psychology*, 26(6), 731–750.

Schraube, E. (2022, in press). Technology and the practice of everyday living. In H. J. Stam & H. Looren de Jong (Eds.), *The Sage handbook of theoretical psychology*. 1–22.

Vygotsky, S. L. (2004). Introduction: The fundamental problems of defectology. In R. W. Rieber & D. K. Robinson (Eds.), *The essential Vygotsky* (pp. 153–175). Kluwer Academic/Plenum Publishers.

6
AGENCY IN BEHAVIOR SETTINGS

A mindshaping perspective on ecological psychology

Miguel Segundo-Ortin and Annemarie Kalis

6.1 Introduction

In this chapter, we aim to examine the account of individual agency that Harry Heft advances in relation to Barker's theory of behavior settings. Our main hypothesis is that the mindshaping view put forward by Victoria McGeer (2015, 2021) provides useful tools for understanding agency as an individual feature that is nonetheless situated in the context of behavior settings.

The structure of this chapter is as follows. In section 6.2, we provide the background on eco-behavioral science, focusing on the main characteristics of behavior settings. In section 6.3, we analyze Heft's interpretation of this notion, as well as his concerns with understanding the relationship between behavior settings and individual agency. Even though we believe that Heft's approach offers promising suggestions to build a situated theory of agency, we find his proposal wanting. Subsequently, in section 6.4, we will develop the outline of a situated account of agency that explains how behavior settings shape individual agency without determining it. To do so, we will draw from McGeer's mindshaping perspective on agency. As we will show, the mindshaping view can complement the Gibsonian approach favored by Heft, giving us the resources needed to understand how agency can be an irreducible feature of individuals and thoroughly situated at the same time.

6.2 A primer on behavior settings

The notion of "behavior setting" was first coined by psychologist Roger Barker (1975, 1978) and his collaborator Herbert Wright to account for the observed variability in children's behavior in different contexts. In 1947, Barker and Wright inaugurated the Midwest Psychological Field Station, a research station devoted to collecting data about the daily behavior of a group of children from Oskaloosa, Kansas. At first, Barker and his collaborators found that the children's actions over their day were structured (e.g., regarding their frequency, distribution, and so on), and assumed that this structure should be a consequence of identifiable social stimuli, such as specific actions or calls by their peers and caretakers (1975, p. 147).[1] Consequently, they thought that by discovering these social stimuli they could formulate laws of behavior.

This assumption, however, proved wrong, as researchers were unable to find social cues that could serve as reliable predictors for the behavioral episodes under scrutiny. Alternatively, Barker and his collaborators noticed a crucial aspect: namely, that the behavior of different children varied less within specific places than the behavior of a single child across different locations.[2] This made the researchers shift their focus from seeking individual social inputs to investigating the characteristics of the places where the behavioral episodes occurred. This was the beginning of what later came to be named "eco-behavioral science":

> We found that we could predict many aspects of children's behavior more adequately from knowledge of the behavior characteristics of the drugstores, arithmetic classes, and basketball games that they inhabited than from knowledge of the behavior tendencies of the particular children. (Barker, 1978, p. 42)

A new hypothesis followed this discovery: if the behavior of children is structured depending on where it takes place, this structure most likely stems from the structure of the place itself. Barker referred to these extra-individual environmental structures as "behavior settings." A behavior setting is a group-level phenomenon that occurs at the scale of lecture theatres, grocery stores, churches, and so on, and that involves individual agents interacting with specific aspects of their environment and peers in a patterned way:

> A behavior setting is a standing behavior pattern *together with* the part of the milieu to which the behavior is attached and with which it has a synomorphic relation … Behavior settings are behavior-milieu phenomena; the milieu is circumjacent to the standing pattern of behavior. (Barker, 1978, p. 27, emphasis in original)

Behavior settings have the following characteristics. First, they occur naturally in the sense of not being created by the experimenter. They have specific locations, both spatially and temporally. They are composed of particular patterns of behavior and specific topological features and objects of the environment. Behavior patterns and environmental features stand in a complementary or "synomorphic" relation. Fourth, there exists a crucial interdependence between the actions of individuals and the behavior settings. On the one hand, behavior settings are generated and maintained by the collective actions of individuals. For instance, although the store may exist physically as a location, it does not exist as a behavior setting if no people purchase items, replace them, etc. On the other hand, the existence of the settings affects the behavior of the individuals as well. They do so in the first place because they make possible the performance of some actions; but they also constrain the actions of their "inhabitants." Crucially, this constraining is sometimes due to the intervention of some inhabitants who correct behavioral deviations of others, but it is often the case that the individuals correct themselves. Lastly, individuals who "inhabit" a behavior setting often play specific roles (the teacher, the waiter), although they can be replaced sometimes (e.g., another person can play the role of teacher). It follows that behavior settings have some degree of flexibility, in the sense that some aspects can be altered without destroying or dissolving it.

As we see it, the theory of behavior settings can be considered a precursor of what we nowadays refer to as "situated cognition" (Gallagher & Varga, 2020; Heft, 2018, 2020; McGann, 2014). Barker's hypothesis is that the behavior of individuals should be accounted for, at least partially, in terms of supra-individual elements of the environment. It follows from his theory that the main unit of analysis for psychologists is no longer the individual's mind, but an extended system that includes both the individual and the characteristics of the behavior setting (including other agents and the *milieu*). In this sense, these extra-individual elements cannot be interpreted as being just the normal ecological backdrop that an agent's internal cognitive machinery needs to achieve goal-oriented action coordination. Rather, they must be seen as constitutive parts of the cognitive machinery itself. Action, so Barker's eco-behavioral science suggests, is irreducibly situated.

6.3 Agency in behavior settings: Heft's proposal

Barker's eco-behavioral approach constitutes a genuine innovation in scientific psychology due to its emphasis on the relevance of the supra-individual structures to understand human behavior. Nonetheless, some authors have criticized Barker for putting too much emphasis on describing the dynamics at the level of behavior settings while at the same time forgetting to account for how individual agency intertwines with the setting's constraints. For instance, it is a fact that behavior settings do not provide strict programs or scripts, and that the same individual can play different roles in the same setting at different moments. Similarly, explanations at the setting level cannot account for the fact that individuals enter, leave, create, and modify settings according to their particular goals.

One of these critical voices is Harry Heft.[3] As he observed:

> [T]he resulting account [of Barker's eco-behavioral science] does not offer predictions at the level of any particular individual. Instead, it provides an analysis of the ecobehavioral resources of a place at an extra-individual level. … A question, then, that Barker needed to confront was how to

understand the relation between behavior settings and the actions of individuals. (Heft, 2001, p. 258)[4]

In order to answer this question, Heft has proposed to take inspiration from J. J. Gibson's ecological psychology (Gibson, 1966, 1979[2015]). One of the core ideas of Gibsonian psychology is that individuals make their way in the world by acting on perceived affordances. Affordances, however, are *not* private entities that exist on the mind of the perceiver. Contrariwise, Gibsonian psychologists hold that the perceptual information available in the ambient array of a location – i.e., the temporally extended structures and patterns present in ambient light within a room – provides individuals with the right kind of perceptual systems with information about the possibilities for actions afforded by the objects therein – whether they can be grasped, reached, if they are throwable, and so on. Thus, when individuals detect this perceptual information, they perceive the objects' affordances. Taking Gibson's ecological psychology as its starting point, Heft proposes to understand agency as the "selective control" that individuals have in perceiving and acting upon affordances (2001, p. 198; see also Reed, 1996).

With this basic definition at hand, the next question concerns how behavior settings relate to individual agency. Importantly, Heft believes that, for human beings, agency is always and everywhere socially situated. This means that "the ways individuals engage the environment, in large measure, grow out of an ongoing developmental history of participation in social practices within their community" (Heft, 2020, p. 814). According to him, if we understand behavior settings as higher-order structures that emerge through the coordinated actions of individuals, we can postulate that "inhabitants" of behavior settings can perceive affordances related to these settings (Heft, 2001, p. 296; Heft et al., 2014).

However, the story is more complicated than it may look at first sight. On the one hand, as Heft acknowledges, behavior settings do not simply afford particular actions to their inhabitants. Instead, they somehow "coerce" how the individuals act. On the other hand, this coercion is not absolute, for individuals can still behave relatively freely within behavior settings. Moreover, they can choose whether or not they want to inhabit them. This leads to the fundamental question of how to develop a unified understanding of agency that covers both individual selective control upon affordances, and the environmental structuring and constraining that takes place in a behavior setting. As Heft puts it: "How can the operations (e.g., control processes) of an autonomous agent in a complex system be conceptualized in a manner that is consistent with the operations of the broader, dynamic system with multiple determinants?" (2001, p. 317). In short, Heft is after a *situated* notion of agency.

To face this challenge, Heft refers to the work of Hutchins (1995) and proposes to understand behavior settings from the point of view of distributed cognition. Distributed cognition is "a framework for thinking about cognition which seeks to understand how the cognitive properties of aggregates emerge from the interaction of component parts" (Hutchins, 2001). When applied to specific cognitive abilities, e.g., the capacity of pilots to remember the range of speeds at which landing is safe, this framework predicts that the cognitive activity is not performed by any single element in isolation. Instead, it emerges from the complex interaction of the different parts of the system – encompassing not only the individual pilots but also other crew members and the artifacts in the cockpit. Following Hutchins, Heft proposes that individual agency emerges[5] within the constraints of a distributed cognitive system that is the behavior setting:

> The individual conceptualized as part of a person-environment system is an *adaptive agent*. Actions reflect an ongoing selective engagement of particular features of a setting, an attunement to some dynamic structures rather than others … . The individual is functionally flexible, adaptively shifting in the focus of intentional action and shifting with respect to contextual frames. In the case of a distributed cognitive system, the individual functions selectively and coordinately to maintain operations that encompass artifacts, representations, and other individuals. (2001, p. 366)[6]

Although we wholeheartedly agree that agency involves adaptation to the situational constraints imposed by behavior settings, it is not clear to us how agency could be conceptualized as an emerging property of distributed cognitive systems. For one thing, Heft (2001, p. 365) recognizes that Hutchins' view is in tension with Gibson's ecological approach, as Hutchins explicitly embraces the view that cognition consists of the manipulation of representations. This tension motivates Heft to interpret distributed cognition and behavior settings through the lens of Dynamical Systems Theory (DST) (pp. 329–322). However, we hold that this second move is also problematic. As noted by Chemero (2009, pp. 96–97) and Beer (2014, p. 135), DST comprises a set of mathematical tools that help us model the behavior of systems that change over time in a lawful way, but these tools do not by itself constitute a theory of cognition. It follows that although cognitive systems can be modeled using DST, DST *alone* cannot tell apart a cognitive system from any other physical system that can also be modeled using the same mathematical formalism (e.g., a hurricane, a pair of pendulums, a neural network, etc.). We hold that the same conclusion follows with respect to agency. Even if DST might be a useful tool to model the behavior of agents, it can't tell us what agency is. Hence, we do not think that DST is the right tool for analyzing the kind of situated "intentional selective operations" that Heft is trying to account for, and which we agree are central for understanding human agency and action.

Second, we have some difficulties with the use of the distributed cognition framework to explain agency. Recall Hutchins' example of pilots remembering the speed range at which landing the aircraft is safe. This cognitive task is explained by combining the cognitive properties of different "aggregates." However, some of these aggregates are themselves agents. The pilots, for example, can choose whether they want to follow the ready-made protocols, or whether they will improvise new techniques to calculate the speeds. Distributed cognition, then, already implies the existence of agents who, together with other agents and specific artifacts, can achieve cognitive tasks. But if agents are required for distributed cognition, it is hard to see how distributed cognition can account for agency in the first place.

These shortcomings motivate us to seek for other resources that could help build a situated theory of agency. The following section is devoted to this task.

6.4 In what sense is human agency situated?

We finished the previous section by claiming that the frameworks of distributed cognition and DST are not adequate to explain in what sense human agency is situated. To repeat, for us the challenge consists of understanding how the individual's agency and the dynamics of behavior settings intertwine. Remember, too, that this relationship is two-fold. When individuals participate in behavior settings, their perception–action gets shaped by the dynamics of the setting. Yet, at the same time, the constraint imposed by the setting is not absolute, for a behavior setting depends on individuals willing to participate and comply with its norms. This analysis opens up two different questions. First, how do behavior settings shape individual agency? And, second, how does the behavior settings framework deal with individual freedom?

Before we provide an answer to these questions, we submit to the reader the idea that agency, far from being a single feature of biological organisms, consists of a set of capacities that together enable individuals to act in a goal-directed way. Among these capacities is the "selective control" that individuals have in perceiving and acting upon affordances, but also others that serve to complement and scaffold this basic capacity, including our abilities to make plans and reflect on the course of our actions. Moreover, what makes our analysis of agency a *situated* analysis is that it understands this set of capacities as being at least partially constituted by socio-normative practices (De Bruin, 2017; De Jaegher & Froese, 2009; Maiese, 2021). These socio-normative practices, however, are anchored to (or situated in) specific behavior settings. Our claim is then that human agency must be understood in relation to behavior settings. Importantly, our proposal echoes more recent ideas put forward by Heft concerning perceptual learning and development (Heft, 2018),[7] but introduces a new element in the discussion: we draw upon McGeer's view of "mindshaping" (McGeer, 2015, 2021) to develop a concrete proposal on how to understand the relationship between human agency and behavior settings.

According to McGeer, a crucial feature of human agency is the fact that it develops within a normative, social context. From birth on, humans shape each other's behavior and thought by means of folk-psychological regulative practices. This can be as basic as a parent telling a child that if they say they want a sandwich, they expect them to eat it. By means of such simple exchanges, parents and caregivers teach children how to believe, desire or act in appropriate ways. Moreover, by becoming enculturated in such mindshaping practices, we don't simply become more prone to correct other people when they violate our expectations, but learn to hold ourselves accountable for norm transgressions too (McGeer & Pettit, 2002). As McGeer puts it:

> The central insight of the mindshaping view is that agents learn to become well-behaved folk-psychological agents, shaping their thought and action to conform to locally relevant norms of recognizable kind-and-context-appropriate agency (where kinds of agents may be differentiated along any of a number of dimensions: gender, class, role, and so on). (2021, p. 1058)

The core idea of the mindshaping view is thus that our folk psychological practice of ascribing beliefs, desires, and intentions to each other and ourselves should be understood, first and foremost, as a *regulative practice*. Its primary function is not, as was traditionally thought, to understand and explain what others do in folk-psychological terms, but to regulate or shape our own minds.[8] It follows that in learning how to engage in folk-psychological normative practices – e.g., learning what "believing something" entails – we learn how to shape our own thought and action to accord with the myriad of norms that are proper to our cultural milieu. These norms involve, among other things, what is appropriate to believe, what is appropriate to desire and intend, and, most importantly, what is appropriate to do in light of one's beliefs and desires. Moreover, the mindshaping view proposes that by learning how to operate within these folk-psychological norms "[w]e learn how to be interpretable, according to those norms – and thereby how to interpret others who shape their thought and behavior likewise" (2021, p. 1050). Therefore, folk-psychological mastery is essential for achieving social coordination in human communities.

There are some specific aspects of the mindshaping view that deserve further consideration. First of all, it does not assume the existence of such folk-psychological states prior to the acquisition of the relevant folk-psychological vocabulary and the norms that regulate its use. Second, the norms that regulate individuals' thought and action are not private entities. Instead, they are publicly shared and negotiated whenever individuals call each other to account. Summing up these features together, McGeer writes: "The regulative view conceptualizes folk-psychology as a fundamentally *interpersonal* (versus individualistic) *mind-making* (versus mind-detecting) enterprise" (2015, p. 261, emphasis in original). Third, the regulative view takes inspiration from Ryle and Dreyfus, as it understands folk-psychological mastery in terms of *know-how*. McGeer makes this point explicit when she compares our ability to think and behave as well-regulated folk-psychological agents with our ability to play chess (2015, p. 263). As she tells us, even though at the beginning we may need to think explicitly of the rules that are at play in chess, mastery is only acquired when we develop the right embodied dispositions to behave according to these rules. In this sense, the regulative view is also explicitly *non-intellectualist*:

> [E]xpert performance depends on rule-abiding (and rule-governed) procedures become embedded in bodily schemas – i.e., motor and cognitive routines (ways of thinking/acting) that just operate in accordance with the rule. This is what makes skilled performance fast, fluid, effortless and intuitive. (2021, p. 1048)

In sum, the idea is that human agency develops within folk-psychological practices that shape our minds by teaching us how our beliefs, desires, and actions are governed by norms. By making folk-psychology a primary regulative enterprise, this view suggests that individuals incorporate into their behavioral repertoire a series of capacities to employ, both in thought and in action, folk psychological normative notions.

We can now come back to our previous proposal that agency consists of a set of capacities that together enable individuals to act in a goal-directed way. Although Heft focused on the capacity of exerting control upon what affordances are perceived and acted, we want to emphasize the additional importance of the capacity of regulating thought and action in normative folk-psychological terms. This second capacity, we believe, is exclusively human, but it serves to scaffold the other, more basic, capacity proposed by Heft.

To see the connection between folk-psychological thinking and ecological psychology consider the proposal advanced by Brancazio and Segundo-Ortin (2020; see also Segundo-Ortin & Kalis, under review) that mastering the use of the concept of "intention" is a useful tool to coordinate our perception and action upon the affordances currently present to achieve distal goals. An example of this is Louise's plan to take a trip to the consulate to renew her visa tomorrow. There are a number of steps she must take care of in order to achieve this, some of which must be attended to in an orderly fashion – e.g., first, she must check the train schedule and see whether it conflicts with her work, after this, she should register the absence in her work roster, then, make sure she can get to the station in time to catch the train, and so on. Successfully carrying out these steps requires one to perceive and take advantage of the relevant affordances in the environment. According to Brancazio and Segundo-Ortin, when individuals learn how to formulate explicit intentions, they develop the capacity to make plans, and, with it, the capacity to exert control upon the affordances they seek to perceive and actualize at each moment in relation to distal goals. Intentional thinking, they hold, is a useful means to link individual perception-action cycles into coherent wholes. Following this view, Segundo-Ortin (2022, pp. 8–9) argues that intentional thinking is also useful for individuals to learn what affordances are appropriate to them to actualize.[9]

This idea, we believe, fits hand in glove with the claim by McGeer that mastery of folk-psychological concepts "shapes how agents perceive the world around them" (2021, p. 1058). Even though she focuses her analysis on how the development of folk-psychological expertise improves our ability to perceive "agency-indicative information" – e.g., people's movements, gestures, facial expressions, etc. – we believe that it also enables us to make better use of the environment's information about affordances. In sum, our claim is that becoming an effective agent involves regulating not only our thought and action but also our perception of affordances in goal-oriented and normative ways.

Now that we have explained in which sense mindshaping scaffolds the development of individual agency in human beings, it is time to come back to the questions we enounced at the beginning of the section: how do behavior settings shape individual agency? And, how does the behavior settings framework deal with individual freedom? By answering these questions, we hope to show that the mindshaping view of folk-psychology can play a valuable role in understanding situated (human) agency.

In responding to these questions, it is important to understand the role that normativity plays in mindshaping. As we mentioned before, the key idea is that individuals learn how to shape and regulate their thought and action (and perception, we add) in accordance with norms. Complying with these norms is essential for making us understandable to others. However, these norms do not "float free." Instead, they are anchored to specific *places* or *behavior settings* outside of which the behavior will be perceived as incomprehensible. This point is highlighted in an exampled put forth by McGeer (2021) concerning rugby. At first sight, it is obvious that learning how to play and appreciate rugby requires developing both a set of athletic skills and a cognitive repertoire to *understand* the game. This involves, first and foremost, an understanding of the rules (knowing them, and, more importantly, knowing how to apply them) but also the capacity to predict what the players are likely to do in different circumstances, as well as the ability to adapt your actions to these foreseen possibilities. However, the point we want to stress here is that both rugby playing and rugby understanding also require

> certain culturally produced and culturally maintained environmental resources: e.g., the ball; the pitch with its various designated zones (e.g., midline, goal line, out lines and so on); even the existence of other players ... exercising rugby know-how depends on the continuing persistence of these cultural practices in the surrounding environment. (p. 1045)

In other words, both rugby-playing and rugby-observing expertise require the existence of behavior settings where these activities make sense.

The important thing to note is that, for McGeer, rugby is not an exception. On the contrary, all kinds of everyday practices are dependent on the existence of culturally produced and culturally maintained behavior settings where the practices make sense. This means that we can only behave as *experts* – understanding and predicting others and making ourselves understandable at the same time – in the context of concrete behavior settings. Acting and thinking as a rugby player only makes sense in a rugby pitch (or something near enough), with other agents that can behave as teammates and opponents, and so on, and, by the same token, acting and thinking as a grocery shopper only makes sense in the context of a store or a market.

This allows us to offer an answer to our first question. As we see it, behavior settings shape individual agency by supporting the learning and practicing of specific folk-psychological norms. These norms concern, first and foremost, how we (and the others) should behave, but also what it is appropriate to believe, desire, and so on. Therefore, some of the capacities that are constitutive of human agency — our capacity to make plans and understand our actions and those of others in folk-psychological terms — only make sense in the context of our participation in particular behavior settings. The norms that make possible expert agency in particular domains only exist insofar as they are anchored to specific behavior settings.

But, moving on to the second question, how does the behavior settings framework deal with individual freedom? As pointed out earlier, the constraints imposed by behavior settings are far from absolute, and the "mindshaping" brought about by participation in behavior settings not only enables agents to adhere to the relevant rules but also to criticize or ignore those rules. In other words, its account of agency is built on the assumption that human beings are not determined by their environment. This is why our folk psychological practices are characterized by an elaborate system containing numerous ways to motivate, prod, rebuke, and sanction those who fail to adhere to folk psychological norms:

> Thus, competent folk-psychologists not only know how to regulate their thought and action in accord with such norms ... they also know how to enter into negotiations about normatively untoward behavior and to offer excuses, explanations, apologies and adjustments when these are seen on all sides to be merited. (2015, p. 266)

Folk psychological practices that are grounded in behavior settings thus enable participants to become "enculturated free agents," in the sense of regulating their behavior and thought in relation to social norms. However, even if rejecting or ignoring folk psychological norms is always a possibility, it must be noted that being comprehensible to others and ourselves is something human beings generally deeply care about (McGeer, 2015). Behavior settings offer the concrete contexts in which we can make ourselves comprehensible to others. So even if individual agents always have the genuine option to violate or ignore norms, the regulative power of behavior settings should not be underestimated.

6.5 Concluding remarks

Following Heft's ecological interpretation of Barker's eco-behavioral science, we have tried to offer a situated account of human agency. At the core of our proposal is the view that agency consists of different capabilities that together enable individuals to act in goal-oriented ways. One of these is the capacity to exert control upon what affordances we perceive and act, as Heft proposes. However, this is not the complete story. Following McGeer, we have argued that agency also encompasses the capacity of thinking and acting according to folk-psychological norms – norms that prescribe, among other things, what is appropriate to believe, what is appropriate to desire and intend, and, most importantly, what is appropriate to do in light of one's beliefs, desires, and intentions. These folk-psychological norms, we have argued, are situated in the sense of being anchored to specific behavior settings outside of which they make no sense. This means that many of the norms we abide by at any specific moment in time belong to the behavior setting where we are. In sum, our claim is that insofar as individual agency is constrained by these norms, and the norms are anchored to behavior settings, individual agency is *situated*.

This proposal, we believe, resonates well with Heft's own position, and in fact tries to extend it. For instance, in a recent paper on behavior settings, he claims that "[i]f children are to function adaptively as social beings in the community whether they develop and live from day to day, they must learn not only where such places are located but also how to participate in them" (2018, p. 100). Following the mindshaping view, we hold that learning how to participate in a behavior setting requires, among other things, making ourselves understandable to others, as well as learning how to understand and predict them. The capacity to think and act according to folk-psychological norms, we claim, is crucial to achieve this. Likewise, to the claim that "the ways individuals engage the environment, in large measure, grow out of an ongoing developmental history of participation in social practices within their community" (Heft, 2020, p. 814), we add that among these practices are those that consist of making sense of ourselves and others in folk-psychological terms.

Furthermore, we hold that this proposal opens up new possibilities for those who, starting from J. J. Gibson's ecological psychology, aim to build a theory of human agency. In particular, we think that investigating the relationship between explicit thinking – particularly thinking that incorporates folk-psychological terms – and direct perception of affordances is a promising research venue. As we have argued, it is not a wild speculation that human beings use explicit intentional thinking to regulate what affordances of the environment they seek to perceive and actualize (Brancazio & Segundo-Ortin, 2020; Segundo-Ortin, 2022). In fact, this idea is in line with the proposal of other Gibsonian theorists, including Sanches de Oliveira et al. (2021) or Reed (1996) of incorporating explicit, linguistically articulated thought into ecological psychology. Even Heft (2020, p. 822) seems to recognize this possibility when he suggests that concepts can contribute to our awareness of social structures and institutions.

An account of agency based on mindshaping is situated in another sense: the folk-psychological norms that shape our individual agency are publicly shared (McGeer, 2015, p. 263). This means that folk-psychological norms only come into play for individuals once they have been learned from others – often, after they have been corrected or called upon for some transgression. Moreover, in line with the emphasis on *know-how* put by McGeer, we can dispute whether norm-abiding behavior requires the representation of norms. For one thing, we often behave in normatively appropriate ways without being able to explain it (see Rietveld, 2008 for different examples of this). And even though we sometimes enounce norms – for instance, when we correct others, or when we justify our actions to others – there is no reason to think that these are acts through which we externalize a previously represented rule or norm. Contrariwise, it is possible that we create a representation of the norm *in situ*, reflecting on what we and others usually do in the same or similar circumstances (Segundo-Ortin, 2022). Therefore, we believe that McGeer's mindshaping framework has all the required ingredients for being fruitful combined with Heft's ecological interpretation of behavior settings, and we look forward to further develop the resulting account of situated agency in the future.

Acknowledgments

This research was supported by the Nederlandse Organisatie voor Wetenschappelijk Onderzoek VIDI Research Project "Shaping our action space: A situated perspective on self-control" (VI.VIDI.195.116). Miguel's contribution was partly supported by a Ramón y Cajal Fellowship from Ministerio de Ciencia e Innovación del Gobierno de España (Award # RYC2021-031242-I).

Notes

1 For Barker, behavior occurs in molar units. These units consist of goal-oriented activities (behavior episodes) with a beginning, a direction, and an end.
2 An example of this is aggressivity. Barker and colleagues found that some children displayed different levels of aggressivity when exposed to different social situations, but these changes were congruent with the places where children were at the different times.
3 A different kind of critical approach has been developed by Wicker (1992, 2002). Unlike Heft, Wicker's solution is thoroughly internalistic.
4 According to Heft, Barker offers a sketch of an answer drawing upon Heider's distinction between "thing" and "medium" (Heft 2001, pp. 258–261). Heft is nonetheless critical of this solution, for he considers that it perpetuates undue dualisms in psychology.
5 The language of "emergence" is explicitly used by Heft: "psychological functions at any given moment emerge from a confluence of multiple dispositions to act expressed in conjunction with the multiple and changing conditions of the environment confronting the individual over time. And considering the active character of animate processes and the changing character of environmental conditions, this is a dynamic, ceaselessly shifting process' (2001, p. 317).
6 In line with Heft, McGann has proposed that agency is in itself distributed (McGann, 2014). As he puts it, "agency is not circumscribed by the organism," rather, he contends, "it is distributed through the physical, and particularly the social, environment in which the organism is operating" (p. 224). To this, he adds, "From such a perspective agency is something that holds in situations" (p. 229).
7 See section 5 for an elaboration of this connection.
8 Importantly, McGeer does not deny the reality of our capacity to interpret and even predict the behavior of others in folk-psychological terms. Instead, she holds that this epistemic capacity is a consequence of our capacity to regulate our own behavior in such terms. In this sense, our capacity for mind-reading is not pre-existing but depends on particular forms of enculturation and is limited to the degree to which we participate in cultural mind-making practices.

9 "For instance, I can deliberate about what it is more appropriate to do if I have a deadline in two days and my friends are asking me out and reach the conclusion that I should stay at home to finish the paper. In this situation, I use self-directed speech to control my attention, focusing on the specific aspects of the environment that are relevant to what I intend to do" (Segundo-Ortin, 2022, p. 8).

References

Barker, R. G. (1975). *Ecological psychology: Concepts and methods for studying the environment of human behavior*. Stanford University Press.

Barker, R. G. (Ed.). (1978). *Habitats, environments, and human behavior: Studies in ecological psychology and eco-behavioral science from the Midwest Psychological Field Station, 1947-1972*. Jossey-Bass.

Beer, R. (2014). Dynamical systems and embedded cognition. In: Frankish, K., & Ramsey, W. (Eds.), *The Cambridge handbook of artificial intelligence* (pp. 128–148). Cambridge: Cambridge University Press.

Brancazio, N., & Segundo-Ortin, M. (2020). Distal engagement: Intentions in perception. *Consciousness and Cognition*, 79, 102897. doi:10.1016/j.concog.2020.102897

Chemero, A. (2009). *Radical embodied cognitive science*. Cambridge, Mass.: MIT Press.

De Bruin, L. C. (2017). First-person folk psychology: Mindreading or mindshaping? *Studia Philosophica Estonica*. 170–183. https://doi.org/10.12697/spe.2016.9.1.07

De Jaegher, H., & Froese, T. (2009). On the role of social interaction in individual agency. *Adaptive Behavior*, 17(5), 444–460. doi:10.1177/1059712309343822

Gallagher, S., & Varga, S. (2020). Meshed architecture of performance as a model of situated cognition. *Frontiers in Psychology*, 11. doi:10.3389/fpsyg.2020.02140

Gibson, J. J. (1966). *The senses considered as perceptual systems*. New York, NY: Greenwood Press.

Gibson, J. J. (1979[2015]). *The ecological approach to visual perception*. New York, NY: Psychology Press.

Heft, H. (2001). *Ecological psychology in context: James Gibson, Roger Barker, and the legacy of William James's radical empiricism*. New York, NY: Psychology Press.

Heft, H. (2018). Places: Widening the scope of an ecological approach to perception–action with an emphasis on child development. *Ecological Psychology*, 30(1), 99–123. doi:10.1080/10407413.2018.1410045

Heft, H. (2020). Ecological psychology as social psychology? *Theory & Psychology*, 30(6), 813–826. doi:10.1177/0959354320934545

Heft, H., Hoch, J., Edmunds, T., & Weeks, J. (2014). Can the identity of a behavior setting be perceived through patterns of joint action? An investigation of place perception. *Behavioral Sciences*, 4(4), 371–393. doi:10.3390/bs4040371

Hutchins, E. (1995). How a cockpit remembers its speeds. *Cognitive Science*, 19(3), 265–288. doi:10.1207/s15516709cog1903_1

Hutchins, E. (2001). Cognition, distributed. In N. J. Smelser & P. B. Baltes (Eds.), *International encyclopedia of the social & behavioral sciences* (pp. 2068–2072). Pergamon. doi:10.1016/B0-08-043076-7/01636-3

Maiese, M. (2021). Mindshaping, enactivism, and ideological oppression. *Topoi*, 1–14.

McGann, M. (2014). Situated agency: The normative medium of human action. *Synthesis Philosophica*, 29(2), 217–233.

McGeer, V., & Pettit, P. (2002). The self-regulating mind. *Language & Communication*, 22, 281–299. 10.1016/s0271-5309(02)00008-3

McGeer, V. (2015). Mind-making practices: The social infrastructure of self-knowing agency and responsibility. *Philosophical Explorations, 18*(2), 259–281.

McGeer, V. (2021). Enculturating folk psychologists. *Synthese, 199*(1), 1039–1063. doi:10.1007/s11229-020-02760-7

Reed, E. (1996). *Encountering the world: Toward an ecological psychology*. Oxford: Oxford University Press.

Rietveld, E. (2008). Situated normativity: The normative aspect of embodied cognition in unreflective action. *Mind, 117*, 973–1001.

Sanches de Oliveira, G., Raja, V., & Chemero, A. (2021). Radical embodied cognitive science and "real cognition". *Synthese, 198*(1), 115–136. doi:10.1007/s11229-019-02475-4

Segundo-Ortin, M. (2022). Socio-cultural norms in ecological psychology: The education of intention. *Phenomenology and the Cognitive Sciences*. doi:10.1007/s11097-022-09807-9

Segundo-Ortin, M., & Kalis, A. (2022). Intentions in ecological psychology: An Anscombean proposal. *Review of Philosophy and Psychology*. https://doi.org/10.1007/s13164-022-00661-x

Wicker, A. W. (1992). Making sense of environments. In *Person–environment psychology: Models and perspectives* (pp. 157–192). Lawrence Erlbaum Associates, Inc.

Wicker, A. W. (2002). Ecological psychology: Historical contexts, current conception, prospective directions. In *Handbook of environmental psychology* (pp. 114–126). John Wiley & Sons, Inc.

7
BEHAVIOR SETTINGS, ENABLING CONSTRAINTS, AND THE NATURALIZATION OF SOCIAL NORMS

Vicente Raja and Manuel Heras-Escribano

7.1 Introduction: Behavior settings and ecological psychology

We engage in a fairly diverse set of social situations on a daily basis. We attend office meetings, go to concerts, do grocery shopping, or participate in our sport team's practice. All these situations and many others occur at different places and have their own norms, material conditions, affordances, etc. And when we engage in one of these situations, all these elements influence the repertoire of behaviors we exhibit. For instance, we may run and scream in the sport team's practice, but it would often be seen as against the norms in the office meetings. These social situations are the ones Roger Barker named *behavior settings*. In his work, Harry Heft has explored the influence of behavior settings in our psychological lives and also the possible role the concept can play in our psychological sciences. In this chapter, we aim to further explore the path opened by Harry Heft by considering the relationships between behavior settings, social norms, and enabling constraints.

One of the key aspects of Harry Heft's work within the ecological tradition is his emphasis on the importance of *places* to provide a full-blown account of perception and action. The importance of places is central because places, especially in the case of humans, "are nearly always embedded in meaningful, collective social practices" (Heft, 2018a, p. 100). As such, humans carry out their activities in places that are shaped both by their material context, affordances, and social norms and practices. The emphasis of Heft on places and, importantly, on the behavior settings emerging in them aims to expand the scope of ecological psychology toward social practices and events, therefore making the ecological approach relevant for social psychology and the social sciences. Following this line of research, ecological psychology will not only be an approach to the dynamical interactions between organisms and their natural environments, but it will also pay attention to the way social practices,

DOI: 10.4324/9781003259244-8

material culture, and intersubjectivity shape our interactions with the extended sociocultural environment. This attempt to expand ecological psychology toward sociality is shared by other researchers within the ecological tradition. However, the work of Heft combining ecological psychology and behavior settings is the place where we think one can find the best resources for establishing a plausible experimental framework for expanding ecological psychology toward the social realm.

In the following, we want to contribute to this line of research that aims to expand ecological psychology toward the social realm by stressing and complementing some consequences of Heft's proposal. Generally speaking, we think the notion of *enabling constraints* (Raja & Anderson, 2021) may be used to characterize different aspects of behavior settings, and especially those related to the social constructs that constitute them. Using enabling constraints, we can incorporate those constructs, such as norms or practices, in the explanations offered by ecological psychology and the radical embodied approaches to psychology. As we see it, our proposal combining behavior settings and enabling constraints will serve a two-fold purpose. First, as already noted, our proposal will help strengthen Heft's ecological approach to the psychology of the social. In other words, it will help ecological psychology to go beyond the perception-action events in purely natural environments. And second, our proposal will serve to provide an innovative ecological account of the naturalization of normativity that is compatible with the experimental sciences. To do so, we explore the relationship between behavior settings and norms in section 7.2. Then, in section 7.3, we will study the role of enabling constraints as a concept to properly characterize behavior settings and norms within the ecological approach. Afterward, in section 7.4, we will provide some concrete examples of the plausibility of our proposal and will offer a tentative modeling strategy for behavior settings and norms in the context of ecological psychology. Section 7.5 closes our contribution with some concluding remarks.

7.2 On behavior settings and norms

Behavior settings are dynamical structures discovered that emerge in particular places by virtue of equally particular social interactions. The notion of behavior settings was first introduced by Roger Barker and his colleagues in the late 1940s and the early 1950s during observational research that lasted almost three decades in Oskaloosa, Kansas (Heft, 2001; Schoggen, 1989). Barker and colleagues proposed that the interplay both between individuals and among individuals and their environments is patterned due to the set of constraints imposed by the material context, the opportunities of behavior in a given place, the social norms that apply to a given situation, etc. Behavior settings are the dynamical structures that stem out from these interactions taken together. Concretely, Heft (2018a) describes behavior settings as:

> [R]egions in the community [that] could be characterized as emergent, dynamic structures constituted by interdependent, joint actions among

> individuals and features of the material environment (milieu) considered over some extended period of time. (pp. 108–109)

These dynamic structures emerge from collective actions that are constrained by social norms and, Heft adds, they are also regulated by the available affordances (these affordances being parts of milieus). Note that although some of these constraints have developed into material aspects of culture (Baggs et al., 2020), the dynamical structure of behaviors that includes socio-cultural norms and affordances can self-emerge without the need for an explicit internal or external imposition of a set of norms: norms and constraints often stem out from the very interactions among individuals and "[a]s a result, places as behavior settings that afford particular socio-cultural possibilities for human daily life come into existence and are sustained over some duration" (Heft, 2018b).[1] Heft's assertion illustrates the tight connection between behavior settings and places, the latter being the basis for the former. But how do they originate? Again, in Harry Heft's own words:

> Behavior settings literally come into existence in a specifiable location and for some duration of time through the joint actions of their participants supported by affordances. (Heft, 2018a, p. 110)

It would be a mistake, however, to understand behavior settings as containers in which socio-cultural practices and activities occur. Rather than *entering* into a behavior setting, individuals *join* a behavior setting by participating in it. Behavior settings are not areas, but standing patterns of behaviors (joint activities) and milieus. This shows that it is all about the behavioral pattern that emerges from the interaction between the material context, affordances, and norms.

And norms are something to be illuminated in this case. First of all, there is no exhaustive definition of what is understood by socio-cultural norms. Are norms general maxims? Are they in the head or, on the contrary, they are available in the environment just like affordances are? Are norms perceived? If so, which is the information available for norms? A way to answer these questions is by complementing the just presented notion of behavior settings with a recent approach to normativity in the context of unreflective skilled action (Heras-Escribano, 2019; Heras-Escribano & Pinedo, 2018a, 2018b). This approach offers a non-reifiable account of norms in which they can be understood not as sets of entities in the head or in the environment, but as sets of practices that emerge in the forms of life of different communities.[2] Contrary to other approaches to normativity in metaphysics and the philosophy of mind, the proposal of Heras-Escribano and colleagues is based on the post-analytic and pragmatist ideas of authors such as Ryle, Dewey, Sellars, and Wittgenstein. Also, this view of normativity is compatible with naturalism, because since norms are not physical or mental entities, they are not extra elements added to our natural ontology (Heras-Escribano & De Pinedo, 2018b).

One might ask how these norms can be featured in our scientific explanations. As we have said, in this view norms are not reified. This means they are not extra entities in the world that we should search for. They are sets of practices that have a role and an influence in how processes deploy. In this sense, they are not particular mental or environmental *objects* to include in the explanation. However, their influence in human behavior is part of the explanation insofar as social and normative practices exert pressure on the way people act in social environments. As we will see, our proposal is to naturalize such a pressure by understanding social and normative practices as enabling constraints in social situations (section 7.3). Before we do so, it is important to note that Heras-Escribano and Pinedo (2016) applied this non-reifiable view of normativity to the ecological notion of affordance, concluding that social norms can influence our taking of affordances. Furthermore, this view on normativity is fully compatible with Barker's idea of behavior settings as far as they are understood as including social norms, and consequently these norms make crucial contributions to the self-regulating processes that constitute those very behavior settings as dynamical structures of standing patterns.

The combination of behavior settings and the non-reifiable account of normativity is not the only element required to explain the sociocultural realm. Norms are also shaped by non-normative aspects of the material context of human practices, like the already mentioned affordances. At the same time, we change our environment when we need to accommodate a proper norm-following process. In this sense, there is a dialogical relation between materiality and normativity in the socio-cultural realm in which each one of them permeates the other one. In this sense, both affordances and norms impose restrictions and enable opportunities of action for individuals. With this in mind, we want to move from the idea that culture is not in the *head* – that we overcome with behavior settings and our proposal of social normativity – to the idea that culture is not in the *norms*. The sociocultural environment is a complex system; therefore, we need a complex account of our sociocultural interactions (Baggs et al., 2019).

We do not have enough space here to delve into all the intricacies of normativity and social norms. For this reason, we will restrict our analysis to the naturalization of social norms and the way in which we can make them empirically testable despite being neither physical nor mental entities themselves. As hinted earlier, our approach to the naturalization of normativity has its starting point in the notion of constraint. If norms are a kind of constraint, they are suitable to figure within our empirical models of social psychology; therefore, the normative aspects of behavior settings may be experimentally tractable in the same way affordances or dynamics are so in the experimental framework of ecological psychology. For this reason, it is possible to combine such an experimental framework with behavior settings in order to provide an ecologically-inspired approach to the social realm. To do so, we propose the centrality of the notion of *enabling constraint* developed by Raja and Anderson (2021). We turn to it now.

7.3 Enabling constraints and behavior settings

The notion of enabling constraint used here was first developed in the context of mechanistic explanations (Anderson, 2015a).[3] Concretely, it was an alternative to the common notion of constitution in the literature on mechanisms. Classical mechanistic explanations of a target system decompose it to localize functions in the causal organization of its components. These explanations take constitution as the fundamental relationship between a system and its parts: the lower-level parts are constitutive of the higher-level whole system and the causal organization of the parts explains the behavior of the whole system (Bechtel, 2009; Craver, 2008; Craver & Darden, 2001). A classic example of this kind of explanation may be found in the neurophysiology of the visual system, concretely in the stimulus-direction selectivity of the dendrites of Starburst Amacrine Cells (SACs) in the mammalian retina (Tauchi & Masland, 1984). The dendrites of SACs implement a mechanism, so the mechanistic story goes, that allows the visual system to detect the directions of motion in the visual field. However, as Anderson (2015a) points out, this mechanism crucially depends on the activity of other non-SAC cells, such as bipolar cells connected to them. In this sense, the direction-detection mechanism cannot be explained just by the appeal to the lower-level components of the higher-level SAC system. Moreover, bipolar cells do not seem to *constitute* SACs in any meaningful sense of the term. This is the context in which Anderson (2015a) proposes that the role of bipolar cells in the direction-detection mechanism of SACs' dendrites is not one of constitution but one of *enabling constraint*: bipolar cells limit the degrees of freedom of the activity of SACs' dendrites and, precisely by virtue of that limitation, allow them to be direction sensitive in the way they are.[4]

Enabling constraints therefore appear as a notion that helps characterize systemic relationships that go beyond the straightforward constitution relation typical of mechanistic explanations. Raja and Anderson (2021) provide the general definition of the concept as:

> **Enabling constraint** = $_{Df}$ A positive constraint between S and $\{X\}$ that results in strictly functional outcome(s) for S. (p. 214)

In this definition, S is the system and $\{X\}$ is the set of factors impacting S. Thus, an enabling constraint is a limitation (therefore a constraint) that some x of $\{X\}$ impose on S making it exhibit a functionality that would be absent without the limitation (therefore enabling). There are examples of this kind of constraints in the life sciences. For instance, the anatomical limitations of human knees act as enabling constraints for bipedal locomotion. Healthy human knees have just one degree of freedom (i.e., they can bend only in one way), but this limitation in bending is precisely what allows for the motor control of bipedal locomotion. A knee able to bend in all ways, like a wrist, would be impossible (or at least way more difficult) to control. In a different context, morphological constraints due to developmental ontogenesis enable the influence of particular evolutionary pressures on particular organisms. Holekamp et al. (2013), for instance, claim that the superior manual dexterity of primates with respect to carnivores makes the former sensitive to evolutionary pressures via modified use of hands to which the latter are blind. In this sense, development of morphology acts as an enabling constraint on evolution.

These are just two examples among many others, but the reader may ask: what does this have to do with behavior settings and norms? We think the notion of enabling constraint can be very productive to characterize the way behavior settings influence the behavior of the individuals that join them. Also, in the particular case of the sociocultural norms at play in those behavior settings, they can also be regarded as enabling constraints both for the individuals joining the behavior settings and for the behavior settings as such. In the spirit of Heras-Escribano and Pinedo (2018a, 2018b), these norms are not entities of the system, but activities that constraint the system. And the same applies to behavior settings.

The first case to be considered is the enabling and constraining role of behavior settings on individual behavior. Following Heft's definition above, the interdependent joint actions of individuals in a shared environment are what make the dynamic structures of behavior settings emerge. Once these dynamic structures have emerged, the question is whether and how they influence the very individual behaviors that constitute them. Take, for instance, the behavior setting of an office meeting between co-workers. The place of such behavior setting can be a meeting room of the company. In the meeting room, the participants may be seated in relatively comfortable chairs around a big table. Most of them will be carrying some papers, a laptop, a phone, a coffee, etc. They will be discussing some issues relevant for the company that have most likely been decided and scheduled beforehand. They will go through these topics in a fairly linear fashion: first the summary of the last year's results, then some new product ideas, then a discussion about hiring for a new department, etc. Most of the participants will remain seated for the whole meeting and will take turns to talk. If some of them are presenting some data necessary for the discussion, they will take the first turn in each of the scheduled issues. If there is a hierarchy between participants (e.g., CEO, project managers, other staff, and so on) their turn taking will be adapted. Most of them will be paying attention to the participant talking. Or at least pretending to do so. The participants will not be playing with their phones or wearing their headphones during the meeting. There will be little chats both before the meeting officially starts and also after it ends. Even in the case of heated discussions, they most likely remain within generally civilized parameters. There will be agreements and disagreements, and so on.

We could continue describing different aspects of this behavior setting, but we think the general idea is well illustrated. The plurality of material, behavioral, social, and normative factors that leads to the emergence of behavior settings makes them challenging to model in the context of psychology. Crucial for this challenge is the realization that not all these factors operate homogeneously within the behavior setting. Think, for instance, in the moment one of the participants takes her turn and starts talking about an important company report. For this to occur, many different factors converge. Some of them are physiological and anatomical, like the machinery involved in the production of speech. Some other factors are perceptual, like her visual capacity to see the pages in which the report is written down. Reading, of course, also involves some skills. All these factors play a very specific role in the motor control of her talking. She literally has the skills to move her body and face in such a way as to produce the appropriate noises for her speech. In principle, we should be able to model these movements and the perceptual information that constraints them with the typical tools used in ecological psychology, such as dynamical systems theory.

However, other aspects of her talking behavior in the company meeting does not seem to straightforwardly fall into physiology, anatomy, perceptual information, or skills.[5] For instance, and despite having the physiology, anatomy, and skills to scream and to whisper, the participant will control her speech so it is not too loud or too quiet. The volume of her voice will be enough to be heard without problems but not loud enough as to be unpleasant. Similarly, and again despite having the physiology, anatomy, and skills to do so, the participant will probably not step on the table and dance while presenting the report. The normative constraints imposed by the behavior setting, as opposed to physiology, anatomy, or skills, are the driving forces that explain, at least in part, the volume of the speech and the sitting, non-dancing behavior. Note that screaming and dancing would be perfectly appropriate for other behavior settings, such as concerts or parties, but not for a company meeting. This fact highlights the enabling character of these constraints. Social norms allowing screaming and dancing likely enable several of the expected outcomes of concerts or parties. However, the same norms would be just mere limitations for the aims of a company meeting: proper communication, calm deliberation, etc. In this sense, the social norms that constrain voice volume and dancing in the behavior setting of a company meeting are not just mere limitations, but limitations that enable the success of the behavior setting. The social norms at play in behavior settings are, in two words, enabling constraints.

7.4 Modeling behavior settings and norms

So far, we have provided a phenomenological[6] description of an example of a behavior setting (a company meeting). We think there is nothing too controversial in what we have described in this particular instance of behavior setting. We also think this kind of description might be applied to any other behavior setting. At the same time, there is nothing especially insightful, other than identifying the normative aspects of the particular behavior setting with enabling constraints. Understanding different aspects of behavior settings in terms of enabling constraints is conceptually fruitful, as it allows for a more fine-grained analysis of each situation. Again, we think this descriptive strategy can be applied to all behavior settings. However, if the concept of enabling constraint is to be really productive for the research on behavior settings, a mere conceptual re-organization of the field will not be enough. Enabling constraints should be a tool to model behavior settings and norms within the general modeling framework of psychology and, more concretely for our and Heft's work, in the framework of ecological psychology. This is the core issue: how to use enabling constraints to model behavior settings and norms?

First of all, a reminder of what typical models of behavior are in ecological psychology may be beneficial for the reader. Take, for instance, a navigation behavior in a sparsely crowded environment. An agent (a person) can locomote toward an object through that environment. This object can be identified as the *goal* of the navigation. While moving around, the agent will be avoiding some of the other objects in the environment. These other objects can be identified as the *obstacles* in the navigation. This kind of navigation behavior has been modeled within the ecological literature by Brett Fajen and William Warren (2003; see also Warren, 2006). Leaving technical details aside, Fajen and Warren's model captures the agent's change of steering in the environment as she locomotes toward the goal while avoiding obstacles. This behavior is formalized with a dynamical model in which the approach toward the goal and avoiding of the obstacles is modeled in terms of the closing or the opening of the angle formed by the agent's steering direction and the position of the goal or the obstacle, respectively (Figure 7.1). The variables of the model are those angles and the steering itself. These variables represent the quantitative aspects of the behavior that change in time as it evolves.

The model also has parameters that characterize the limitations of all the different aspects of the behavior. The two parameters featured in Figure 7.1, damping (b) and stiffness (k), refer to the limitations of the motor system itself. They characterize, for instance, how fast and smoothly the motor system of the agent is able to change its steering either to avoid an obstacle or to better approach to a goal. But these are not the only parameters featured in the model. Some other parameters limit the influence of environmental information in the steering behavior of the agents. It seems clear that, for the agents to properly change their steering in a given environment, they need to be perceptually aware of those steering angles they need to open or close depending on whether they face an obstacle or a goal. For many agents, this perceptual information is visually available (e.g., Wilkie & Wann, 2003).[7] However, not all the available perceptual information influences behavior to the same extent. For instance, the angle between the agent's steering direction and the position of several obstacles may be simultaneously available in the agent's visual field. Nevertheless, not all these angles equally affect the changes in steering behavior. Generally speaking, closer obstacles affect this change more than further away ones. To model this fact, Fajen and Warren (2003) include weighting parameters for the influence of perceptual information about obstacles and goals in their behavioral model.

Once the usual modeling strategy of ecological psychology is described, the next step consists in arriving at two realizations. The first realization is that we have already been talking about constraints. The limitations in the changes of behavior imposed by parameters are indeed constraints. In other words, parameters are the typical way in which natural constraints are included in ecological models.[8]

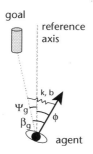

FIGURE 7.1 Relationship between agent's steering direction and the position of the goal in the ecological model of navigation (Fajen & Warren, 2003). The vector of the agent's steering direction, ϕ, and the position of the goal, ψ_g, form an angle β_g. Steering changes toward the goal (i.e., the closing of the β_g angle) are modeled using the equation of a damped mass-spring and its two typical parameters for damping (b) and stiffness (k). The case of the obstacle is similar with the only difference that steering changes open the respective β_i angle (from Warren, 2006, p. 374, figure 7).

Physiological and anatomical constraints, for instance, and the ones that limit the speed and smoothness of the changes of agents' steering while navigating an sparsely crowded environment. In this sense, the damping and stiffness terms of Fajen and Warren's model stand for these constraints.

The second realization is that the notion of enabling constraint provides ecological psychology with the opportunity to straightforwardly relate behavior settings and norms with the parameters of their models of behavior. The social and normative constraints of behavior settings present limitations to behavior that enable concrete practices in different social situations. Think of the notion of canonical affordance, for instance (Costall, 2012). Canonical affordances are those typical affordances objects offer to perceivers in everyday social environments. For example, although in principle a chair affords many things to an agent (e.g., stepping on it, throwing it away, turning it upside down, and so on), the canonical affordance of chairs in most social environments is sitting. In most of these contexts, canonical affordances are enforced neither by the physiology or the anatomy of agents nor by their material environment. On the contrary, canonical affordances are the product of normative constraints in the social environment. In this sense, if ecological psychologists want to develop a model of behavior that includes canonical affordances, such normative constraints may be part of the model in the form of parameters that limit behaviors in different ways. In other words, the parameters of the model may refer both to natural and social/normative limitations of the behavior of interest. In the case of Fajen and Warren's model of navigation, for instance, it is possible to think of a social situation in which a goal is not available for particular agents – e.g., they cannot enter a particular meeting room. Although the agents may have the capacity and skill to get into the room, they might have their access denied for some reason. In this sense, a possible goal (e.g., the door of the room) may be unavailable for an agent such that it does not feature as a goal but as an obstacle in the model.

One can think of a parameter modulating these dynamics within the navigation model. A parameter that, depending on several normative aspects of the situation, allows for changing goals into obstacles or vice versa when the dynamics of the behavior requires so.

This discussion on the conceptual relationship between the normative constraints of behavior settings and the parameters of the dynamical models used by ecological psychologists brings us back to the central statements we want to make in this chapter. First, as we proposed in the previous section, the social and normative limitations imposed by behavior settings in the behavior of the agents that join them are enabling constraints. Second, constraints are parameters or hyperparameters – i.e., parameters that limit the change of other parameters – of the ecological models of behaviors. And therefore, the influence of behavior settings in the activities of the agents that join them can be modeled through the parameters of the typical ecological models of behavior. For this reason, we think the conceptual combination of behavior settings and enabling constraints provides a plausible, sounding methodological route to incorporate Harry Heft's insights regarding social psychology into the experimental research carried out by ecological psychologists.

We are very aware we are proposing a speculative hypothesis. We cannot say that the kind of modeling we have just detailed is currently pursued within ecological psychology. However, some recent works are beginning to characterize social situations that can be considered behavior settings and are incorporating similar ideas. For instance, based on the navigation example we have been using in this chapter, recent work by William Warren models the navigation behavior of crowds both when a group of people follow a leader and when there is no clear leader in the crowd (Rio et al., 2018; Warren, 2018). At least in the cases of crowds following a leader, it seems clear that we are modeling a behavior setting, that is, an emergent, dynamic structure constituted by interdependent, joint actions among individuals. To model this kind of setting, Warren and colleagues expand the model of individual navigation previously developed by Fajen and Warren (2003) including new variables for the members of the crowd and their alignment to both steering direction and speed of the leader. Like the variables of the previous model, the changes of these new variables are also limited by some parameters. For instance, a parameter limits the influence of the leader on the behavior of each member of the crowd depending on how far away from the leader each member is. The further away the leader is, the lesser her influence is. Eventually, if the leader is too far away, there is no influence at all. Thus, what this parameter is quite literally quantifying is whether an agent is *joining* a behavior setting or not. The value of the parameter expresses whether a concrete behavior setting (i.e., a crowd following a leader) is constraining the behavior of an individual agent or not. One can imagine other parameters expressing the way leaders are selected and the way different social norms may affect this selection. In this sense, although these models are not providing full-fledged models of behavior settings, we think they are pointing to the right direction. And that is the direction we have tried to develop in this work.

7.5 Conclusion

We think the work of Harry Heft is crucial if we want to pursue an ecological psychology capable of responding to wider psychological questions regarding social situations and normative behavior. In this chapter, we have selected one of the notions to which Heft has paid more attention in his career, the notion of behavior setting. We have explored the different natural and social factors that make behavior settings emerge and we have tried to characterize them in terms of enabling constraints. We do think enabling constraints offer two fundamental benefits in order to understand behavior settings and their normative components. First, by conceptualizing behavior settings in terms of enabling constraints, we achieve a more nuanced description of the different components of the settings. Brains and norms, for instance, have different influences in the emergence of behavior settings and enabling constraints allow us to highlight such a difference. And second, enabling constraints provide us with a way to operationalize behavior settings and norms such that they can feature as parameters in the ecological, dynamical models of behavior. By doing so, and in the spirit of Heft's work, we are closer to explaining sociality and to naturalizing normativity within the ecological approach to psychology.

Notes

1 This is in line with James Gibson's question of how can behavior be regular without being regulated (1979/2015, p. 215). We think that the definitions of behavior setting and place open the door to an ecological explanation of sociality partly because behavior settings and ecological psychology share the same spirit regarding self-organization.
2 We do not want to make the stronger claim that *all* norms *must* be like this as we remain open to the possibility that some norms in some contexts have different environmental or organismal sources (Baggs et al., 2020; De Pinedo, 2020; Raja & Chemero, 2020). However, we focus on sociocultural norms as sets of practices that emerge in the forms of life of different communities because we take them to be of chief importance for behavior settings.
3 The name "enabling constraint" has also been used to address the nature of self-organization both regarding the relationship between evolution and development (Salthe, 1993) and in the general case (Juarrero, 1999).
4 It is important to point out that there are other possible solutions to understand the relationship between bipolar cells and SACs. One of them consists in giving up the idea that the direction-detection mechanism is restricted to SAC's dendrites and then describing a wider mechanism that includes bipolar cells as one of its constituents. We do not have space to address this alternative possibility here, but Anderson (2015b) does it explicitly and details the benefits of the enabling constraint strategy.
5 As the reader will see, these other aspects are the social and normative constraints of behavior settings. For our analytical strategy, these (enabling) constraints are sources for the emergence of behavior settings different from physiology, anatomy, perceptual information, skills, etc. It is important to point out that these sources for the emergence

of behavior settings are completely alien to each other. We think they are most likely connected in many interesting ways. For the sake of clarity, however, we will maintain the analytical strategy of differentiating them.
6 By "phenomenology," we do not refer to the philosophical tradition. Rather, we use the term as it is used in physics when experts talk about "particle phenomenology," for instance.
7 Although, in principle, the same perceptual information could be available through a different sensory modality, e.g., touch/haptics (Lobo et al., 2019).
8 Note that other constraints might be implicitly or explicitly included in the model due to the very modeling activity. Modelers must make decisions regarding the variables they will consider, the parameters they will include, the way the collective variable of the system is characterized, the simplification assumptions of the model, etc. These decisions always constraint the model applicability and explanatory power. For the sake of brevity and clarity, we will not address these issues in this chapter.

References

Anderson, M. L. (2015a). Beyond componential constitution in the brain: Starburst Amacrine Cells and enabling constraints. In T. Metzinger & J. M. Windt (Eds.), *Open MIND*: 1(T). Frankfurt am Main: MIND Group. doi:10.15502/9783958570429

Anderson, M. L. (2015b). Functional attributions and functional architecture. In T. Metzinger & J. M. Windt (Eds.), *Open MIND*: 1(T). Frankfurt am Main: MIND Group. doi:10.15502/9783958570757

Baggs, E., Raja, V., and Anderson, M. (2019). Culture in the world shapes culture in the head (and vice versa). *Behavioral and Brain Sciences*, *42*, E172. doi:10.1017/S0140525X19001079

Baggs, E., Raja, V., & Anderson, M. (2020). Extended skill learning. *Frontiers in Psychology*, *11*, 1956. doi:10.3389/fpsyg.2020.01956

Bechtel, W. (2009). Constructing a philosophy of science of cognitive science. *Topics in Cognitive Science*, *1*, 548–569.

Costall, A. (2012). Canonical affordances in context. *Avant*, *3*(2), 85–93.

Craver, C. F. (2008). *Explaining the brain: Mechanisms and the mosaic unity of neuroscience*. Oxford: Oxford University Press.

Craver, C. F., & Darden, L. (2001). Discovering mechanisms in neurobiology: The case of spatial memory. In P. K. Marchamer, R. Grush, & McLaughlin (Eds.), *Theory and method in the neurosciences*. Pittsburgh: University of Pittsburgh Press.

De Pinedo García, M. (2020). Ecological psychology and enactivism: A normative way out from ontological dilemmas. *Frontiers in Psychology*, *11*, 1637.

Fajen, B. R., & Warren, W. H. (2003). Behavioral dynamics of steering, obstacle avoidance, and route selection. *Journal of Experimental Psychology: Human Perception and Performance*, *29*, 343–362.

Heft, H. (2001). *Ecological psychology in context: James Gibson, Roger Barker, and the legacy of William James's radical empiricism*. Psychology Press.

Heft, H. (2018a). Places: Widening the scope of an ecological approach to perception–action with an emphasis on child development. *Ecological Psychology*, *30*(1), 99–123.

Heft, H. (2018b). Places as emergent dynamic structures in everyday life. *ENSO Seminar Series*. Retrieved from http://www.ensoseminars.com/presentations/past27/

Heras-Escribano, M. (2019). *The philosophy of affordances*. Cham: Palgrave Macmillan.

Heras-Escribano, M., & Pinedo-García, D. (2018a). Affordances and landscapes: Overcoming the nature–culture dichotomy through niche construction theory. *Frontiers in Psychology*, *8*, 2294.

Heras-Escribano, M., & Pinedo-García, M. D. (2018b). Naturalism, non-factualism, and normative situated behaviour. *South African Journal of Philosophy, 37*(1), 80–98.

Heras-Escribano, M., & de Pinedo, M. (2016). Are affordances normative? *Phenomenology and the Cognitive Sciences, 15*(4), 565–589.

Holekamp, K. E., Swanson, E. M., & Van Meter, P. E. (2013). Developmental constraints on behavioural flexibility. *Philosophical Transactions of the Royal Society B, 368*, 20120350.

Juarrero, A. (1999). *Dynamics in action: Intentional behavior as a complex system*. Cambridge, MA: The MIT Press.

Lobo, L., Nordbeck, P. C., Raja, V., Chemero, A., Riley, M. A., Jacobs, D., & Travieso, D. (2019). Route selection and obstacle avoidance with a short-range haptic sensory substitution device. *International Journal of Human-Computer Studies, 132*, 25–33.

Raja, V., & Chemero, A. (2020). In favor of impropriety. *Constructivist Foundations, 15*(3), 213–216.

Raja, V., & Anderson, M. L. (2021). Behavior considered as an enabling constraint. In F. Calzavarini & M. Viola (Eds.), *Neural mechanisms: New challenges in the philosophy of neuroscience* (pp. 209–232). New York: Springer.

Rio, K. W., Dachner, G. C., & Warren, W. H. (2018). Local interactions underlying collective motion in human crowds. *Proceedings of the Royal Society B, Biological Sciences*. doi:10.1098/rspb.2018.0611

Salthe, S. N. (1993). *Development and evolution: Complexity and change in biology*. Cambridge, MA: The MIT Press.

Schoggen, P. (1989). *Behavior Settings: A revision and extension of Roger G. Barker's Ecological Psychology*. Stanford, CA: Stanford University Press.

Tauchi, M., & Masland, R. H. (1984). The shape and arrangement of the cholinergic neurons in the rabbit retina. *Proceedings of the Royal Society of London B, 223*(1230), 101–119. doi:10.1098/rspb.1984.0085

Warren, W. H. (2006). The dynamics of perception and action. *Psychological Review, 113*(2), 358–389.

Warren, W. H. (2018). Collective motion in human crowds. *Current Directions in Psychological Science, 27*(4), 232–240.

Wilkie, R., & Wann, J. (2003). Controlling steering and judging heading: Retinal flow, visual direction, and extraretinal information. *Journal of Experimental Psychology: Human Perception and Performance, 29*(2), 363–378.

8
VALUES, AFFORDANCES, AND AGENCY

Giving heft to ecological accounts

Bert H. Hodges

8.1 Introduction

Harry Heft has been a singular voice in ecological psychology for over three decades. He has not been alone. Many others, including some of those contributing to this volume, have worked with him to enlarge and enrich the promise of an ecological approach to acting, perceiving, thinking, and feeling that emerged from the work of Gibson (1966, 1979), Barker (1968), and others. But while many have contributed to the chorus, Harry's part has been distinctive and distinguished, a solo of sorts. Rather than begin with his publications, I begin with a question he asked several ecological researchers over coffee the first week I met him: *do you think a person can directly perceive righteousness?* The stunned silence that met his question testified to its audacity, prompting only one unthinking reply, which demonstrated the negativity bias of psychologists (Krueger & Funder, 2004): 'I don't know about righteousness, but you certainly can perceive self-righteousness!"

Part of what shocks about such a question is that it suggests that something that deserves the name *righteousness* exists to be perceived. Ecological researchers tend to view psychology as a natural science (Reed, 1996), and many have thought that a naturalistic view of existence requires a commitment to there being nothing that is properly labeled right or wrong, meaningful or meaningless, beautiful or ugly (Deacon, 2012). If one focuses on claims that ecological psychology is a psychology of natural laws (Raja, 2019), then it is not easy to see how it has anything to say about acting, perceiving, thinking, or feeling being right, or not right. They simply are what they are. However, meaning and value are central to Gibson's ecological account (1966, 1979). As Heft (2007, p. 102) elegantly concluded: "we live individually and collectively in a world of meanings and values." Many others concur and propose this conviction should be central for the ecological sciences

DOI: 10.4324/9781003259244-9

(Costall & Still, 1989; Hodges & Baron, 1992; Kadar & Effken, 1994, 2005; Reed, 1988, 1996; Sanders, 1997; Still & Good, 1998).

8.2 Affordances reconsidered

One of Gibson's most audacious and famous claims is that animals, humans included, perceive meanings and values directly. However, Gibson (1966) felt the need to disguise values and meanings as *affordances*, given behaviorism's antipathy to meaning, but the coined term served to help him relocate values and meanings. Affordances are what the environment "offers the animal, what it *provides* or *furnishes*, either for good or ill" (1979, p. 127). Meaning is neither a subjective projection of some animate agent(s), nor is it a property of some object. Rather, the environment, as a whole, is providential; it is there for the agent(s), providing what is needed, so that the agent(s) can do something valuable, that can be judged "good or ill." Those wishing a more formal definition may find Gibson's characterization of affordances disappointing, but it affords more than many ecological researchers and theorists have granted.

One underappreciated dimension is that affordances are systemic, relational, and social (Costall, 1995; Heft, 2020). A fine example of this is found in Gibson's (1979) proposal of what a postbox affords for humans, at least canonically (Costall, 2012). Heft, more than anyone, has worked to unpack this example, which he has shown requires engaging a *postal system,* which "is not an entity to be perceived in its entirety" (Heft, 2020, p. 821), but is a "conceptual awareness of a dynamic social structure ... [that] is real, rather than imagined" (Heft, 2017, p. 138). He goes on to claim that this requires an approach to meaning and value that is "grounded" in everyday perceiving and acting, and "rooted in *engagement* with the environment" (p. 138, italics added). In and of itself, a postbox affords little or nothing of interest to most humans. Its affordances as a place to deposit letters emerge within a set of social practices.

To extend Heft's insights, it is worth noting the systemic complexity of the environment required for postboxes to come into existence. Postal systems are nested within larger, literate, law-abiding societies, where people care about and trust each other enough, to send letters, checks, or advertisements, using strange metal boxes. Systems of such complexity are never perceived whole; thus, placing a letter in a postbox is an act of prospective faith. It is *not* about momentary perception, memory, or imagination. It is *not* a guess, an inference, or a prediction. Rather, the act is warranted by practical, personal, communal knowledge (Polanyi, 1958). As Heft (2017, p. 139) notes: "When individuals engage in social practices they do not infer 'the rules' of social life by applying intellectual processes to scattered observations but instead [by] functioning adeptly and normatively in particular social situations," which is "characteristic of skilled action" (Heft, 2017, p. 139).

In this regard, participating in a postal system is not unlike speaking a language. Language is vast, systemic, and dynamic. It is not perceptually comprehensible as an entity; thus, it is not something that is bounded by a skull, confined to genetic codes, or encapsulated in a set of rules that linguists can discover and decode. Rather, it is an ongoing, unfolding set of social and physical practices in which most humans participate for most of their lives. Language in some abstract sense is not learned; rather, very particular local practices are engaged and enacted that continue to expand and evolve as members of the community travel in wider circles of social relations over longer periods of time (Wray & Grace, 2007). Conversing with others has its own affordances (e.g., the joy of a friendly conversation), and and like a postal system, it gives birth to many other affordances. Humans learn to participate in one or more linguistic communities in which they have a stake; they participate in patterns of actions with others that care about each other – as family, friends, teammates, traders, competitors, and even enemies (Graeber & Wengrow, 2021; Hodges, 2017; Tomasello, 2008). Words, apart from relationships, are impotent, as are postal boxes apart from social systems.

A second aspect of Gibson's account is that affordances are an offering to animate agents. Affordances create opportunities that may invite, or even demand, actions by agents, but they do not force actions. Affordances are not stimuli. Gibson described his ecological approach to action and perception as moving from a stimulus psychology to a values-realizing one (Hodges, 2022; Reed, 1988). Affordances demand agency. The first of Heft's (1989) papers I remember reading focused on the need for intentionality in perceiving. Agents engage in action, making perceiving possible. Animate agents offer affordances to their environmental habitats, just as those habitats provide what is necessary for agents to exist and function effectively. Together, habitats and agents form self-sustaining *niches*, ways of life so rich that it takes multiple disciplines for humans to begin to appreciate their complexity and directedness. More about agency shortly, but first, the relation of affordances and values must be clarified.

A third aspect of Gibson's description suggests that affordances are not values themselves, except in a limited sense. Affordances are offerings that provide what agents need to engage in perceiving and acting that realizes values. Affordances open pathways for situated agents to move in good, or not so good, directions; this is what makes them *meaningful*. Hodges and Baron (1992) proposed that values cannot be localized in what a particular object, situation, or event affords. Rather, values are ecosystem defining; they are the larger scale goods that define the proper functioning of the ecosystem(s) and that constrain the fields of action for animate activity within it. What gives warrant for acting, perceiving, feeling, or thinking in some specific setting is whether the direction and manner of those activities open further possibilities for action that will sustain and enrich the niche and the ecosystems of which it is a part. Values are constraints on affordances, and affordances that are engaged appropriately can contribute to realizing values. In this sense, affordances can be partial realizations of values (Hodges & Baron, 1992, p. 263).

Having considered the centrality of meaning and values to Gibson's ecological approach, particularly his proposal that affordances are what animate agents perceive most directly, I want to elaborate this in two directions, each inspired by themes in Heft's work. First, ecological values-realizing theory (Hodges & Rączaszek-Leonardi,

2022) is briefly described, leading to an oft-asked question: what about cultural differences? Heft has often reminded psychologists of the importance of attending to culture (Heft, 2013b). Second, I highlight the social nature of perceiving and acting – a persistent concern of Heft (2001, 2007, 2017, 2020) – with special attention to the nature of language. In doing so, the critical importance of *agency* to Gibson's ecological account emerges. How should it be characterized, and what are its implications for responsible action?

8.3 Values, ecosystems, and cultures

In one of Heft's (2011) many interesting chapters, he explores how behavior is directed and situated by focusing on Edwin Holt's (1915, 1931) idea of the "recession of the stimulus." Rather than seeing behavior as a reaction to local and immediate stimuli, Holt sees it as a free and purposive reaching out *toward* a stimulus, which becomes the object of inquiry and examination, and a source of bodily organization and directed movement. The object of inquiry, or stimulus, need not be an object, per se, but is the entire situation into which the agent acts. As the object of action, the *situation is as much a constituent of the activity* as the organismic processes of the agent (Holt, 1915, p. 55; cited in Heft, 2011, p. 196). Thus, the purposes of actions are often directed far away, and far ahead, toward a much more extensive and complex ensemble of factors than the immediate circumstances in which actions unfold. The significance of local and immediate stimuli recedes; actions are now located on a much larger stage, and in a longer running play. It may be that these larger scale constraints guiding action, which seem to be deeply recessed from the moment and the place of action, are what is most important in understanding what action is and what it means.

Heft (2011) uses his discussion of Holt to explore the nature of *situations*, the fact that "the meaning of any action cannot be adequately addressed until it is properly situated within some environment-organism functional unit," such as Barker's (1968) "behavior setting," and Lewin's (1942) "time-field-units." To Heft's insights, I add the following proposal: the most "recessed" constraints on acting, perceiving, feeling, and thinking are *values*. In a deep and important sense, the objects of inquiry, the "stimuli" that psychological acts reach for, are – at their most recessed – values. Values, in this accounting, are not properties of individual agents, or social groups, or environmental objects or events. Rather, values are the boundary conditions of ecosystems that give definition to the system, and that provide constraints that necessarily guide and evaluate fields of action within the system.

If values constrain fields of action, then they are constitutive of psychological acts, such as perceiving. As Gibson (1979) put it: "The visual system *hunts* for comprehension and clarity (p. 219). Perceiving gets wider and finer, and longer and richer and fuller as the observer explores (p. 255) … without ever reaching a limit" (p. 253). On this ecological account of perceiving, visual, auditory, and haptic systems are not primarily goal oriented, rule-following, or even law-governed. This is *not* to say that exploratory actions (i.e., perceiving) are never goal-directed or rule-following, or that they occur in some domain beyond the constraints of natural laws. However, ecological values-realizing theory (Hodges, 2007b, 2009; Hodges & Baron, 1992; Hodges & Rączaszek-Leonardi, 2022) *does* claim that the looking, listening, and manipulating of animate agents are reaching out for something that is more encompassing (more recessed, in Holt's terms) than goals or rules, or even laws. Laws define what is physically possible, but values recruit and harness laws into functional acts. When animate agents are looking, listening, manipulating, locomoting, and so on, they are hunting for values. Actions seek *clarity* (e.g., variations that differentiate better and worse ways to move), *coherence* (e.g., invariants that provide patterns and pathways toward what is good), *comprehensiveness* (e.g., explorations and constructions that expand the reach of invariances, i.e., skills), and *complexity* (e.g., encounters with violations of assumed invariants, provoking incoherence and re-clarification, i.e., creativity).

Actions are constrained by many more values than the four just mentioned. The ecological task is to identify tasks and skills, settings and situations, with the intention of exploring the most prominent values that give shape and purpose to those skills and situations. Modest, but promising, efforts have been made in a number of domains, including social interaction (Hodges & Geyer, 2006; Hodges et al., 2014); perception-action skills, such as driving (Hodges, 2007b; Hodges & Rączaszek-Leonardi, 2022) and carrying (Hodges, 2017; Hodges & Lindhiem, 2006); language (Hodges, 2007a, 2009, 2014b; Hodges & Fowler, 2010); timing (Zhang et al., 2019); reasoning (Hodges, 2019); and development (Hodges, 2014a; Hodges & Baron, 1992; Rączaszek-Leonardi & Nomikou, 2015).

Ecological values-realizing theory (Hodges & Baron, 1992; Hodges & Rączaszek-Leonardi, 2022) can be summarized as follows. All psychological acts, whether perceiving, acting, thinking, or feeling, are constrained by multiple values that are heterarchically related to each other. Driving, for example, is constrained by the values of accuracy, tolerance, speed, safety, freedom, equality, justice, stability, flexibility, comfort, efficiency, and economy, among others. To claim that values are heterarchically related means that they cannot be ranked on a permanent basis. Speed, comfort, and stability may take the lead in some driving situations, but that can suddenly shift, with accuracy, justice, and safety becoming "most important," setting the parameters for other values.

Values are obligatory constraints; if speed, comfort, accuracy, freedom, and safety, for example, are not attended to and enacted sufficiently, driving will cease, or the driving ecosystem will deteriorate. If all driving were like bull-riding, the discomfort would severely limit those willing to participate; if driving did not move people more quickly from one place to another, the safety, accuracy, or freedom of movement would matter little. Observing that values are obligatory to the existence of a driving ecosystem makes clear that values are not just rules (e.g., roadways, signals, speed limits); rules can be changed, but values cannot. Values are also not laws like those that govern the mechanics, forces, and frictions that make driving possible; values are "more recessed" constraints than laws are. Although both are obligatory, value-constraints are often more elastic than law-governed ones.

A person may fail to drive justly, accurately, or safely *sometimes in some places*, without the field of action immediately collapsing. Nevertheless, perceiving and acting that persists in failing to realize values will threaten freedom of action and will degrade ecosystem potentials.

Since they define the ecosystem and the fields of action within that system, values provide the criteria by which psychological acts can be judged. What counts as good driving, or good traffic rules, or good vehicle design is evaluated in terms of values. Does it contribute to safety, accuracy, comfort, justice, efficiency, and all the other values that make driving a *common good*? When goals are adopted, or rules are formulated, or when changes to goals or rules are proposed, it is values that provide the basis for *legitimating* a practice or a particular set of acts; it is also the basis for *critique*. The working hypothesis of ecological values-realizing theory is that across time and task, all the values are equally important as constraints. The heterarchical nature of values means they function as a *cooperative tension*; no one value is ever maximized because all the values mutually constrain each other. Values work in concert to enable each value to be realized; in the long run, for example, justice, truth, freedom, and social solidarity constrain each other in ways that make complex communal and individual actions possible. In the short run, values-realizing activity is *frustrating*, in a sense not unlike physical systems that are "subject simultaneously to very many different physical requirements that they cannot possibly satisfy fully" (Beek et al., 1992, p. 91). Tradeoffs may seem essential, but the dynamics of the cooperative tension always works to make them unnecessary or temporary.

A question frequently asked about ecological values-realizing theory is: how do values relate to cultural differences? Most people, including social scientists, view values as personal or social preferences or prejudices, and point to differences across cultures as evidence in favor of that view. How does an ecological view address the different conceptions and practices of cultures spanning geography and history? An ecological account does not claim that values are universals that are invariant across time or location, but it also pushes back on subjectivism (i.e., values answer to individuals) and relativism (i.e., values answer to cultures) with the claim that individuals and cultures answer to values. If subjectivism were the case, coherent cultural practices and traditions would be impossible (Midgley, 1993); societies only exist if individuals acknowledge the claims of something larger than themselves as grounding legitimate agreement and disagreement with others. If cultural relativism were the case, then cultures would have no basis for self-critique, for development, growth, and creativity. New forms and functions within cultural practices would be unable to emerge and be evaluated as worthy of acceptance. Furthermore, constructive engagement with other cultures would not be possible. Learning from other individuals and cultures would be pointless since goodness had been assigned to individual autonomy or cultural superiority.

Pointing to individual or cultural differences as a way of denying the validity and power of values is somewhat like pointing to illusions and ambiguities as an argument against an ecological approach to perceiving. Gibson (1966) repeatedly had to remind his interlocutors of the enormous skill and success of perceptual systems in guiding bodily activities of animate agents. Humans, as cultures and individuals, have been intermingling, interacting, and learning from each other for millennia. The ways of life of countless species are entangled with others in ecosystems (Van Dijk, 2021). These encounters between individuals and cultures can be difficult and deadly, but the interactions are almost never zero-sum. There is nearly always the possibility of learning from, and with, each other, and of finding common goods that can be shared. Perceiving and acting with others is sometimes easy, but more often it is hard, painful, and patient work.

Ecological values-realizing theory claims that values cannot be reduced to any given culture's current appropriation of their claims. Hodges and Geyer (2006) explored what it means to be truthful in tense and awkward situations, briefly addressing cross-cultural differences. They noted different ways that Chinese, German, and American cultures have balanced relations between social solidarity, trust, honor, and truth. Germans think Americans are not serious enough in their truth claims; Chinese think Americans are insensitive to others and not true to the situation; and Americans think Chinese are far too loose in their utterances, so accuse them of lying. Hodges and Geyer suggest that the dialogical tensions among values that can be observed across cultures can also be found *within* cultures, across varying situations. Truth and other values, they suggested, are more complex than any culture's norms. The heterarchical relation among values pushes back on cultural preferences that try to rank values as more or less important, or that circumscribe who and what is included within their scope (e.g., equality prevails, so long as one is male, white, a landowner). Values reveal themselves over time, but it requires persistent engagement and attention. One is trapped within one's own subjectivism or one's cultural assumptions only to the extent that one fails to engage with others with enough care and humility to learn.

As I write this, Slavic and European cultures are staring each other down, seemingly about a country along their borderlands, but at a deeper level, about their aspirations to expand and enrich their ways of life. Such confrontations are often attributed to different values, but an ecological approach suggests that it is the larger ecology of values that provides hope for negotiation, reconciliation, and joint efforts. The problem in working out how such encounters can be constructive rather than destructive is that it demands a willingness to confront one's own inadequacies in attending to and enacting values such as justice and freedom, rather than only drawing attention to the "blind spots" of others.

Graeber and Wengrow (2021) provide fascinating historical examples of cultural encounters that challenged their participants to "rethink" their assumed understanding and embodiment of values such as freedom, truth, and justice. In the 17–18th centuries, Indigenous Americans encountered Europeans who came as settlers to the "new world," while some Americans travelled and lived in Europe, each culture taking the measure of the others' ways. Europeans were shocked that Americans viewed them as "slaves" (e.g., they constantly bowed to the wishes of kings, captains, and nobles), who were selfish, quarrelsome, and uncaring in their actions toward others. By contrast, European military and religious invaders were often deeply impressed with the hospitality, eloquence, and generosity of the "savages" that they had come to subdue or convert.

Evidence suggests that Europeans, particularly the French, felt the sting of the critique offered by American ways of life and tried to take its lessons to heart, but with little success. The reasons for this are complex, but the important point for present purposes is that without some common appreciation of what it means to be selfish or charitable, hospitable or quarrelsome, free or enslaved, there could have been no cross-cultural critique and no attempt at self-critique. Without critical self-awareness, there would be no attempts to reform or improve one's ways of acting and perceiving, one's way of life.

This process of critical and appreciative engagement with other cultures or individuals works because of common goods. Furthermore, critical assessment within and across cultures makes it clear that no culture and no individual begins to exhaust the meanings of values. Graeber and Wengrow (2021) note the ferocious dialogue around the value of *equality*. What does it mean: equality of being deserving of care and compassion; equality before the law; equality of condition; equality of opportunity; equality of access to land; equality in political power; equality of freedom to express one's views; equality of caloric intake; or something else? If all of these, are they all equally important? Does equality undermine the uniqueness of individuals or celebrate it? Ecological values-realizing theory proposes that learning how to embody and enact freedom, equality, and other values is an ongoing task for individuals and cultures. As Gibson (1979, p. 253) claimed, we are never done perceiving; it requires ongoing engagement with others, both within and across cultures (Reddy, 2008). The fact that humans argue about values, and how best to realize them, does not demonstrate that values are subjective preferences that do not matter to public action. Real argumentative conversation is not about opinions, but about matters of real substance – what is true, what matters, what should be done? Values are not just ways of talking; rather, language itself answers to values.

8.4 Agency, language, and responsibility

When individuals and groups encounter ways of perceiving and acting that challenge what they think is possible or appropriate, what is possible and appropriate for them to do? How does one find one's way when confronted with navigational or descriptive skills that seem impossible (Heft, 2013b, provides excellent examples), or pronouncements or practices that seem factually wrong or morally abhorrent? How do we perceive and act with skill and wisdom in a populated environment? Heft (2013a, 2013b, 2017, 2020) has repeatedly challenged ecological researchers to face the complexities of social perception and action, cultural agency, and the enduring effects of social and personal histories.

Although it is often not appreciated, one of Gibson's (1966, 1979) key contributions was his focus on the agency of perceivers, that agents are responsible to act in ways that make it possible for them to learn about their environments and alter them in ways that create further affordances. People, he noted, are "subject to the laws of mechanics and yet *not* subject to the laws of mechanics, for they are not *governed* by these laws" (Gibson, 1979, p. 135). Agency extends beyond humans (Heft, 2013b), and may extend beyond the animate and organic into thermodynamics (Hodges, 2022). The freedom and flexibility that are implied in agency emerge only in the context of ecosystem interdependencies, and this is true for humans too (Hodges, 2022). Di Paolo et al. (2018, p. 236) argued that entering the collective life of a community "is an affirmation of individuality, not a loss of it," and Heft (2013a, p. 165) observed that "humans cannot develop skills to operate symbolically without opportunities for engagement with an interlocutor in an environment rich in symbolic meanings." Without engagement and dialogue, agency is undermined.

What does engagement, dialogue, and agency look like in linguistic interactions? One of the mistakes often made in language studies is an excessive focus on speaking and not enough on listening. Fowler (1986, pp. 23–24) claimed that listeners can only understand the vocal-tract gestures of others by "virtue of their sensitivity to the historical and social context of constraint in which the activity is performed," going on to argue that the relation between utterances and what is specified is necessary, "not due to physical law directly, but to cultural constraints that have evolved over generations of language use" (p. 24). If I grow up in an English-speaking community and operate in it for 40 years, is it arbitrary as to what actions I take in response to some utterance? Hardly. It is as natural as breathing. We might do well to adopt Ingold's (2000) suggestion that skills such as conversing be considered as a *dwelling*, which we inhabit, rather than as so many arbitrary rules to be internalized. Understood as a habitation, the directness of language

> lies not in some deductive certainty, but in the subtle social and moral dynamics of real physical bodies, dialogically arrayed, that have directly shared and cared for a set of places and tasks over a common history, working to do the next thing that needs to be done for the good of those places, those tasks, and themselves. (Hodges & Fowler, 2010, p. 246)

As Heft (2017) rightly noted, Gibson intended for ecological theory to address collective, cultural skills and practices, such as conversing. Gibson's own contributions, however, were sparse and suggestive. He acknowledged that conversing allows one "to see through the eyes of another" (Gibson, 1982, p. 412), at least "metaphorically"; however, since it is "mediated" by the speaker who has selected the information rather than the listener, it is only "indirect." What grounds conversing, Gibson suggested, is the optic array and the agency of movement through it, revealing invariants that can be shared across different perspectives. Although two bodies cannot occupy the same position, agents can switch positions, each discovering what the other saw earlier.

Gibson was right to realize that optic, haptic, and auditory arrays afford public information that is potentially shareable, but his claims betray an Enlightenment bias to trust oneself over others. Gibson assumes too easily that we may reverse positions with others and see it from their point of view; often this is impossible or impracticable. Social constraints may keep perceivers in their place, and events – always irreversible – are frequently too short to explore sufficiently to engage in confident action. Communities can know more than any one of the individuals who constitute it. A community of perceivers literally embodies the multiple perspectives necessary to accurate perception, and what I have called *dialogical arrays* allows for a partial sharing of perspectives (Hodges, 2007a, 2009, 2014b). Furthermore, since communities are historical, they allow the detection of events and meanings that would escape the notice of a single perceiver or a cohort of perceivers over their own lifespan.

If I visit a volcanic mountain repeatedly over two weeks to see it for myself, it is not at all clear that I should trust what I have seen rather than the reports of others who have lived in the region for decades. Similarly, a young girl who trusts her mother's descriptions of events rather than her own perceptions is not naïve or gullible, if her trust is based on her prior perception of her mother's skill and commitment to her and her well-being. If one inhabits a social, linguistic community that has reliably shown care and skill in acting and perceiving, is trusting the eyes, ears, or hands of others any less direct that looking, listening, or handling for oneself? All perceiving is selective, but I may prefer another's perspective to my own precisely because I take them to be more skilled or better positioned with respect to the relevant information. Conversing can be less opaque or murky than Gibson feared because it is dialogical. Another person may offer a perspective on current, past, or future events, but the listener(s) can ask further questions, challenge the claims made, and give their own perspective to see how the other responds. Perceiving is dialogical; it is active and engaged, rather than being reduced to passive reception or blind acceptance. Thus, it seems reasonable to suggest that conversing with others is a perception–action system (Hodges, 2007a, 2009). Over a wide range of settings and situations, joint perceiving and acting (as well as feeling and thinking for humans) is likely to afford the richest affordances for both groups and individuals. As inhabitants of linguistic communities, humans are afforded new opportunities for caring and being cared for, and for acting more responsibly in caring for the environments that sustain their existence.

Values, affordances, and agency make possible responsible action. Harry Heft has been an agent of ecological psychology, working to make it more responsible, more just, and more truthful in its accounts of organism-environment relations. Perhaps, one might even say that Harry's contribution to ecological psychology has been to make it more righteous. In any event, it deserves our gratitude.

References

Barker, R. G. (1968). *Ecological psychology: Concepts and methods for studying the environment of human behavior.* Stanford University Press.

Beek, P. J., Turvey, M. T., & Schmidt, R. C. (1992). Autonomous and nonautonomous dynamics of coordinated rhythmic movements. *Ecological Psychology*, *4*(2), 65–95. 10.1207/s15326969eco0402_1

Costall, A. (1995). Socializing affordances. *Theory & Psychology*, *5*(4), 467–481. 10.1177/0959354395054001

Costall, A. (2012). Canonical affordances in context. *Avant*, *3*(2), 85–93.

Costall, A., & Still, A. (1989). Gibson's theory of direct perception and the problem of cultural relativism. *Journal for the Theory of Social Behaviour*, *19*(4), 433–441. 10.1111/j.1468-5914.1989.tb00159.x

Deacon, T. W. (2012). *Incomplete nature: How mind emerged from matter*. New York: W. W. Norton & Company.

Di Paolo, E. A., Cuffari E. C., & De Jaegher, H. (2018). *Linguistic bodies: The continuity between life and language*. MIT Press.

Fowler, C. A. (1986). An event approach to the study of speech perception from a direct–realist perspective. *Journal of Phonetics*, *14*, 3–28. 10.1016/s0095-4470(19)30607-2

Gibson, J. J. (1966). *The senses considered as perceptual systems*. Houghton-Mifflin.

Gibson, J. J. (1979). *The ecological approach to visual perception*. Houghton-Mifflin.

Gibson, J. J. (1982). Notes on affordances. In E. S., Reed, & R., Jones (Eds.), *Reasons for realism* (pp. 401–418). Hillsdale: Lawrence Erlbaum.

Graeber, D., & Wengrow, D. (2021). *The dawn of everything: A new history of humanity*. Macmillan.

Heft, H. (1989). Affordances and the body: An intentional analysis of Gibson's ecological approach to visual perception. *Journal for the Theory of Social Behaviour*, *19*(1), 1–30. 10.1111/j.1468-5914.1989.tb00133.x

Heft, H. (2001). *Ecological psychology in context: James Gibson, Roger Barker, and the legacy of William James's radical empiricism*. Mahwah: Lawrence Erlbaum.

Heft, H. (2007). The social constitution of perceiver-environment reciprocity. *Ecological Psychology*, *19*(2), 85–105.

Heft, H. (2011). Holt's "recession of the stimulus" and the emergence of the "situation" in psychology. In E. P. Charles (Ed.), *A new look at New Realism: The psychology and philosophy of E. B. Holt* (pp. 191–219). Transaction Publishers.

Heft, H. (2013a). An ecological approach to psychology. *Review of General Psychology*, *17*(2), 162–167. 10.1037/a0032928

Heft, H. (2013b). Wayfinding, navigation, and environmental cognition from a naturalist's standpoint. In D. Waller & L. Nadel (Eds.), *The handbook of spatial cognition* (pp. 255–294). American Psychological Association.

Heft, H. (2017). Perceptual information of "an entirely different order": The "cultural environment" in *The senses considered as perceptual systems*. *Ecological Psychology*, *29*(2), 122–145. 10.1080/10407413.2017.1297187

Heft, H. (2020). Ecological psychology as social psychology? *Theory & Psychology*, *30*(6), 813–826. 10.1177/0959354320934545

Hodges, B. H. (2007a). Good prospects: Ecological and social perspectives on conforming, creating, and caring in conversation. *Language Sciences*, *29*(5), 584–604. 10.1016/j.langsci.2007.01.003

Hodges, B. H. (2007b). Values define fields: The intentional dynamics of driving, carrying, leading, negotiating, and conversing. *Ecological Psychology*, *19*(2), 153–178. 10.1080/10407410701332080

Hodges, B. H. (2009). Ecological pragmatics: Values, dialogical arrays, complexity, and caring. *Pragmatics & Cognition, 17*(3), 628–652. 10.1075/p&c.17.3.08hod

Hodges, B. H. (2014a). Rethinking conformity and imitation: Divergence, convergence, and social understanding. *Frontiers in Psychology: Cognitive Science, 5*, 726. 10.3389/fpsyg.2014.00726

Hodges, B. H. (2014b). Righting language: A view from ecological psychology. *Language Sciences, 41*(Pt A), 93–103. 10.1016/j.langsci.2013.08.010

Hodges, B. H. (2017). Carrying, caring, and conversing: Constraints on the emergence of cooperation, conformity, and language. *Interaction Studies: Social Behaviour and Communication in Biological and Artificial Systems, 18*(1), 26–54. 10.1075/is.18.1.02hod

Hodges, B. H. (2019). Resisting knowledge, realizing values, and reasoning in complex contexts: Ecological reflections. *Theory & Psychology, 29*(3), 291–310. 10.1177/0959354319852423

Hodges, B. H. (2022). Values define agency: Ecological and enactive perspectives reconsidered. *Adaptive Behavior.* https://doi.org/10.1177/10597123221076876

Hodges, B. H., & Baron, R. M. (1992). Values as constraints on affordances: Perceiving and acting properly. *Journal for the Theory of Social Behaviour, 22*(3), 263–294. 10.1111/j.1468-5914.1992.tb00220.x

Hodges, B. H., & Fowler, C. A. (2010). New affordances for language: Distributed, dynamical, and dialogical resources. *Ecological Psychology, 22*(4), 239–254.

Hodges, B. H., & Geyer, A. (2006). A nonconformist account of the Asch experiments: Values, pragmatics, and moral dilemmas. *Personality and Social Psychology Review, 10*(1), 2–19. 10.1207/s15327957pspr1001_1

Hodges, B. H., & Lindhiem, O. (2006). Carrying babies and groceries: The effect of moral and social weight on caring. *Ecological Psychology, 18*(2), 93–111. 10.1207/s15326969eco1802_2

Hodges, B. H., & Rączaszek-Leonardi, J. (2022). Ecological values theory: Beyond conformity, goal-seeking, and rule-following in action and interaction. *Review of General Psychology, 26*(1), 86–103. 10.1177/10892680211048174

Hodges, B. H., Meagher, B. R., Norton, D. J., McBain, R., & Sroubek, A. (2014). Speaking from ignorance: Not agreeing with others we believe are correct. *Journal of Personality and Social Psychology, 106*(2), 218–234. 10.1037/a0034662

Holt, E. B. (1915). *The Freudian wish and its place in ethics.* Henry Holt.

Holt, E. B. (1931). *Animal drive and the learning process: An essay toward radical empiricism* (Vol. 1). Henry Holt.

Ingold, T. (2000). *The perception of the environment: Essays in livelihood, dwelling, and skill.* Routledge.

Kadar, E. E., & Effken, J. A. (1994). Heideggerian meditations on an alternative ontology for ecological psychology: A response to Turvey's (1992) proposal. *Ecological Psychology, 6*(4), 297–341. 10.1207/s15326969eco0604_4

Kadar, E. E., & Effken, J. A. (2005). From discrete actors to goal-directed actions: Toward a process-based methodology for psychology. *Philosophical Psychology, 18*(3), 353–382. 10.1080/09515080500177358

Krueger, J. I., & Funder, D. C. (2004). Towards a balanced social psychology: Causes, consequences, and cures for the problem-seeking approach to social behavior and cognition. *Behavioral and Brain Sciences, 27*(3), 313–327. 10.1017/S0140525X04000081

Lewin, K., & Cartwright, D. (1942). Field theory and learning in social sciences. Field theory in social science, selected theoretical papers, 212–230.

Midgley, M. (1993). *Can't we make moral judgments?* St. Martin's Press.

Polanyi, M. (1958). *Personal knowledge: Toward a post-critical philosophy of science*. University of Chicago Press.

Raja, V. (2019). J. J. Gibson's most radical idea: The development of a new law-based psychology. *Theory & Psychology*, 29(6), 789–806. 10.1177/0959354319855929

Reddy, V. (2008) *How infants know minds*. Harvard University Press.

Reed, E. S. (1988). *James J. Gibson and the psychology of perception*. Yale University Press.

Reed, E. S. (1996). *Encountering the world: Toward an ecological psychology*. Oxford University Press.

Rączaszek-Leonardi, J., & Nomikou, I. (2015). Beyond mechanistic interaction: value-based constraints on meaning in language. *Frontiers in Psychology*, 6, 1579. 10.3389/fpsyg.2015.01579

Sanders, J. T. (1997). An ontology of affordances. *Ecological Psychology*, 9(1), 97–112.

Still, A., & Good, J. (1998). The ontology of mutualism. Ecological Psychology, 10(1), 39–63. 10.1207/s15326969eco1001_3

Tomasello, M. (2008). *Origins of human communication*. MIT Press.

Van Dijk, L. (2021). Affordances in a multispecies entanglement, *Ecological Psychology*, 33(2), 73–89. 10.1080/10407413.2021.1885978

Wray, A., & Grace, G. W. (2007). The consequences of talking to strangers: Evolutionary corollaries of socio-cultural influences on linguistic form. *Lingua*, 117(3), 543–578.

Zhang, M., Lu, A., & Hodges, B. H. (2019). Lifting, tasting, and carrying: The interaction of magnitude and valence effects in time perception. *Acta Psychologica*, 193, 1–10. 10.1016/j.actpsy.2018.11.010

9
YOUNG PEOPLE'S RESPONSES TO THE EARTH'S AFFORDANCES OF REGENERATION

Louise Chawla

9.1 Affordances of natural processes

This chapter explores the notion of "slow-motion affordances" when people farm, garden, or restore abandoned or degraded land – and the land responds. The "good farmer" and "constant gardener" are familiar figures in literature, who embody people's relationship with the land when they seek to maintain its healthy functioning at the same time as it yields flowers, fruit, vegetables, grains, and livestock for practical use. Between tilling the soil, planting seeds, and harvesting crops, there are months of waiting – so that part of the relationship between a person and place consists of learning the rhythms that guide the land's responses. More recently, people practice ecological restoration to repair degraded ecosystems. In this case, it may take many years before native species flourish again. Always, there is uncertainty, as outcomes depend on the weather and countless other interdependencies of living systems.

According to the ecological psychologist James Gibson (1986, p. 127), who coined the term "affordance," "The affordances of the environment are what it *offers* the animal, what it *provides* or *furnishes*, either for good or ill." It means the functional significance of an object, event, or place for an individual, such as nectar for a bee or sweet fruit for a person (Heft, 2001, p. 123). As a relational term, affordances depend on the capabilities, motivations, and memories of individuals as much as the features of the environment. The term is usually applied to immediately perceptible possibilities. Farming, gardening, and ecological restoration are full of affordances of this kind, such as a shovel that affords digging and soil that can be turned; but they also involve affordances that require learning over time, such as whether a sapling will grow into a tree that bears fruit. These possibilities for growth and change are this chapter's main interest, with a focus on restorative processes when people work with the purpose of reclaiming habitats for diverse plants and wildlife.

DOI: 10.4324/9781003259244-10

When the psychologist Joachim Wohlwill (1983, p. 7) considered how to differentiate the domains of "natural" and "man-made," he noted that the natural environment is commonly defined as "the vast domain of organic and inorganic matter that is not a product of human activity or intervention" and "the organic processes that permeate the world of nature and have come to known as the *ecosystem*." Yet, he observed, these are fuzzy categories, as large stretches of "natural" environments bear the imprint of human activity. Besides immediate uses of the environment for hunting, foraging, and building, humans have taken advantage of the earth's slow-motion affordances since time immemorial. Prehistoric groups altered their environment to increase the abundance of food producing plants and game (Stuart-Smith, 2020, pp. 116–118); and by 10,000 B.C., people were establishing agricultural settlements. In the late 19th and early 20th centuries, landscape architects like Frederick Law Olmsted and Jens Jensen began to recreate native forests, wetlands, and prairies, aided by the emerging science of ecology (Ryan & Grese, 2005). Their work reflected a rising awareness that species could be driven to extinction by excesses of environmental exploitation, including the eradication of their habitats by the axe and plow. Today, the Society for Ecological Restoration (n.d.) defines its mission as "to sustain biodiversity, improve resilience in a changing climate, and re-establish an ecologically healthy relationship between nature and culture."

Like farming and gardening, ecological restoration is an example of humans working with organic processes to imprint their aims on "natural" landscapes: yet these landscapes remain different than built spaces in inherent ways. Among the distinctions, Wohlwill (1983), noted, are change and intricate complexity. Natural landscapes are in constant diurnal and seasonal change, and these changes reflect complex ecosystem interdependencies of climate, weathers, waters, landforms, vegetation, wildlife, and human interactions: complexities that humans can detect to some degree, depending on their level of engagement and attention to a particular environment, but only partially. As Wohlwill observed, these dynamics of change require "an extension of our approach to perception, so that it encompasses the dimension of time and of change occurring over extended periods of time" (p. 23).

In the moment, people can notice the possibilities that natural environments afford to shape the earth for human ends, but long-term affordances are learned through extended observation and cultural teaching. For example, a person can see immediately that building a dam of rocks across a stream slows the water; but when this principle is applied in check-dams of rocks to slow hillside erosion, these practices reflect cultural learning that has been passed down for generations. For children, who are engaging with new nature spaces and organic elements for the first time, there is the excitement of first-time discoveries; but when children participate in farming, gardening, and restoration work, they are being initiated into cultural practices. Therefore, social interactions and the transfer of cultural values, beliefs, and knowledge are inherent parts of these experiences.

9.2 Understanding young people's experiences of restoration work

As climate change disrupts the ancient adjustments between land, air, and water that created a habitable planet for humans and other species, and as growing human populations and consumption press wild species into smaller and smaller territories, the term "regeneration" has become a rallying call. As it is used by the environmental activist Paul Hawken (2021) in his book *Regeneration: Ending the Climate Crisis in One Generation*, the word signifies that it is not enough for humans to stop doing harm to the earth by no longer emitting greenhouse gases or destroying wild habitats: the damage already done requires action to sequester carbon back into the earth and restore lost habitats. Restoring degraded land and recreating biodiverse habitats are central to this work.

Through surveys and their own narratives, adult volunteers in ecological restoration say that they find many sources of satisfaction in their work (Grese et al., 2000; Miles et al., 1998; Schroeder, 2000). Repeatedly, they report that they find meaning in acting responsibly toward the Earth and benefiting current and future generations. They feel less helpless about what is happening in the world. They find learning about nature fascinating. They enjoy working with others, accomplishing tangible shared goals, meeting new people, making new friends, and developing a sense of community. Some develop a deep attachment to their site. People appreciate the peace and beauty they find at restoration sites, and some experience a sense of spiritual connection with all life. They enjoy working outdoors, find that the work is good for their physical health, and report personal growth such as increased self-confidence.

When children and teens participate in restoration work, how do they experience their engagement? Much less is known about this question. To gather insights, this chapter reviews studies of programs that involved young people in regenerating native ecosystems in their communities. It is guided by four questions: *what did children and teens do as they engaged with the land? What did they witness as the land responded? What did this interaction mean to them?* And because they worked with others in groups, *how did they experience the social aspect of this work?*

Why do these questions matter? When millions of young people took to the streets during the Climate Strikes of 2019, they voiced their fear and anger over the planetary changes that threaten life on earth and, in their terms, rob them of their future. A recent ten-nation survey of 10,000 young people aged 16–25 suggests how widely these emotions are shared (Hickman et al., 2021). Three-quarters believed the future is frightening, and 65% agreed that governments are failing them. Unless young people feel hope that they can contribute to creating a better world, and that they are not alone in their concerns and efforts to take action, they risk falling into denial, despair, or apathy (Ojala, 2016). A recent review compared practices that increase young people's sense of connection with nature with practices that help them cope constructively with environmental fears and worries (Chawla, 2020). One of the practices that appeared in both bodies of research was involving young people in working together with others to protect and restore natural areas. Activities of this kind increased young people's connection with nature *and* constructive coping with alarming environmental information. Because ecological restoration falls in this intersecting space, this chapter seeks to understand what young people say and do when they participate. Are the earth's affordances for regeneration a meaningful part of their experiences?

9.3 Reviewing young people's experiences of restoration activities

Three main criteria guided the selection of studies to answer this chapter's questions about what young people do during restoration projects, what they witness in the land, what interactions with the land mean to them, and how they experience the social side of restoration work. (1) Young people knowingly contributed to increasing local biodiversity. (2) The study provided information about what young people perceived, did and felt as they engaged with the land. (3) The age range for study participants was early childhood through 18. Because no previous reviews of this material emerged, the starting date for publications was left open.

To gather studies that met these criteria, it was necessary to cast a wide net. In searching for relevant articles, books, book chapters, and dissertations on citation databases, many different search terms were tried. Figure 9.1 lists key words and

---

Key words that yielded useful results:

I. child* OR teen* OR "young person" OR "young people" OR youth OR adolescent was combined with the following successive sets of key words:

 1. "ecological restoration" OR "habitat restoration" OR "environmental restoration" OR "ecosystem restoration" OR "restoration ecology"

 2. "ecological regeneration" OR "habitat regeneration" OR "environmental regeneration" OR "ecosystem regeneration"

 3. "habitat renewal" OR "environmental renewal" OR "ecosystem renewal"

 4. reforestation OR afforestation OR rewilding OR "prairie restoration" OR "grassland restoration" OR "stream restoration" OR "marine restoration" OR "watershed restoration"

II. schoolyards OR "school grounds" AND biodiversity
III. "conservation education"
IV. "civic ecology"
V. "restoration education"

Citation databases where useful results were found: Academic Search Premier, ERIC, GreenFILE, Web of Science, World Cat

---

FIGURE 9.1 Search process to identify publications about young people's experiences of ecological restoration practices

citation databases that yielded useful results. When abstracts failed to provide enough information to determine whether studies fit the selection criteria, the full study was consulted. As relevant studies were identified, their reference lists were scanned for potential additions. During this search process, eight studies emerged. Three studies were added that were already in the author's collection of child-environment research, but not picked up by the key word search, for a total of 11 studies. The texts broke into two groups: six about ecological restoration on school grounds and five about restoration projects on community lands beyond school. Because these categories were distinct in several ways, this chapter focuses on the experiences of young people who contributed to the restoration of local biodiversity beyond their school grounds.

This search process revealed that young people's experiences of participating in restoration projects do not form a well-defined area of investigation. Publications about young people in restoration work often used general key words such as "place-based education," "education for sustainability," "service-learning," or "environmental education," where they were buried under thousands of studies with other interests. When they surfaced, they were usually simple program descriptions that explained how programs were organized and the roles young people played. Although some quoted a few young participants, they did not give young people's experiences systematic attention. When studies assessed outcomes for young people, they usually used predetermined measures of environmental knowledge, youth development, or social learning, without considering how young people related to the land itself. In contrast, the five publications reviewed below include insights into young people's experiences as they envisioned or witnessed changes in natural areas.

All five texts applied qualitative methods, with three including quantitative measures. Each study was analyzed through a first level of summarizing basic content, followed by thematic coding (Saldaña, 2009). Four tables were created under the heading of the four research questions that guided this review, and passages relevant to each question were identified and recorded. When findings were similar across studies, they were grouped under shared themes. For details about each study's sample and methods, see Table 9.1.

9.4 Restoring biodiverse habitat on community lands

Sedawi et al. (2019) and Howard and Kern (2019) studied stream restoration activities with Indigenous children: in a Bedouin village in the Negev Desert in Israel, in the first case, and in the territories of two Native American tribes in the Pacific Northwest, in the second case. In both cases, students learned about a local stream and planned for its restoration, but stopped short of participating in the restoration work. Nevertheless, both studies are noteworthy. In the Bedouin village, the Hebron Stream had become so polluted and hazardous that students had to observe the first stages of reclamation work from a distance; but to understand what their reclaimed stream could look like, they visited healthy,

TABLE 9.1 Qualitative Studies of Habitat Restoration on Community Lands

Study	Location and Duration	Research Methods
Moras (1999)	Three alternative high schools in northern California environmental restoration learning programs for 67 at-risk students with seven teachers One academic year	• Site visits and observations • Surveys with students and teachers • Focus groups with students and teachers
Fridriksson (2012)	Selected classrooms in the Kamloops School District, British Columbia, Canada 83 students in grades 3–7 who raised salmon in classroom tanks for release in the Tranquille River October–May during one school year	• Participant observation • Student drawings and writings • Students' guided reflective writing the morning after they released their salmon • Follow-up interviews with six students within a week of the release
Linden (2016)	High school south of Portland, Oregon Eight students in an environmental science-based conservation corps program Six-week curriculum	• Participant observation • Pre- and post-tests of students' ecological understanding • Retrospective pre-/post-surveys of students' sense of nature connection and general self-efficacy • Student interviews
Sedawi et al. (2019)	Village school in the Negev Desert, Israel 107 Bedouin students, followed through grades 5–6 (60 girls, 47 boys) Two-year place-based education curriculum	• Pre- and post-drawings by students • Semi-structured pre- and post-interviews with students
Howard and Kern (2019)	STEM summer camp on tribal lands in the Pacific Northwest (STEM = Science Technology Engineering & Math) Native American children in grades 4–9 Four-day program	• Vignettes based on participant observation • Analysis of the students' videotaped presentations of their stream restoration models, presentation transcripts, and physical models

biodiverse streams in other parts of Israel. As a result, their original negative and pessimistic view of their local stream changed to an optimistic understanding of the stream's possibilities. On the tribal lands, when the Native American students presented their final models for stream restoration, they showed how to integrate

Western science-based techniques with Native cultural practices. Their reconciliation of these two traditions opened the way for an authentically cross-cultural curriculum for future programs.

Because three studies included young people's experiences as they engaged with the land to restore native biodiversity, they will be examined here in detail. One study bridged school and community: Fridriksson (2012) explored how 8–12 year olds made meaning out of the eight-month process of raising salmon in classroom fish tanks for spring release in the Tranquille River in British Columbia. Moras (1999) and Linden (2016) used a combination of qualitative and quantitative methods to investigate the impact of community-based ecological restoration activities on at-risk high school students in Oregon and California.

9.4.1 Engaging with the land

The representative of "the land' that engaged children in British Columbia were Coho salmon, as part of a program to increase the salmon population in a regional river. Each participating class watched someone mix salmon milt and eggs in their classroom tank in early October, and from then until May, it was the students' responsibility to monitor the water temperature and keep the tank clean. When the salmon fry emerged, students fed them four times a day. During a day-long field trip to the Tranquille River in May, they released the fry into the river, took a guided walk to learn about the forest and river ecosystem, enjoyed free play in nature, and participated in a simulated stream activity to learn how to protect the watershed.

Students in the Oregon high school had selected a conservation corps internship to earn environmental science credits toward graduation. During the six week program, they spent two days a week working in teams of two or three to complete restoration projects in their community. Their work included planting trees and rare native plants on public land, maintaining established plant communities at various Wetlands Conservancy sites, and canoeing on the Willamette River to a recently reclaimed industrial site to remove invasive weeds. Students in northern California attended three high schools. At one, they did creek clean-up, water quality monitoring, planting and enhancing Monarch butterfly habitat along the creek banks, and educational outreach about the creek's importance. A second high school participated in Project HAWK, adding to this project's legacy that had already turned 30 acres along a local creek into an environmental education center for kindergarten through grade 12 students. A third high school had recently redirected its efforts from wilderness habitat restoration to organic community gardening, but it still involved some students in tree planting and stream clean-up and restoration.

9.4.2 Perceiving landscape changes

Children in British Columbia followed the salmon in their classroom tanks from fertilized eggs, to eggs with eyes, to alevin that stayed at the bottom of the tank in gravel nests – still attached to the yolk sacs that were their source of food, to fry that swam about and hunted for their food. They studied and drew pictures of the fish at each stage of development. On the release day, each child carried a plastic bag with a few fish to the river and let them swim free with words of encouragement.

Half of the students in the high school internship in Oregon said that the most important thing they learned was to notice the local ecology of animals, trees, native and invasive plants, and the ecosystem functions that species served. One boy described his new awareness of details:

> Before I just saw it as a wetland, sometimes I saw animals in there, now I see all the plants and what the water's doing, what's in the water, the color the water is, you know. If I'm with someone I point out what I see. Most commonly the red-winged blackbird is the most obvious thing in the city. (Linden, 2016, p. 92)

A few students in the three northern California high schools referred to the growth they observed in their plantings.

More often, however, the high school students talked about perceiving their own accomplishments. Gibson (1986) noted that this is the other side of engaging with affordances: as animals use affordances in their environment, they simultaneously learn about the properties of the environment *and* their own potential for action and accomplishment. Both facets of experience run through the high school students' accounts – as in the following student's statement. "Well, we were able to turn a desolate area into a butterfly habitat and take all the trash out of there" (Moras, 1999, p. 183). In the words of a girl in Oregon, "I learned that we *can* do it, just cause we're little people doesn't mean we can't make a big change" (Linden, 2016, p. 100). In Oregon, students' scores on a quantitative measure of their general sense of efficacy increased significantly over the program's course; and most California students believed that they gained greater confidence in problem solving.

A number of high school students put their accomplishments in an extended ecological time frame. As a California student said:

> There's a lot of stuff that needs to be done out there. It takes more than just our lifetimes, because you plant the trees and trees live a lot longer than we do, right? And we're not even close to being done out there. (Moras, 1999, p. 197)

Regarding the challenge of watershed restoration, another concluded:

> Yeah, it shows you that with a problem that large, all you can do is take a step. That's what we've done. It's taught me that. All you can do is take a step. You can't expect it to be solved overnight. (p. 183)

9.4.3 The meaning and value of biodiverse areas

Students in British Columbia developed a strong sense of responsibility for their classroom salmon. Many reported feeling satisfaction that they were able to help "something that we all know needed our help" (Fridriksson, 2012, p. 46). Many students echoed the statement: "The experience made me feel happy and helpful because you get a good feeling knowing you gave something a better chance at life and living" (p. 47). When students did reflective writing the morning after they released the fish, many reported complex feelings. As one said, "When we released the fry in the Tranquille River, I was happy, sad, and worried at the same time" (p. 50). On the positive side, "The salmon finally get to be where they belong in the wild, and they are free and able to explore" (p. 51). Yet at the same time, as a student confessed: "I was sad because I have known these fish for a long time, I will miss them so much, and I love them so much" (p. 50). A number of students expressed apprehension: "I'm a little bit scared because we all weren't sure what would happen to them and we don't even know if they are alive right now" (p. 50). A few students were able to put the experience in an ecosystem perspective:

> It's kind of sad, but not crazy sad, because other things need food. It is part of the food chain, the salmon will need to eat things like bugs, maybe other really small fish, and bears and other predators need to eat too so it's just kind of how life goes with them. (p. 51)

The at-risk high school students in California and Oregon had histories of skipping school; but in both locations their attendance improved significantly. In California, 98% of the students surveyed said that getting outside in nature motivated them to come to school. One of the reasons they gave was a sense of responsibility: "I feel the fish, plants, and animals were relying on us to take care of them" (Moras, 1999, p. 176). Students in Oregon made similar statements: "There's the *wow*, our soul is with these creatures too, and we're supposed to take care of them" (Linden, 2016, p. 84). In Oregon, every student's score for nature relatedness increased in their retrospective survey; and in California, students said that they came to understand the importance of watershed restoration through their hands-on activities, increased environmental knowledge, and cooperation with other watershed protectors in their community.

9.4.4 Social aspects of restoration work

Raising and releasing salmon in British Columbia was a social experience, and students often used the word "we" when they wrote and talked about it; but this was not an aspect of the program that Fridriksson (2021) explored. For the high school students, social connections were central. When students in Oregon were asked to score different aspects of their program, they rated "belonging" highest, in the sense of social inclusion and acceptance. When students in California answered a survey question about whether the program made them feel more connected to their community, 63 out of 65 said that it did. For these students who had failed in conventional classrooms, being acknowledged for accomplishing something beneficial for their community was a new experience. "Instead of looking down on us, you know," one explained, "they're looking up and realizing we are doing something and we're helping preserve the environment" (Moras, 1999, p. 173). According to another, "It makes you feel like you're wanted again" (p. 73). In the words of a third, "I'm helping out the community so I feel like I'm part of it" (p. 68). At both sites, students noticed their growth in interpersonal skills and their ability to work with others.

Teamwork was an essential part of the programs in both California and Oregon, and it contributed to the students' sense of belonging. "It's easier to make goals when there's a team," explained a student in Oregon.

> If it was me by myself making a goal I wouldn't be so on top of things with myself, but because I'm working with people, I feel like I need to get the work done, and I should get the work done, and I *can* get the work done with all their help. (Linden, 2016, p. 89)

Students in both places recognized that their teachers facilitated accepting and supportive team dynamics.

9.5 Discussion

This review of research that investigated young people's experiences when they participated in restoring biodiverse ecosystems was motivated by concern about how children and adolescents navigate an uncertain environmental future, and how adults can support them in finding pathways to constructive hope: hope that balances acknowledging threats such as climate change and biodiversity loss with belief in the value of working for a better future. As the introduction to this chapter explained, involving young people in working together with others to protect and restore natural areas was one of the practices that appeared at the intersection of two bodies of research: one examining how to increase young people's sense of connection with nature; and the other, how to encourage constructive coping with environmental fears (Chawla, 2020). Ecological restoration is a prime example of working with others for the benefit of the natural world; therefore, this review sought to understand how restoration activities might contribute to these outcomes.

The idea of affordances provides a useful relational perspective to study partnerships between people and the land because it acknowledges the environment itself as a significant actor. When people engage in ecological restoration (or farming or gardening), they see the immediate effects of their actions, as well as long-term changes. The land and its plants and animals is a living thing in dialogue with human participants, and outcomes depend on the ecology of a place as much as human intention. The study of affordances requires fine-grained observation of what people do in a location and what the environment enables them to accomplish, relative to the properties of the place and people's goals and capabilities. It is a lens for recording what people do, how the environment responds, and the emotions they express. When people work together, observing whether they support each other becomes another dimension to observe – the social affordances that people bring to an activity. To probe deeper into the meaning of engagement, it is valuable to supplement observation with qualitative approaches like interviews, focus groups, and participants' writing and drawings. Although none of the five studies reviewed here adopted ecological psychology and the concept of affordances as its theoretical framework, all but one combined observation with open-ended qualitative measures. Therefore, they offer glimpses into young people's experiences of working with nature and each other.

The studies by Sedawi et al. (2019) and Howard and Kern (2019) showed that even just studying a local natural area and learning how it could change for the better can have a positive impact – even without an opportunity to help make these changes happen. Almost all of the Bedouin children in Israel came to see the stream that ran through their village in a new light, as an ecologically valuable resource that could become a source of beauty and clean water for their community. When the Native American children in the Pacific Northwest discovered that the stream they studied was part of their tribal history and identity, they demonstrated how to bring together Western science and traditional practice to reclaim this place as a resource for their people.

By working on restoration projects in their communities, students in British Columbia, Oregon, and California also came to recognize that the rivers, streams, wetlands, and other natural habitats that they encountered were vital resources. In terms of opportunities to observe natural cycles of change over time, the Canadian children in Fridriksson's (2012) study had eight months to follow each stage of their fishes' development and notice the fishes' movements and habits, In contrast, the high school students were transported to sites beyond their school to complete tasks assigned by community partners and then leave. Student said that they enjoyed being out in nature, learning about it and observing plants and animals there, but they primarily spoke about laboring to complete their assigned tasks. Witnessing nature's regenerative forces requires extended time, so it is not surprising that they had much less to say about this facet of ecological restoration compared to the experience of work itself. Along with the sense of competence that they expressed as they discovered that they could organize and complete challenging tasks successfully, they often referred to their relations with their work teams and communities. For these at-risk students, feeling accepted and supported by their teammates, teachers, and community partners was highly meaningful.

Regarding this chapter's question about whether engaging in restoration work can enable young people to face the risks of climate change and biodiversity loss with constructive hope, none of the studies reviewed here asked this question in exactly this way. In part, this result may reflect the fact that four of these studies were completed before accelerating public awareness about the risks of climate change and the youth-led Climate Strikes in late 2019. Nevertheless, can ingredients of hope be found in the restoration experiences that young people reported? In his book *The Necessity of Experience*, the ecological psychologist Edward Reed (1996) asserted that hope "is not a subjective feeling but an objective property of our encounters with the world" (p. 153). "Hope means that a goal is achievable," he wrote – provided the goal does good rather than harm to the world. "In present terms, hope is part of our experience when we detect information that tells us how to reach a goal" (p. 153). The studies presented here are filled with descriptions of young people engaging with nature and each other, and their expressions of the satisfaction they found in completing tasks competently, feeling supported as they worked, and helping other living things and their communities. In each study, they indicated that the restorative activities that they envisioned, or actually took, were pathways toward meaningful environmental goals. These are ingredients of hope, according to Reed's definition.

Surprisingly, this extended search for publications that systematically examine young people's experiences during restoration projects, including their awareness of the land, yielded few studies. Although people like Hawken (2021) consider working for the regeneration of the Earth one of the most compelling responsibilities of our time, there has been little research interest in how young people experience opportunities to participate. There may be useful evaluations in the gray literature of environmental organizations that enlist youth in restoration work; but based on this present search of published books, articles, and graduate theses and dissertations, how young people experience restoration work, including the land itself, has been rarely studied. Going forward, the studies gathered here demonstrate the value of combining observation with qualitative and quantitative measures. Observation creates opportunities to view young people's encounters with restoration sites and communication with their co-workers through the fine-grained lens that the concept of affordances invites. Qualitative approaches allow young people to explain in their own words how they experience these social and environmental relationships. Quantitative measures determine how representative their experiences are. The studies gathered here suggest that young people's experiences of restoration work deserve increased research attention.

References

Chawla, L. (2020). Childhood nature connection and constructive hope: A review of research on connecting with nature and coping with environmental loss. *People and Nature*, 2, 619–642. doi:10.1002/pan3.10128

Fridriksson, K. E. (2012). *Not just something you put in a frying pan and give to your family: Children's meaning making and salmon restoration*. M.A. thesis in Environmental Education and Communication. British Columbia, Canada: Royal Roads University.

Gibson, J. J. (1986). *The ecological approach to visual perception*. Lawrence Erlbaum Associates. Originally published in 1979.

Grese, R. E., Kaplan, R., Ryan, R. L., & Buxton, J. (2000). Psychological benefits of volunteering in stewardship programs. In P. H. Gobster & R. B. Hull (Eds.), *Restoring nature* (pp. 265–280). Island Press.

Hawken, P. (2021). *Regeneration: Ending the climate crisis in one generation*. Penguin Books.

Heft. H. (2001). *Ecological psychology in context*. Lawrence Erlbaum Associates.

Hickman, C., Marks, E., Pihkala, P., Clayton, S., Lewandowski, E., Mayall, E., Wray, B., Mellor, C., & van Susteren, L. (2021). Climate anxiety in children and young people and their beliefs about government responses to climate change: A global survey. *Lancet Planetary Health, 5*(12), e863–e873. doi:10.1016/S2542-5196(21)00278-3

Howard, M., & Kern, A. (2019). The role of story and place in Indigenous science education: Bigfoot in a youth-designed ecological restoration plan. *Cultural Studies of Science Education, 14*(4), 915–935.

Linden, S. J. (2016). *Connecting to nature, community, and self: A conservation corps approach to re-engaging at-risk youth in science education*. M.Sc. thesis, Portland State University, Oregon. Proquest Dissertations Publishing, 10141878.

Miles, I., Sullivan, W. C., & Kuo, F. E. (1998). Ecological restoration volunteers: The benefits of participation. *Urban Ecosystems, 2*, 27–41.

Moras, P. S. (1999). *Characteristics of environmental restoration, service-learning projects in selected California watersheds and the perceived gains by participating at-risk high school students and their teachers*. Ed.D. thesis in Education, University of La Verne, California. Dissertation and Thesis 6.1. https://digitalcommons.unomaha.edu/slcedt/61

Ojala, M. (2016). Young people and global climate change: Emotions, coping, and engagement in everyday life. In N. Ansell, N. Klocker, & T. Skelton (Eds.), *Geographies of global issues: Change and threat: Geographies of children and young people 8* (pp. 1–19). Springer Science + Business Media. doi:10.1080/00958964.2015.1021662

Reed, E. S. (1996). *The necessity of experience*. Yale University Press.

Ryan, R. L., & Grese, R. E. (2005). Urban volunteers and the environment: Forest and prairie restoration. In P. F. Barlett (Ed.), *Urban place: Reconnecting with the natural world* (pp. 173–188). MIT Press.

Saldaña, J. (2009). *The coding manual for qualitative researchers*. Sage Publications.

Schroeder, H. W. (2000). The restoration experience: Volunteers' motives, values, and concepts of nature. In P. H. Gobster & R. B. Hull (Eds.), *Restoring nature* (pp. 247–264). Island Press.

Sedawi, W., Ben Zvi Assaraf, O., & Reiss, M. J. (2019). Regenerating our place: Fostering a sense of place through rehabilitation and place-based education. *Research in Science Education*. doi:10.1007/s11165-019-09903-y

Society for Ecological Restoration. (n.d.). *Mission and vision*. Retrieved 6 February 2022 from https://www.ser.org/page/MissionandVision

Stuart-Smith, S. (2020). *The well-gardened mind: The restorative power of nature*. Scribner.

Wohlwill, J. F. (1983). The concept of nature: A psychologist's view. In I. Altman & J. Wohlwill (Eds.), *Behavior and the natural environment* (pp. 5–37). Plenum Press.

10
HUMANIZING ECOLOGICAL PSYCHOLOGY

Heft's incorporation of the sociohistorical into perceiving and acting

Kerry L. Marsh and Benjamin R. Meagher

10.1 Introduction

Harry Heft is in equal measure a psychological theorist, philosopher, historian, and humanist ... who also manages to carefully spotlight important areas to direct empirical efforts. His most notable empirical contributions are arguably in wayfinding and navigation, affordance research, and behavior settings. In this chapter, however, we largely focus on how important his ideas have been (and continue to be) for "socializing affordances" (Costall, 1995), and for bringing a sociohistorical viewpoint to environments. In many ways, he has *humanized* ecological psychology, bringing a strongly social and developmental perspective to perceiving and acting. His voice was most important at times in which ecological psychology's great empirical success incorporating universal dynamical and movement principles led some to believe that any appeal to *human* contexts might detract from detailing principles that cut across all living things. That Heft was onto something(s) important is particularly clear in the second decade of the 21st century – it's easy to see that the imprint Heft was making on the field, particularly surrounding social and developmental theorizing (Rączaszek-Leonardi et al., 2018; Rietveld & Kiverstein, 2014; van Dijk & Rietveld, 2017) and others whose work is reflected in this volume.

In this chapter, we discuss the importance of Heft's theorizing to the social psychological literature in particular, how his ideas have deepened our understanding of place, and his insightful critiques on some current issues in environmental psychology literature, particularly on restorative spaces. Throughout this chapter, we discuss our research on affordances in social contexts and indoor spaces, and on restorative environments – much of this work influenced by publications, talks, and correspondence with Harry Heft.

10.2 Affordances in the social world

As Heft notes, perception-action is coupled to structure at the level of affordances and at the level of places within which such affordances are nested. It is particularly in the area of social affordances that his viewpoint has been most urgently needed. When researchers began to tackle what possibilities for action *others* afford an individual, there were significant challenges regarding the scale at which to define such possibilities and how to begin to specify the information that perceivers might be detecting. One approach to affordances was to focus on specifying information at the level of the individual, akin to detection of stable features of actors such as gender (Marsh et al., 2006). Some stable personality traits, transient states, and physical features of the target of perception might convey to the perceiver the target's capabilities for and openness to the perceiver's potential actions, and thus whether the target can be pulled into cooperative, joint action by the perceiver, or is vulnerable to unilateral actions by the perceiver, with good or ill intent (Marsh et al., 2006; McArthur & Baron, 1983). Thus, earliest approaches to social affordances focused on individual-level features (McArthur & Baron, 1983) and found dynamic visual information was sufficient to veridically specify many important features. For instance, research on kinematics revealed that figures in motion depicted only in points of light provide sufficient information for a perceiver to detect the sex of a walker (Runeson & Frykholm, 1983), and research on face perception illustrated that people were sensitive to the cardiodal transformation that faces undergo in aging (Alley, 1988; Zebrowitz, 1997). However, research examining social affordances at the level of the individual actor had a rather limited scope, given its a-contextual and non-relational nature. In such an approach there was no focus on fit between a perceiver and actor, which is essential to the affordance concept. As Heft emphasizes throughout his writings, crucial affordances arise from the "*collective actions of individuals.*"

The synergistic approach to social affordances (Marsh et al., 2006; Riley et al., 2011) moves closer to Heft's perspective. It focuses on how two or more individuals operate as an emergent coordinative structure with unique possibilities for actions. As a consequence of environmental constraints that put demands on the individual's capabilities, these new higher order units of perceiving and acting emerge – the social synergy of a "we." Inspired by research on shifting between different affordance modes in completing solo actions such as stair climbing or grasping objects with one versus two hands (van der Kamp et al., 1998; Warren, 1984), research from this perspective quantified the affordance boundaries that delimited *solo versus social* interaction and described the dynamics of shifts between modes. The work established that the system had multistability, that is, regions of action where both solo and joint action affordances were present, and other regions without multiple action possibilities. For example, work by the first author and collaborators verified that perceivers could readily detect when they reached the limits of their own capabilities and would thus be aware of when they would be able to (or be required to) shift between solo and cooperative action

(Richardson et al., 2007). Participants were asked to consider a variety of planks that ranged widely in size from short to long; all planks could be carried only by grasping the ends. The longest planks could only be carried jointly, whereas the shortest could only be comfortably moved solo. Action and perception-only experiments determined that a relational measure capturing fit between the dyads' capabilities (arm spans) and the plank length (called a dimensionless pi number; van der Kamp et al., 1998) could precisely determine the point at which a social synergy – cooperative joint action – emerged.

From the perspective of Heft's writings, perhaps our most important finding was the phenomena of hysteresis. Hysteresis means that the trajectory by which one reaches a current place of action, for instance, the sequence of preceding actions leading up to reaching the critical pi number, matters for what actions will follow. One reoccurring theme of Heft's writings is that history matters, not only the longer time scale of a child's development but also the shorter time scale preceding a current action. Thus, for Heft, history should be a critical aspect of studying affordances; history should change the way one attends to a task. In our experiments, history of immediate actions were manipulated by presenting planks in continuous sequences from smallest to largest or in order of reversed size. In the trial in which participants moved planks of wood of decreasing size, the initial planks were of necessity moved jointly, whereas when the sequence was in ascending order, the initial planks were moved solo. During a third trial in which pieces were presented in random order, the point at which people shifted between solo and joint action adhered quite closely to the critical pi number (a quantification of one's action capabilities – arm span – considered against plank length). This pi number presumably reflected the most optimal mode of efficiently moving planks. But in the multistable area around that pi number, presenting the planks in ascending versus descending order mattered. There was a history effect, or "hysteresis" such that there was a stickiness of the current trajectory of action. For instance, if planks were presented in order from largest to smallest, dyads consistently continued joint action somewhat past the point at which solo action became a possibility: history mattered.

10.3 Embedding affordances within higher order structures

Although the synergistic approach to understanding social affordances moves substantially beyond the individual approach in incorporating emergent dynamical principles and methods – and thus history – it is only a modest step toward realizing the promise of Heft's theorizing, which argues not merely that affordances be embedded in interactional dynamics, but within higher order structures more broadly. Heft (2018, p. 99) suggests that perception-action practices are nearly aways coupled in "human societies to dynamic structure at the level of places within which affordances are nested." The trajectory of Heft's developing ideas on how sociocultural context should be incorporated into ecological psychology started in the late 1980s with the recognition that "properties of objects take on affordance properties in relation to embodied skills" (Heft, 2013), but by the time of his tour de force volume of 2001 he was well on his way to proposing more fundamental reconceptualization of the ecological niches, "places" that affordances were incorporated into (Heft, 2001). Along the way he significantly changed the direction of research on environmental description, he pulled Roger Barker's classic work on behavior settings back from the brink of obscurity in social psychological circles, and finally he incorporated Barker's ideas into a broader approach to understanding "places" with particular sociocultural meaning. We discuss each of these ideas in turn.

Heft revolutionized the domain of environmental description in his application of the affordance concept (Heft, 1988, 1997). Although most environment description to that point largely focused on describing forms, such as noting the trees and a grassy field edged by hedges within a landscape, or describing stairs, chairs, and other physical features of a built environment, Heft suggested that environments should be described in terms of their functional significance for an individual (Heft, 1988). Heft illustrated this in his reanalysis of the detailed observational record from Barker and Wright's (1951) study, *One Boy's Day*. Voluminous observational records were produced in the course of Roger Barker and associates' meticulous in-depth observations of 20 children in the everyday settings of a small town in the Midwest. Although their initial focus was to understand how predominant theories of the era explained behavior (e.g., stimulus-response principles), they largely found that children's behavior was substantially determined by situation types: this best explained both consistencies and differences between children's behaviors. Barker discovered that behavior "tended to be congruent with respect to some *higher order dynamic units of the environment* constituted by the joint actions of the individuals and the material features ('milieu') at some locale" (Heft, 2018, p. 107). Within this context, Heft analyzed the record of a seven-year old boy's behavior in settings outside the home, throughout an entire day in April, 1949. He created an exhaustive list of all of the boy's transactions with environmental features, such as coasting on his bike down an incline, or hitting a stone with a baseball bat. Heft then categorized each action that the boy was doing with regard to *affordances* that features of the environment reflected. This revealed *commonalities* between behaviors that superficially would appear to be different (appeared in different geographic areas, and occurred with different environmental forms), but along a more meaningful way dimension – reflecting behaviors capitalizing on the affordance of "climb-able-on," for instance. The research also uncovered important *distinction*s in environmental features that otherwise would have been hidden with conventional environmental description approaches, wherein all trees would be categorized together for instance. Not so for an affordance categorization: whereas "swing-on-able" included an instance when the boy swung on a low hanging branch of a particular tree, other trees that lacked a roughly vertical appendage/outcropping of sufficient height and strength to afford grabbing and swinging for a boy of this height were irrelevant to this category.

Heft's use of the affordance concept in developing a functional taxonomy for children's environments (1988) substantially affected environmental psychology, particularly those concerned with the design of children's outdoor spaces, because it offered "a way of thinking about environments that is psychologically meaningful" (Heft, 1988, p. 36). With some exceptions (Jongeneel et al., 2015; Sporrel et al., 2017), the experimental literature pursuing rigorous ways to test hypotheses in this realm has lagged Heft's leadership. Although Heft's writings suggest rather deeply complex and challenging conceptual issues, the first steps toward developing testable hypotheses are inevitably more concrete, smaller steps in that direction, where one forgoes some of the rich nuance and complexity of his ideas in exchange for experimental control. For instance, our own work (Meagher & Marsh, 2011, 2015, 2017) has attempted to examine indoor spaces with fairly simple affordance profiles in which we vary not only the affordance structure of interior spaces (rooms) but vary the experiences preceding participants' exposure to those rooms. Our intuition was that much of the language that people use to describe their psychological and aesthetic reactions to built spaces are an amalgamation of affective reactions (pleasure or discomfort) intertwined with intuitive awareness of affordances in that space. Thus, terms such as spacious, cavernous, cramped, and cozy imply not strictly how much square footage is available in a room, but whether the room has "more" or "fewer" affordances that are inviting. In our experiments, we found for instance, that rooms that are functional, that is, had furniture arranged to provide more affordances, were viewed as more spacious and attractive than when the same room's furniture was arranged to constrain actions.

We have also incorporated history by varying participants' preceding experiences – evoking different modes of travel (skateboarding, walking, or bike riding), or inducing different social states before assessing responses to rooms. In each experiment, the rooms that participants responded to (in real space, or virtual space) differed in affordances that were relevant to the mindset evoked by their preceding history of acting. In some experiments, their travel before entering the room involved biking versus walking, in other experiments, their immediate psychological experiences involved social rejection, or social engagement with others. We tested whether the thumbprints of that immediately preceding history mattered with regard to how they responded in entering a room that say, would have been constraining for bike travel, or a room that was arranged to provide more vs. fewer possibilities for social interaction. However, our work has been somewhat constrained in ways that Heft has noted are significant limitations in environmental psychology, which relied extensively on still photograph depictions of environment. Although some of our experiments involved manipulating the affordance structure of actual rooms that participants walked around and rated in real time, pragmatic constraints and experimental control meant that some experiments depicted 2D spaces, and some experiments used more immersive and dynamic 3D virtual experiences. Moreover, although these studies offer some first steps toward systematically demonstrating how affordances-based reactions to an indoor space are affected by sociohistorical variables, none of these were spaces in which *other people* were even present.

Moreover, as Heft (2007) notes, experimental contexts are unusual "places" that differ from more naturally occurring places. One of the most important contributions of Heft's writings to social psychology has been to explicate and extend Roger Barker's notion of behavior settings that occur in everyday life. Interestingly, Heft's writings foreshadow an increase in social psychologists' call for a need to develop a social psychology of situations (Rauthmann et al., 2020; Reis, 2008). However, research seeking to describe environments unfortunately has been either atheoretical (Guillaume et al., 2016; Lee et al., 2020), dependent on cognitive schemas (Kelley et al., 2003) or uses "affordances" in a way substantially uninformed by Heft's work (Neuberg et al., 2010; Pick & Neuberg, 2022). The most serious recent attempts to develop a taxonomy of social situation are those from the latter category, who use affordances framed from an evolutionary perspective (Brown et al., 2015). However, their conceptualization of affordances diverges in crucial ways from the canonical ecological literature on affordances. By affordances the evolutionary theorists mean *any* opportunities or barriers that an environment or setting has that allow one to achieve higher level, fundamental evolutionary motives – for mate retention, safety, nurturing others, for disease protection, and so forth (Neuberg et al., 2010; Pick & Neuberg, 2022). The emphasis on a specific possibility for *action*, grounded in information that veridically specifies the affordance to a perceiver, is lacking throughout such good-intentioned efforts. Rather "affordance" is largely used as a placeholder for "useful for achieving a goal." Contrary to Heft's view, affordance is conceptualized very statically, and lacks the crucial potential to specify information that can be detected since this requires specification of a possibility for action with a *specific* person, involving *a specific* history of the perceiver, under *specific* circumstances.

Perhaps the root of the problem is that social psychologists do not have a language to adequately elucidate what the material environment (including people) *is*. As a consequence, there is essentially no exploration of the crucial relationally-defined understanding of environment and animal fit that follows from Gibson's work. In contrast, Heft's view of *how humans are in environments* is illustrated by John Dewey's comment that people are not merely in an "environment as coins are in a box" (Costall, 2017). Rather we are embedded in an environment and ourselves extend out into our environments in substantive ways (Meagher, 2020); indeed, even deciding where an organism ends and the environment begins is an arbitrary, false distinction (Järvilehto, 1998). Heft believes that, as Costall said (2017, p. 227) in citing Dewey, that we are in an environment "as a plant is in the sunlight and soil. It is of them, continuous with their energies, dependent upon their support." Thus for environments that include other people, affordances must be studied in that entangled of a manner.

Heft's thinking is true to that value, and this is particularly evident in his explication (Heft, 2007, 2017, 2018, 2020a, 2020b; Heft et al., 2014) of Roger Barker's notions of behavior settings, or 'places' in Heft's more readily-accessible, recent terminology. In "socially constituted places," Heft writes, "place and individual are mutually constitutive. To identify a certain locale as a place of significance for an animal means, for example, that some subset of its features sustain or promote the animal's well-being … In the case of social-constituted settings, a participant's actions are among the factors that constitute the dynamic, collective structure that *is* that place" (Heft 2007). Some subsets of such settings meet the full set of criteria for what meets the formal definition of being a behavior setting (Barker & Schoggen, 1973; Heft, 2001).

Behavior settings are locales or activity settings (such as a plaza, or park, or 24-hour transit center) that have definite geographic and temporal boundaries (Heft, 2001). Thus, "baseball game" is not a behavior setting (nor is an urban plaza, nor a park), but the real ecological event of a *particular* baseball game occurring between two professional baseball teams at a particular stadium on a particular day and time *is* a behavior setting. The components needed for a behavior setting includes relevant "milieu" of objects, equipment and other physical structures (a field, bats, gloves, ball, etcetera) that support the behaviors, and people who fill various roles and help maintain the quasi-stability (e.g., when violation of the rules, or disruptions such as a streaker on the field occur). Explicitly or implicitly, behavior settings strongly convey to someone entering the setting what behavior is normative and what behavior is inappropriate. As Heft describes in many papers (from at least 2001 through 2020), it is very much the collective activities of the participants that define the behavior setting. Although each individual's behavior impacts the setting, the setting exists independent of any particular individual's experience of the setting, with the *interdependencies* of the involved participants (baseball players, coaches, refs, audience) the most critical feature of the behavior setting.

Little research has examined what information is available for a perceiver to distinguish behavior settings, with the exception of a paper by Heft et al. (2014). One study in this paper involved making a number of observations of the trajectories and movements of actors in different behavior settings (e.g., a basketball game, ice cream shop, bank). Simulations were then created that displayed only the collective movements of agents based on those observations. Two experiments using the simulations confirmed that many of the behavior settings could be accurately detected by perceivers from the simulations, and one experiment revealed distinctions between what activities were viewed as appropriate for different behavior settings. These studies provide an exciting first start to developing other testable hypotheses regarding behavior settings. Some promising questions that could be explored involving using quantitative measures to see if certain behavior settings are similar or different from each other in meaningful ways. Key distinctions might include the degree of constraint or freedom for inhabitants of a place, degree of differentiation of roles in the setting, and degree to which constraint/freedom interacts with subgroups – perhaps those who feel more excluded, or those differing in power. New video analysis techniques could quantify how behavior settings not only differ in density of people to space, overall frequency of "turnover" of people in a space, and nestedness of activity (fractality), but also allow for analysis of overall speed and acceleration tendencies (and variability of these in different regions of the place), and particularly, degree to which movements of some participants are constrained to certain locations (e.g., clients) and others not (workers).

10.4 Restorative spaces

In environmental psychology today, there are few concepts more widely discussed than *restorative spaces,* the idea that being in particular physical environments can improve psychological wellbeing. Overwhelmingly, theorizing on this topic has tended to focus on the unique qualities of natural environments (i.e., "green spaces") believed to evoke positive responses in humans. These frameworks tend to argue either for an evolved, instinctual positive emotional response to savannah-like features in the environment (Ulrich, 1983), or to low-level visual properties that ease cognitive processing (Kaplan, 1995). In either case, restoration is conceived of as something that happens to an individual as a product of their presence in a particular type of physical space.

Heft (2021), in contrast, has advocated for an ecological account of restoration by drawing on and extending the work of Wohlwill (1983) to highlight how natural and built environments tend to differ. Although one ecological perspective suggests that perhaps natural environments tend to have more affordances overall than built environments (Brymer et al., 2020), Heft is skeptical about this possibility. Rather he suggests that natural environments will likely have fewer normativity constraints, and may more readily allow people to fashion new actions on the spot (Heft, 2021). In addition, the structures of natural environments will likely have more variation in scale whereas built environments are typically designed to optimize the ability of people of certain body sizes to do certain activities. As Heft notes, however, finding the potential affordances of less-constructed places may require more exploration, and thus engage more of a sense of agency than built environments.

From this perspective, the phenomenological experience of restoration that people have from natural environments may therefore come from the range of affordances available within these places, or the sense of freedom and exploration required to uncover affordances. This pragmatic view of restoration de-mystifies the natural world and emphasizes the active role of the perceiver in the experience. In other words, the environment does not itself *cause* the individual to more relaxed, peaceful, or at ease. Rather, it affords certain perceptual and motoric actions that, when realized by an actively engaged individual, can lead to new and more positive psychological experiences.

Inspired by Heft's ideas, Kerry Marsh is currently exploring the number and nature of affordances that come to mind when people walk nature trails versus sidewalks around the downtown of a small town (Jiang et al., 2022). Benjamin Meagher has explored two implications for Heft's pragmatic view on restorative environments. First, psychological restoration is the product of a single person-environment system: it depends on the relationship between the setting and the occupant. As a result, restorativeness is not a property of a setting, but is equally dependent on the history, motives, and behavioral tendencies of the occupant. Second, if restoration is not an instinctual response to savannah-like green space, that means certain built environments, when designed to afford an adequate range of behavioral activity, can also have the capacity to be restorative. Work by the second author has explored how homes (Meagher, 2016b) and religious spaces (Meagher, 2016a, 2018) can also potentially facilitate desired emotional states, provided there is appropriate fit between the motives of the occupant and the design of the setting. For example, Meagher (2018) investigated how the construct of *perceptual mystery,* the extent to which an environment promotes continued engagement and discovery (Kaplan & Kaplan, 1989) in church design influences the frequency of religious emotions (e.g., awe) during worship. Importantly, these environmental properties enhanced the restorative experiences only of congregants with specific religious motives for engagement (i.e., Quest orientation; Batson, 1976). Similarly, Meagher (2016b) found that restorative design features in homes and undergraduate residence halls were particularly valuable for the individuals most likely to need and use those features: people high in neuroticism, who need to use their environments to help regulate emotional experiences. Thus, an affordance-rich environment is not guaranteed to provide benefits to an occupant. Instead, it also depends on an active occupant, discovering and realizing these behavioral opportunities.

10.5 The role of conceptual knowledge in perceiving and acting in social places

Heft is among a small group of ecological psychologists who have not avoided the challenge of integrating processes traditionally in the cognitive realm into ecological psychology, and he has done so in his lectures and publications for a decade. Reflective processes "involve stepping outside of the ongoing flow of perception-action circumstances, even momentarily, to think reflexively about some object or event ... acts of reflecting are indexed with reference to an abstract, conceptual, temporal dimension" (Heft, 2020b, p. 197). Not surprisingly, it is primarily theorists who have an interest in sociocultural issues who by necessity have had to address symbolic representational processes (language) or other "conceptual" knowledge (i.e., reflection, cognition, or memory).

The reason Heft does not avoid such issues is because he is unabashedly focused on *uniquely human* "ways of living." As he has stated (Heft, 2020a), his intention is to integrate sociocultural dimensions into ecological psychology and yet remain consistent with the meta-theoretical commitments of the field. Consistent with direct perception tenets he rejects that people's understanding of socially-constituted places is driven by cognitive structures – schemas, described as "intra-subjective processes by which individuals mentally construct or impose representational structure" (Heft 2020a, p. 818). Nevertheless, he acknowledges the importance of stored, shared symbolic meanings – language, or abstracted conceptual knowledge (Heft, 2020a).

However, Heft illustrates how the development of symbolic abstractions (words) and schemas *follow* from direct perception processes and as a consequence of children developing in a culture of shared social practices (Heft, 2017). Children are guided to attend to what affordances in a situation are normative and what actions are obligated, and over time they develop attunement to some affordances over others in a place. Moreover, "the language used by those around the child can direct attention both incidentally and intentionally to particular features" (Heft, 2017, p. 135). This is particularly crucial for features of the environment whose meaning would be completely unclear to someone with no cultural context. The classic example from Gibson that Heft elaborates (Heft, 2020a, 2020b) is developing awareness of the affordances of a postal box. Although a solitary alien would be unable to detect the social affordances of a mailbox in isolation, the collective activities with regard to the postal box are publically detectable. And even though the postal box is but a small part of a postal system which has extensive hidden components, Heft uses example of the "occluding edge effect" to explain how people have an awareness of the existence of environmental structure that over even some extended time may be hidden (Heft, 2020b). It is through experience with some aspect of an extended complicated social system that our schemas and concepts arise, Heft notes: "habits and skills stem from prior participation in social practices involved in making use of the postal system. *The concept of a postal system emerges* from participation in those social practices" (Heft, 2020a, p. 823, my emphasis). Moreover, "the use of a term such as *postal* system consolidates and fixes actions and observations by way of predication" (Heft, 2017, p. 138). What is notable about how Heft integrates the role of cognitive structure into people's understanding of places is that he stays true to the fundamental understanding that cognition *emerges as a consequence* of extended and complex actions and guided perceptual attunement.

In contrast, the social psychological literature on situations and environments takes as a *starting point* abstracted knowledge for understanding different situations. However, from an ecological perspective of Heft and others (Heft, 2020a) cognitive structures are a *downstream consequence* of our shared experiences acting and perceiving in socially constituted settings, scaffolded by our interactions with others. Borrowing an analogy once used by Timo Järvilehto in a talk in the 2000s, viewing schemas or language as the cause of our understandings of such situations (rather than emerging concurrent with perception and action) is a bit like putting the last piece in a jigsaw puzzle, and seeing that piece as the cause of the unified whole that comprises the intertwined pieces.

10.6 Conclusion

In at least three distinct areas of psychology – social, developmental, and ecological – and at least one cross-disciplinary domain – environmental psychology, Harry Heft's work has been revolutionary. His work has substantially changed how researchers' think about what environments are, how we navigate through them, and what psychological processes are core to our connection to environments. His work has improved the normativity of ecological psychologists pursuing questions that acknowledge the sociohistorical and cultural dimensions of perception-action. If one mark of a scientist's impact is an increased generativity of research studying concepts they promoted, then by all measure Heft's work has been of high impact indeed. This volume cannot do full justice to his impact because it occurs at a point in time when not only are Heft's ideas continuing to evolve but some fields of research, most notably social psychology, have only a beginning awareness of his work.

References

Alley, T. R. (Ed.). (1988). *Social and applied aspects of perceiving faces*. Erlbaum.
Barker, R. G., & Schoggen, P. (1973). *Qualities of community life: Methods of measuring environment and behavior applied to an American and an English town*. Jossey-Bass.
Barker, R. G., & Wright, H. F. (1951). *One boyas day; a specimen record of behavior*.
Batson, C. D. (1976). Religion as prosocial: Agent or double agent? *Journal for the Scientific Study of Religion, 15*, 29–45.
Brown, N. A., Neel, R., & Sherman, R. A. (2015). Measuring the evolutionarily important goals of situations: Situational affordances for adaptive problems. *Evolutionary Psychology, 13*, 1–15. doi:10.1177/1474704915593662
Brymer, E., Araújo, D., Davids, K., & Pepping, G.-J. (2020). Conceptualizing the human health outcomes of acting in natural environments: An ecological perspective. *Frontiers in Psychology, 11*. doi:10.3389/fpsyg.2020.01362.
Costall, A. (1995). Socializing affordances. *Theory & Psychology, 5*, 467–481.
Costall, A. (2017). 1966 and all that: James Gibson and bottom-down theory. *Ecological Psychology, 29*(3), 221–230. doi:10.1080/10407413.2017.1330121
Guillaume, E., Baranski, E., Todd, E., Bastian, B., Bronin, I., Ivanova, C., ...Funder, D. C. (2016). The world at 7:00: Comparing the experience of situations across 20 countries. *Journal of Personality, 84*, 493–509. doi:10.1111/jopy.12176
Heft, H. (1988). Affordances of children's environments: A functional approach to environmental description. *Children's Environments Quarterly, 5*, 29–37.
Heft, H. (1997). The relevance of Gibson's ecological approach to perception for environment-behavior studies. In G. T. Moore & R. W. Marans (Eds.), *Advances in environment, behavior, and design*, Vol. 4 (pp. 71–108). Plenum.
Heft, H. (2001). *Ecological psychology in context: James Gibson, Roger Barker, and the legacy of William James's radical empiricism*. Erlbaum.
Heft H. (2007). The social constitution of perceiver-environment reciprocity. *Ecological Psychology, 19*, 85–105.
Heft, H. (2013, July). *The concept of place in ecological psychology and why it matters*. Paper presented at the International Conference on Perception-Action 13, Estoril, Portugal.
Heft, H. (2017). Perceptual information of "an entirely different order": The "cultural environment" in the senses considered as perceptual systems. *Ecological Psychology, 29*, 122–145. 10.1080/10407413.2017.1297187
Heft, H. (2018). Places: Widening the scope of an ecological approach to perception–action with an emphasis on child development. *Ecological Psychology, 30*, 99–123. 10.1080/10407413.2018.1410045
Heft, H. (2020a). Ecological psychology as social psychology? *Theory & Psychology, 30*(6), 813–826. doi:10.1177/0959354320934545

Heft, H. (2020b). Revisiting 'The discovery of the occluding edge and its implications for perception' 40 years on. In J. B. Wagman & J. J. C. Blau (Eds.), *Perception as information detection: Reflections on Gibson's ecological approach to visual perception*, 1st ed. (pp. 188–204). Routledge/Taylor & Francis Group.

Heft, H. (2021). Perceiving "natural" environments: An ecological perspective with reflections on the chapters. In A. R. Schutte, J. C. Torquati, & J. R. Stevens (Eds.), *Nature and psychology: Biological, cognitive, developmental, and social pathways to well-being*. Nebraska Symposium on Motivation, Vol. 67 (pp. 235–273). Springer International Publishing.

Heft, H., Hoch, J., Edmunds, T., & Weeks, J. (2014). Can the identity of a behavior setting be perceived through patterns of joint action? An investigation of place perception. *Behavioral Sciences, 4*, 371–393.

Järvilehto, T. (1998). The theory of the organism-environment system: I. Description of the theory. *Integrative Physiological and Behavioral Science, 33*, 321–334. 10.1007/bf02688700

Jiang, S., Ott, A., Burt, C., & Marsh, K. L. (2022, June). *Salience of affordances in natural versus built environments*. Poster presented at the International Society of Ecological Psychology, Hattiesburg, MS.

Jongenee, D., Withagen, R., & Zaal, F. T. J. M. (2015). Do children create standardized playgrounds? A study on the gap-crossing affordances of jumping stones. *Journal of Environmental Psychology, 44*, 45–52.

Kaplan, R., & Kaplan, S. (1989). *The experience of nature: A psychological perspective*. Cambridge University Press.

Kaplan, S. (1995). The restorative benefits of nature: Toward an integrative framework. *Journal of Environmental Psychology, 15*(3), 169–182. doi:10.1016/0272-4944(95)90001-2

Kelley, H. H., Holmes, J. G., Kerr, N. L., Reis, H. T., Rusbult, C. E., & Van Lange, P. A. M. (2003). *An atlas of interpersonal situations*. Cambridge University Press.

Lee, D. I., Gardiner, G., Baranski, E., & Funder, D. C. (2020). Situational experience around the world: A replication and extension in 62 countries. *Journal of Personality, 88*(6), 1091–1110. doi:10.1111/jopy.12558

Marsh, K. L., Richardson, M. J., Baron, R. M., & Schmidt, R. C. (2006). Contrasting approaches to perceiving and acting with others. *Ecological Psychology, 18*, 1–37.

McArthur, L. Z., & Baron, R. M. (1983). Toward an ecological theory of social perception. *Psychological Review, 90*(3), 215–238.

Meagher, B. R. (2016a). Perceiving sacred space: Religious orientation moderates impressions of religious settings. *Environment and Behavior, 48*(8), 1030–1048. doi:10.1177/0013916515581626

Meagher, B. R. (2016b). There's no place like a neurotic's home: Neuroticism moderates the prioritization of restorative properties in home environments. *Journal of Individual Differences, 37*(4), 260–267. doi:10.1027/1614-0001/a000213

Meagher, B. R. (2018). Deciphering the religious orientation of a sacred space: Disparate impressions of worship settings by congregants and external observers. *Journal of Environmental Psychology, 55*, 70–80. doi:10.1016/j.jenvp.2017.12.007

Meagher, B. R. (2020). Ecologizing social psychology: The physical environment as a necessary constituent of social processes. *Personality and Social Psychology Review, 24*(1), 3–23. doi:10.1177/1088868319845938

Meagher, B. R., & Marsh, K. L. (2011). Judgments of interior spaces: The role of affordances. In E. P. Charles & L. J. Smart (Eds.), *Studies in perception and action XI: Sixteenth international conference on perception and action*, Vol. 11 (pp. 163–167). Psychology Press.

Meagher, B. R., & Marsh, K. L. (2015). Testing an ecological account of spaciousness in real and virtual environments. *Environment and Behavior*, 47, 782–815. doi:10.1177/0013916514525039

Meagher, B. R., & Marsh, K. L. (2017). Seeking the safety of sociofugal space: Environmental design preferences following social ostracism. *Journal of Experimental Social Psychology*, 68, 192–199. doi:10.1016/j.jesp.2016.07.004

Neuberg, S. L., Kenrick, D. T., & Schaller, M. (2010). Evolutionary social psychology. In S. T. Fiske, D. Gilbert, & G. Lindzey (Eds.), *Handbook of social psychology* (pp. 761–796). John Wiley.

Pick, C. M., & Neuberg, S. L. (2022). Beyond observation: Manipulation circumstances to detect affordances and infer traits. *Personality and Social Psychology Review*, 26, 160–179.

Rączaszek-Leonardi, J., Nomikou, I., Rohlfing, K. J., & Deacon, T. W. (2018). Language development from an ecological perspective: Ecologically valid ways to abstract symbols. *Ecological Psychology*, 30, 39–73. 10.1080/10407413.2017.1410387

Reis, H. T. (2008). Reinvigorating the concept of situation in social psychology. *Personality and Social Psychology Review*, 12, 311–329. 10.1177/1088868308321721

Richardson, M. J., Marsh, K. L., & Baron, R. M. (2007). Judging and actualizing intrapersonal and interpersonal affordances. *Journal of Experimental Psychology: Human Perception & Performance*, 33, 845–859.

Rietveld, E., & Kiverstein, J. (2014). A rich landscape of affordances. *Ecological Psychology*, 26, 325–352. doi:10.1080/10407413.2014.958035

Riley, M. A., Richardson, M. J., Shockley, K., & Ramenzoni, V. C. (2011). Interpersonal synergies. *Frontiers in Psychology*, 2. doi:10.3389/fpsyg.2011.00038

Routhmann, J. G., & Sherman, R. A. (2020). The situation of situation research: Known and unknown. 29, 473–480.

Runeson, S., & Frykholm, G. (1983). Kinematic specification of dynamics as an informational basis for person-and-action perception: Expectation, gender recognition, and deceptive intention. *Journal of Experimental Psychology: General*, 112, 585–615.

Sporrel, K., Caljouw, S. R., & Withagen, R. (2017). Gap-crossing behavior in a standardized and a nonstandardized jumping stone configuration. *PLOS ONE*, 12, e0176165. 10.1371/journal.pone.0176165

Ulrich, R. S. (1983). Aesthetic and affective response to natural environment. In I. Altman & J. F. Wohlwill (Eds.), *Human Behavior & Environment*, Vol. 6 (pp. 85–125). Plenum.

van der Kamp, J., Savelsbergh, G. J. P., & Davis, W. E. (1998). Body-scaled ratio as a control parameter for prehension in 5- to 9-year-old children. *Developmental Psychobiology*, 33(4), 351–351.

van Dijk, L., & Rietveld, E. (2017). Foregrounding sociomaterial practice in our understanding of affordances: The skilled intentionality framework. *Frontiers in Psychology*, 7. doi:10.3389/fpsyg.2016.01969

Warren, W. H. (1984). Perceiving affordances: Visual guidance of stair climbing. *Journal of Experimental Psychology: Human Perception and Performance*, 10(5), 683–703.

Wohlwill, J. F. (1983). The concept of nature: A psychologist's view. *Human Behavior & Environment: Advances in Theory & Research*, 6, 5–37.

Zebrowitz, L. A. (1997). *Reading faces: Window to the soul?* Westview Press.

11
UNDERSTANDING THE CHILD'S ENVIRONMENT

Justine Hoch

11.1 Introduction

Harry Heft has spent 45 years (and counting) thinking about the environment. During his notable academic career, Heft wrote scores of articles and chapters and multiple books about ecological psychology, environmental psychology, and the reciprocal relations between the environment and perception-action systems. Throughout these works, Heft persuasively argues that the way psychologists conceptualize and describe the environment has consequences for behavioral analysis, especially in the context of human development. In this chapter, I expand Heft's argument and consider how new modes of child-centered descriptions of the environment are changing the way that researchers think about behavior and development.

11.2 Approaches to environmental description

From the inception of developmental psychology, researchers have studied how the environment shapes child development (for reviews, see Evans, 2006; Wohlwill & Heft, 1987). For example, researchers have examined relations between children's access to books and the development of literacy (Payne et al., 1994), children's access to toys and motor development (Saccani et al., 2013; Valadi & Gabbard, 2020), and children's access to outdoor green space and cognitive development (Dadvand et al., 2015). To study the effects of environmental variation on development, researchers must first choose how to describe the environment. But, as Heft (1988) argues, all methods of description have fundamental – often unexamined – consequences for the way researchers think about the environment and therefore its relation to behavior. Below, I briefly summarize Heft's argument for describing the environment in terms of its functional features, rather than its forms, and the benefits of a function-based approach to description for behavioral analysis.

11.2.1 The traditional approach: Formal description

Most researchers use "form-based" language to describe children's environments (Heft, 1988). That is, researchers typically describe the environment in terms of the forms of the objects, surfaces, and other things in the surrounds that are available to children. A form-based description of a child's home might quantify the books on the child's shelves (Payne et al., 1994), the types of toys in the child's playroom (Saccani et al., 2013; Valadi & Gabbard, 2020), or even pixels of green space in satellite images of the child's neighborhood (Dadvand et al., 2015). Because form-based environmental descriptions rely on everyday terminology (e.g., "books," "toys," or "green"), such descriptions are convenient and easily understood.

A key characteristic of a form-based approach is that environmental features are described independently from – rather than in relation to – an individual. That is, books, toys, and green spaces can be described without referring to any particular child. This approach to description is especially common in studies comparing "enriched" and "impoverished" environments where the type of environment is defined by the things that are (or are not) available. Because form-based environmental features exist independently from the individual, they are typically conceptualized as external stimuli that are passively perceived and processed by the individual. In this way, form-based descriptions emphasize the distinction between the individual and the environment and often imply that behavior and development are the linear result of environmental stimulation (Heft, 1979; Wohlwill & Heft, 1977).

11.2.2 The Heft approach: Functional description

In contrast to a "form-based" approach, Heft (1988) argues for the utility of a "function-based" approach to environmental description. This approach is based on James Gibson's (1979) concept of "affordances." According to Gibson, affordances are possibilities for action that are jointly determined by the fit between the individual and the environment and are what make the environment functionally significant to an individual. Thus, rather than describing the environment in terms of its forms (e.g., objects, doorways, and stairs), a functional approach classifies environmental features in terms of the common activities they support. For example, an object smaller than an individual's hand affords *grasping* (Fagard, 2000), a doorway that is wider than an individual's body dimensions affords *passage* (Franchak et al., 2012), and a stair that is a certain height relative to an individual's leg length and balance control affords *climbing* (Warren, 1984).

A key characteristic of a functional approach is that it describes features of the environment in relation to a specific individual, rather than in isolation. For example, the ceiling affords climbing for a spider but not for a human, and a heavy bag of groceries affords lifting for a parent but not for an infant. Because functional environmental features are relations, not forms, they are conceptualized as dynamic properties that are objectively real and perceptible but are only realized when an individual acts in the environment. In this way, a function-based approach to description emphasizes the interdependence between the individual and the environment and implies that an individual's experience of the environment is both a product of and an influence on behavior and development (Heft & Wohlwill, 1987).

11.2.3 Benefits of functional description for behavioral analyses

Heft argues that function-based descriptions of the environment have several benefits for behavioral analysis. First, describing environmental features in a functional manner – in terms of the activities that they afford to individuals – provides a richer, more meaningful account of the available environmental resources than the traditional form-based approach. For example, a form-based description of a playground might label the types of equipment available for play (e.g., slide, ladder, monkey bars) as if the physical features have the same meaning for all children. But these environmental features may not be equally meaningful for all children – playground equipment might offer very different opportunities for action to preschool and grade school students who differ in size, strength, and coordination (Adolph & Berger, 2006; Gibson, 1992). A three-year old might use the slide as a tent or canopy, a six-year old as a surface to slide down, and a nine-year old as a steep path for walking. In contrast, because functional descriptions are specified in relation to an individual (e.g., equipment that affords swinging for a particular child), they can capture the same functional meaning for individuals who share the same abilities to exploit the relevant affordances.

Second, functional descriptions may be preferable to form-based descriptions because they better reflect an individual's immediate experience of the environment. According to Gibson (1979), the affordances of environmental features are equally salient (if not more salient) than their forms. That is, individuals more readily perceive whether something is in within arms' reach or will fit into the palm of their hand than its shape or size. Moreover, because functional features of the environment may be especially salient to children who have limited experience categorizing and labeling forms (Heft, 1988), functional descriptions might capture children's perceptual experience more accurately than form-based descriptions.

Third, because functional descriptions are based on behavior, they allow common properties to be identified among different environmental forms, whereas form-based descriptions are mutually exclusive. For example, a small stone cannot also be a paper plane, but both objects afford throwing. Thus, functional descriptions may reveal environment-behavior relations that are overlooked by form-based descriptions.

Finally, functional environmental descriptions might be especially useful for describing children's environments because, unlike form-based descriptions, functional descriptions capture development. Form-based descriptions call attention to features of the environment that are stable and static (e.g., a ball is always a ball, and a staircase is always a staircase). But, because functional descriptions are defined relationally, they allow the meaningful features of the environment to change in relation to an individuals' developmental status. Despite their consistent forms, balls and staircases provide new opportunities for action as pre-mobile infants transition to crawling and walking. Thus, as infants gain new skills and new means of gathering information, new affordances emerge (Heft, 1989). In other words, as infants develop, the environment also develops (Adolph, 2019). In this way, functional descriptions prompt researchers to think about the significance of environmental features for specific individuals and to recognize that the environment has a developmental dimension.

11.3 New ways to describe children's environments

In recent years, developmental psychologists have embraced powerful, new recording methods to document the ecology of children's everyday experiences (de Barbaro & Fausey, 2022; Franchak, 2020). Like the functional approach to environmental description, these ecologically inspired methods aim to capture the meaningful features of children's physical and social environments as they change over development. For example, head-mounted cameras and head-mounted eye-trackers record the accessible environment from the child's first-person point of view. Wearable sensors track the movements of the eyes, head, and body record the exploratory actions that support environmental perception. And improvements in recording technologies and data sharing enable researchers to capture children's experiences at scale and in context. In the following sections, I provide illustrative examples that show how recent advances in environmental description are changing the way that researchers think about children's behavior and development.

11.3.1 The first-person point of view

Since 2010, developmental researchers have made considerable progress in documenting children's environments from the first-person point of view (Franchak & Adolph, 2010; Franchak et al., 2011; Sullivan et al., 2021). Typically, developmental researchers document children's environments using third-person camera views. As with form-based descriptions, third-person camera views capture the environment independently from an individual child. For example, a camera on a tripod or held in a researcher's hand might capture the toys on the floor, a parent's facial expression, and parts of the ceiling as a child plays at home. But, because they are recorded from the vantage point of an outside observer, third-person camera views tend to capture the same features of the environment regardless of a child's age, posture, or developmental status, and they tend to capture larger portions of the environment than can be viewed by a child at any given time (Smith et al., 2015). Consequently, third-person camera views may give the erroneous impression that the documented environmental features are simultaneously or equally accessible to all children.

In contrast to third-person camera views, "headcams" and head-mounted eye trackers enable researchers to document the environment as it is seen by children. Headcams are light-weight cameras that record children's field of view as they move and play (for review, see Smith et al., 2015). Head-mounted eye trackers also capture children's field of view, but they have a second camera that points in toward the eye and allows researchers to record children's point of gaze (for review, see Franchak, 2017). Like function-based descriptions, recordings from the first-person point of view are relational. That is, they record the parts of the environment that are visible to a specific child in a specific posture and at a specific developmental timepoint. Thus, instead of describing the potential environment – the stuff in the room that may or may not ever be in view, headcams and head-mounted eye trackers record the accessible environment – the stuff that is in view and accessible for learning (Smith et al., 2015).

Recordings from the first-person point of view reveal surprising discoveries about the contents of infants' visual environments. For example, although ecological psychologists have long argued that looking is an embodied process (Gibson, 1979), data from headcams and head-mounted eye trackers demonstrate the extent to which infants' visual worlds are constrained by their size, body position, and abilities. Headcam data, for instance, show that two-month-olds see faces more frequently than do 15-month-olds (Jayaraman et al., 2015). These differences are likely explained by infants' developing motor skills (two-month-olds cannot yet sit and spend a lot of time on their backs, whereas 15-month-olds can sit up and walk) and the fact that caregivers hold younger infants more often than older infants (Franchak, 2019). Accordingly, very young infants' visual worlds are filled with faces because their views are limited by their posture, and adults frequently put their faces into young infants' field of view. As infants gain postural and locomotor skills, their views are less constrained (Adolph & West, 2022), and infants see more hands and objects as they spend more time engaging with their surrounds (Fausey et al., 2016). Thus, first-person recordings reveal that developmental constraints structure infants' visual environments and carve the world into ordered training datasets that may support learning and generalization (Smith et al., 2018).

In addition to documenting change over developmental time, recordings from the first-person point of view reveal that real-time changes in the accessible environment shape infants' opportunities for learning. Head-mounted eye tracking, for example, shows that while crawling, infants mostly see the ground in front of their hands. To see the objects or people in the room, infants must stop to sit or stand up. In contrast, while walking, infants can see the whole room even while moving (Franchak et al., 2018; Kretch et al., 2014). These real-time changes in infants' visual ecology have consequences for environmental exploration: although infants rarely fixate and then go to a new destination (only 32% of crawlers' and 16% of walkers' locomotor bouts), crawlers are more likely to do so when starting from sitting or upright postures compared to prone postures (Hoch et al., 2020). Infants' locomotor posture also shapes what they choose to explore: compared to walking infants, crawling infants are more likely to fixate and travel to objects on the floor, but less likely to fixate and travel to objects that are higher off the ground (Hoch et al., 2020).

Recordings from a first-person point of view also reveal surprising discoveries about where infants don't look. Infants guide locomotion over precarious ground mostly using visual information from the periphery of their field of view. They step over things in their path and even walk over narrow bridges while pointing their gaze at their goal, not at the ground under their feet (Franchak et al., 2011; Kretch & Adolph, 2017).

Perhaps the most surprising discovery is that infants and children rarely look at others' faces. Despite decades of research focused on what infants learn from face-to-face interactions with their caregivers (Kaye & Fogel, 1980; Tronick & Cohn, 1989), headcam recordings from children at home show that faces are only in view for five minutes per hour by the time infants reach 11 months of age (Jayaraman et al., 2015). Likewise, head-mounted eye-tracking data show that freely mobile 12-month-old infants spend less than 5% of the time looking at their caregivers' faces during free play (Franchak et al., 2018). These real-world visual statistics are challenging long-held assumptions about developmental mechanisms. For example, head-mounted eye tracking data show that inattention to faces – long held to be a signature characteristic of atypical social interactions – is not unique to autistic children (Yurkovic-Harding et al., 2022). Both autistic and neurotypical two- to four-year-olds ignore their parent's face. While playing with their parents in a room filled with toys, children in both groups look at their parent's face only 1% of the time. Thus, although lack of eye contact is a robust diagnostic marker of autism, data recorded from the first-person point of view suggest that it is no more a behavioral mechanism for autistic or neurotypical social interaction than itchy spots are a mechanism for chicken pox (Adolph & West, 2022).

Child-centered recordings also provide new insights into problems researchers once considered intractable. For example, centuries of researchers and philosophers puzzled over the problem of reference in language learning – that is, how infants learn that a particular word maps onto a particular object or feature in the visual scene (Quine, 1964; Yu & Smith, 2012). From a third person point of view, the problem indeed appears extremely difficult – children's environments are littered with objects that could potentially be the referent of a spoken word. However, looking at the environment from the infant's point of view reveals that the problem is not as difficult as it seems (Yurovsky et al., 2013). Parents typically label the objects in infants' hands (Custode & Tamis-LeMonda, 2020; West & Iverson, 2017; Yu & Smith, 2012), and – because infants' arms are short – hand-held objects loom large in infants' field of view and block out other competing objects (Smith et al., 2011). Thus, the coincident timing of action, word, and the salience of the referent makes tractable the previously "intractable" problem of ambiguous word referents. Moreover, day-long recordings collected over months reveal that parents' words are often repeated in the same places in the home in the context of daily routines (Roy et al., 2015; Tamis-LeMonda et al., 2019). In this way, child-centered recordings can uncover previously undetected structure in the environment.

11.3.2 Lab versus life

Researchers have always known that learning and development occur in the context of children's everyday environments. But until relatively recently, limitations in recording technologies hampered researchers' abilities to collect objective, rigorous descriptions of children's environments outside of a laboratory setting. Although developmental researchers collected film and audio data in the 1930s and 1940s (Gesell, 1946; McGraw & Breeze, 1941), the unwieldy size and limited recording durations of the original cinematic technologies made them impractical for use outside of the lab for extended periods of time (Adolph, 2016). Instead, many descriptions of children's everyday environments were generated from narrative vignettes (Barker & Wright, 1951; Darwin, 1877), observer ratings (Bradley et al., 2001; Heft, 1979), and self-report (Saccani et al., 2013; Valadi & Gabbard, 2020).

However, advances in recording technologies – notably, small, lightweight, wearable cameras and sensors with large storage capacities – enable researchers to accurately capture children's real-life physical and social environments (for review, see de Barbaro, 2019). For example, both first- and third-person video cameras record infants' access to objects (Fausey et al., 2016; Herzberg et al., 2022). Wearable audio recorders (e.g., LENA) capture language input and ambient noise over extended periods of time (Zimmerman et al., 2009). Wearable inertial sensors capture full-day recordings of infants' body position and time in motion (Franchak et al., 2021). And wearable tags use radio-frequency identification to measure proximity between infants and caregivers (Salo et al., 2021) and track the locations of each child in a classroom relative to their teachers and peers (Messinger et al., 2019).

Data collected in children's everyday environments reveal heterogeneity that is not observed in controlled laboratory settings. For example, many lab-based studies examine infants' interactions with a small set of standardized objects for relatively short periods of time (Hoch et al., under review). But at home, where infants have full access to toys and household objects, they interact with 41–99 unique objects in only two hours (Herzberg et al., 2022). Similarly, caregivers' language to infants during lab-based tasks dramatically differs from language recorded during everyday routines (Tamis-LeMonda et al., 2017). During structured play, caregivers talk constantly, and language input is consistently dense from one minute to the next. But in the context of daily life, language input fluctuates and is interspersed with long periods of silence. And although researchers typically observe children's social interactions with one partner, proximity data recorded in the classroom show that each child has a different network of peers and that some children are in social contact tens to hundreds of times more than others

(Messinger et al., 2019). By documenting the diversity of children's everyday experiences, new recording technologies are inspiring new hypotheses about the mechanisms that support learning and development in context (de Barbaro & Fausey, 2022).

Recordings of children's daily lives are extremely rich and generate vast amounts of data. Leveraging these recordings requires innovations in infrastructure and policy frameworks that enable researchers to openly share and annotate large datasets (Mendoza & Fausey, 2021). For example, the SAYCam corpus uses collaborative coding to tag 415 hours of naturalistic, longitudinal headcam recordings from three children (Sullivan et al., 2021). To identify videos of interest, large teams of coders with differing expertise tag videos based on their locations, objects, activities, and the people and body parts in view. In a similar vein, online data-sharing platforms such as the Databrary video library (databrary.org), enable researchers to collectively gather data from more diverse contexts (e.g., geographic, socioeconomic) than any one research team could do on their own (Adolph, 2020; Gilmore & Adolph, 2019; MacWhinney, 2000). For example, the Play & Learning Across a Year (PLAY) project uses Databrary to collect one hour of natural free play from 900+ infants and mothers across the USA (play-project.org). This dataset will also include video tours of the home, digital recordings of ambient noise, detailed demographic information, and data from parent questionnaires (Soska et al., 2021). Because the PLAY and SAYCam datasets will be openly shared, they will enable researchers to generate and validate developmental theories using high-quality data collected in a diverse range of environmental contexts.

11.4 Conclusion

Heft (1988) argues that all methods of description highlight some features of the environment while neglecting others. Accordingly, researchers must carefully consider the consequences of their chosen descriptive method for behavioral analysis. By taking inspiration from a functional approach to environmental description, new technologies that capture meaningful features of the environment, reflect the individual's immediate experience, relate to behavior, and capture development are advancing our understanding of children's environments.

References

Adolph, K. E. (2016). Video as data: From transient behavior to tangible recording. *APS Observer, 29*, 23–25.
Adolph, K. E. (2019). An ecological approach to learning in (not and) development. *Human Development, 63*, 180–201.
Adolph, K. E. (2020). Oh, behave! *Infancy, 25*, 374–392.
Adolph, K. E., & Berger, S. E. (2006). Motor development. In D. Kuhn & R. S. Siegler (Eds.), *Handbook of child psychology*, 6th ed., Vol. 2, Cognitive Processes (pp. 161–213). New York: Wiley.

Adolph, K. E., & West, K. L. (2022). Autism: The face value of eye contact. *Current Biology*, *32*(12), 577–580.

Barker, R. G., & Wright, H. F. (1951). *One boy's day: A specimen record of behavior*. New York: Harper Brothers.

Bradley, R. H., Corwyn, R. F., McAdoo, H. P., & Garcia Coll, C. (2001). The home environments of children in the United States part 1: Variations by age, ethnicity, and poverty status. *Child Development*, *72*(6), 1844–1867.

Custode, S. A., & Tamis-LeMonda, C. (2020). Cracking the code: Social and contextual cues to language input in the home environment. *Infancy*, *25*, 809–826.

Dadvand, P., Nieuwenhuijesen, M. J., Esnaola, M., Forns, J., Basagana, X., Alvarez-Pedrerol, M., ... , Sunyer, J. (2015). Green spaces and cognitive development in primary schoolchildren. *Proceedings of the National Academy of Sciences*, *11*(26), 7937–7942.

Darwin, C. (1877). A biographical sketch of an infant. *Mind*, *2*, 285–294.

de Barbaro, K. (2019). Automated sensing of daily activity: A new lens into development. *Developmental Psychobiology*, *61*, 444–464.

de Barbaro, K., & Fausey, C. (2022). Ten lessons about infants' everyday experiences. *Current Directions in Psychological Science*, *31*(1), 28–33.

Evans, G. W. (2006). Child development and the physical environment. *Annual Review of Psychology*, *57*, 423–451.

Fagard, J. (2000). Linked proximal and distal changes in the reaching behavior of 5- to 12-month-old human infants grasping objects of different sizes. *Infant Behavior and Development*, *23*, 317–329.

Fausey, C. M., Jayaraman, S., & Smith, L. B. (2016). From faces to hands: Changing visual input in the first two years. *Cognition*, *152*, 101–107. doi:10.1016/j.cognition.2016.03.005

Franchak, J. M. (2017). Head-mounted eye tracking. In B. Hopkins, E. Geangu, and S. Linkenauger, *The Cambridge encyclopedia of child development* (pp. 113–116). Cambridge, UK: Cambridge University Press.

Franchak, J. M. (2019). Changing opportunities for learning in everyday life: Infant body position over the first year. *Infancy*, *24*(2), 187–209.

Franchak, J. M. (2020). The ecology of infants' perceptual-motor exploration. *Current Opinion in Psychology*, *32*, 110–114.

Franchak, J. M., & Adolph, K. E. (2010). Visually guided navigation: Head-mounted eye-tracking of natural locomotion in children and adults. *Vision Research*, *50*, 2766–2774. doi:10.1016/j.visres.2010.09.024

Franchak, J. M., Celano, E. C., & Adolph, K. E. (2012). Perception of passage through openings cannot be explained geometric body dimensions alone. *Experimental Brain Research*, *223*, 301–310.

Franchak, J. M., Kretch, K. S., & Adolph, K. E. (2018). See and be seen: Infant-caregiver social looking during freely mobile play. *Developmental Science*, *21*, e12626.

Franchak, J. M., Kretch, K. S., Soska, K. C., & Adolph, K. E. (2011). Head-mounted eye tracking: A new method to describe infant looking. *Child Development*, *82*, 1738–1750.

Franchak, J. M., Scott, V., & Luo, C. (2021). A contactless method for full-day, naturalistic motor behavior using wearable inertial sensors. *Frontiers in Psychology*, *12*, 701343.

Gesell, A. (1946). Cinematography and the study of child development. *The American Naturalist*, *80*, 470–475.

Gibson, E. J. (1992). How to think about perceptual learning: Twenty-five years later. In H. L. Pick, P. van den Broek, & D. C. Knill (Eds.), *Cognition: Conceptual and methodological issues* (pp. 215–237). Washington, DC: American Psychological Association.

Gibson, J. J. (1979). *The ecological approach to visual perception*. Boston, MA: Houghton Mifflin.

Gilmore, R. O., & Adolph, K. E. (2019). Open sharing of research video: Breaking down the boundaries of the research team. In K. L. Hall, A. L. Vogel, & R. T. Croyle (Eds.), *Strategies for team science success: Handbook of evidence-based principles for cross-disciplinary science and practical lessons learned from health researchers* (pp. 547–583). Cham: Springer.

Heft, H. (1979). Background and focal environmental conditions of the home and attention in young children. *Journal of Applied Social Psychology, 9*(1), 47–69.

Heft, H. (1988). Affordances of children's environments: A functional approach to environmental description. *Children's Environment Quarterly, 5,* 29–37.

Heft, H. (1989). Affordances and the body: An intentional analysis of Gibson's ecological approach to visual perception. *Journal of the Theory of Social Behavior, 19*(1), 1–30.

Heft, H., & Wohlwill, J. F. (1987). The physical environment and the development of the child. In D. Stokols & I. Altman (Eds.), *Handbook of Environmental Psychology,* Vol. 281–328. New York: Wiley.

Herzberg, O., Fletcher, K. K., Schatz, J. L., Adolph, K. E., & Tamis-LeMonda, C. (2022). Infant exuberant object play at home: Immense amounts of time-distributed, variable practice. *Child Development, 93,* 150–164.

Hoch, J. E., Hospodar, C. M., Alves, G., & Adolph, K. E. (under review). What factors encourage infants to move? Effects of environmental factors, social factors, and months of walking on infants' locomotor practice.

Hoch, J. E., Rachwani, J., & Adolph, K. E. (2020). Where infants go: Real-time dynamics of locomotor exploration in crawling and walking infants. *Child Development, 91,* 1001–1020.

Jayaraman, W., Fausey, C. M., & Smith, L. B. (2015). The faces in infant-perspective scenes change over the first year of life. *PLoS One.* doi:10.1371/journal.pone.0123780

Kaye, K., & Fogel, A. (1980). The temporal structure of face-to-face communication between mothers and infants. *Developmental Psychology, 16*(5), 454–464.

Kretch, K. S., & Adolph, K. E. (2017). The organization of exploratory behaviors in infant locomotor planning. *Developmental Science, 20,* e12421.

Kretch, K. S., Franchak, J. M., & Adolph, K. E. (2014). Crawling and walking infants see the world differently. *Child Development, 85,* 1503–1518.

MacWhinney, B. (2000). *The CHILDES project: Tools for analyzing talk,* 3 ed. Mahwah, NJ: Erlbaum.

McGraw, M. B., & Breeze, K. W. (1941). Quantitative studies in the development of erect locomotion. *Child Development, 12,* 267–303.

Mendoza J. K., & Fausey, C. (2021). Quantifying everyday ecologies: Principles for manual annotation of many hours of infants' lives. *Frontiers in Psychology, 12,* 710636.

Messinger, D. S., Prince, E. B., Zheng, M., Martin, K., Mitsven, S. G., Huang, S., ..., Song, C. (2019). Continuous measurement of dynamic classroom social interactions. *International Journal of Behavioral Development, 43*(3), 263–270.

Payne, A. C., Whitehurst, G. J., & Angell, A. L. (1994). The role of home literacy environment in the development of language ability in preschool children from low-income families. *Early Childhood Research Quarterly, 9*(3), 427–440.

Quine, W. (1964). *Word and object.* MIT Press.

Roy, B. C., Frank, M. C., DeCamp, P., Miller, M., & Roy, D. (2015). Predicting the birth of a spoken word. *Proceedings of the National Academy of Sciences, 112,* 12663–12668. doi:10.1073/pnas.1419773112

Saccani, R., Valentini, N. C., Pereirra, K. R. G., Muller, A. B., & Gabbard, C. (2013). Associations of biological factors and affordances in the home with infant motor development. *Pediatrics International, 55,* 197–203.

Salo, V. C., Pannuto, P., Hedgecock, W., Biri, A., Russo, D. A., Piersiak, H. A., & Humphreys, K. L. (2022). Measuring naturalistic proximity as a window into caregiver-child interaction patterns. *Behavior Research Methods, 54*, 1580–1594.

Smith, L. B., Jayaraman, S., Clerkin, E., & Yu, C. (2018). The developing infant creates a curriculum for statistical learning. *Trends in Cognitive Sciences, 22*, 325–336. doi:10.1016/j.tics.2018.02.004

Smith, L. B., Yu, C., & Pereira, A. F. (2011). Not your mother's view: The dynamics of toddler visual experience. *Developmental Science, 14*, 9–17. doi:10.1111/j.1467-7687.2009.00947.x

Smith, L. B., Yu, C., Yoshida, H., & Fausey, C. M. (2015). Contributions of head-mounted cameras to studying the visual environments of infants and young children. *Journal of Cognition and Development, 16*(3), 407–419.

Soska, K. C., Xu, M., Gonzalez, S. L., Herzberg, O., Tamis-LeMonda, C. S., Gilmore, R. O., & Adolph, K. E. (2021). (Hyper)active data curation: A video case study from behavioral science. *Journal of eScience Librarianship, 10*, e1208.s.

Sullivan, J., Mei, M., Perfors, A., Wojcik, E., & Frank, M. C. (2022). SAYCam: A large, longitudinal, audiovisual dataset recorded from the infant's perspective. *Open Mind: Discoveries in Cognitive Science, 5*, 20–29.

Tamis-LeMonda, C. S., Kuchirko, Y., Luo, R., & Escobar, K. (2017). Power in methods: Language to infants in structured and naturalistic contexts. *Developmental Science, 20*, e12456. doi:10.1111/desc.12456

Tamis-LeMonda, C. S., Custode, S., Kuchirko, Y., Escobar, K., & Lo, T. (2019). Routine language: Speech directed to infants during home activities. *Child Development, 90*, 2135–2152. doi:10.1111/cdev.13089

Tronick, E., & Cohn, J. (1989). Infant-mother face-to-face interaction: Age and gender differences in coordination and the occurrence of miscoordination. *Child Development, 60*(1), 85–92.

Valadi, S., & Gabbard, C. (2020). The effect of affordances in the home environment on children's fine-and gross-motor skills. *Early Child Development and Care, 190*(8), 1225–1232.

Warren, W. H. (1984). Perceiving affordances: Visual guidance of stair climbing. *Journal of Experimental Psychology: Human Perception and Performance, 10*, 683–703.

West, K. L., & Iverson, J. M. (2017). Language learning is hands-on: Exploring links between infants' object manipulation and verbal input. *Cognitive Development, 43*, 190–200.

Wohlwill, J. F., & Heft, H. (1977). Environments fit for the developing child. In H. McGurk (Ed.), *Ecological factors in human development*. Amsterdam: North Holland.

Wohlwill, J. F., & Heft, H. (1987). Environmental cognition in children. In D. Stokols & I. Altman (Eds.), *Handbook of environmental psychology* (pp. 175–204). New York: Wiley.

Yu, C., & Smith, L. B. (2012). Embodied attention and word learning by toddlers. *Cognition, 125*, 244–262. doi:10.1016/j.cognition.2012.06.016

Yurkovic-Harding, J., Lisandrelli, G., Shaffer, R. C., Dominick, K. C., Pedapati, E. V., Erickson, C. A., … , Kennedy, D. P. (2022). Children with ASD establish joint attention during free-flowing toy play without face looks. *Current Biology, 32*(12), 2739-2746.

Yurovsky, D., Smith, L. B., & Yu, C. (2013). Statistical word learning at scale: The baby's view is better. *Developmental Science, 16*(6), 959–966.

Zimmerman, F. J., Gilkerson, J., Richards, J. A., Christakis, D. A., Xu, D., Gray, S., & Yapanel, U. (2009). Teaching by listening: The importance of adult-child conversations to language development. *Pediatrics, 124*(1), 342–349.

12

TOWARD A PSYCHOLOGICAL ECOLOGY

Harry Heft

12.1 Introduction

On the opening page of *Midwest and Its Children: The Psychological Ecology of an American Town*, Barker and Wright (1955/1971) explain what they mean by the phrase in the subtitle, "psychological ecology":

> The term *ecology* comes from a Greek word meaning 'home,' or 'homeland.' In the biological sciences, ecology refers to the study of the relations between homelands or habitats of plants and their functions, structures, and population characteristics. The present study is a *psychological analogue of this conception of ecology*. (p. 1, emphasis added)

The phrase "psychological ecology" aptly captures the focus of much of my scholarly work which has been to explore what an ecological approach would mean for the science of psychology.[1]

An ecological science requires an in-depth familiarity with the relations among living things and their habitats as they mutually exist apart from experimental interventions. Such an effort *presupposes* a terminology that captures the basic phenomena and the entities of the domain of study, whether they be plants or animals, *prior to* the application of abstract formulations or classifications. Such a terminology is foundational to any domain of the life sciences. It typically precedes, as well as continues to accompany, experimental efforts. An ecological science asks in a given domain of study: what is "there" in the environment, and how are those things interrelated?

It struck me at an early point in my studies that, for the most part, the science of psychology lacked a terminology for the environment that was adequate to the ways in which humans *experience* and *engage* their everyday world. Early in its

DOI: 10.4324/9781003259244-13

history, psychology eschewed the "ordinary language" that individuals use in daily discourse to refer to the environment – what Heider (1958) called a "common-sense psychology" – and instead embraced terminology from the physical sciences and geometry. I was interested in finding ways to rectify that step because of the problems it created for psychology. I turned initially for guidance to a group of psychologists – principally Lewin, Gibson, and Barker – who attempted to ground psychological research in everyday experience.

The languages of sensory stimulation and of geometric forms as referents for the environment that I learned about in my training in perception and developmental psychology seemed too remote from how we experience the environment.[2] Those referents raised the prospects of a terminology that was largely artificial in comparison to experienced realities of everyday life. And even worse, employing that terminology in the science of psychology to describe the "real" environment seemed to necessitate claims that the environment individuals *do* experience is located "in the head" as a wholly private *construction*. Such a position made little sense to me in addition to be antiquated from a functionalist, Darwinian point of view where adaptation and attunement to the immediate surround are the hallmarks of organismic functioning, *and* for a species such as ours that is intensely social from the outset of life.

Moreover, in the absence of an environmental terminology that is attuned to human functioning, applied efforts to design and ameliorate everyday environments in order to support human development and welfare were greatly handicapped. An ecological language commensurate with human everyday life seemed much in need in the design fields as well.

Psychology, like other life sciences, would seem to require, then, a sustained and continuing effort to detail the on-going relations of its primary subject (*Homo sapiens*) and its habitats. But what is historically quite remarkable about scientific psychology overall, particularly in the wake of the Darwinian revolution, is how few psychologists seemed to have recognized the necessity for an account of the ecology of human domains, even as such efforts had been proceeding apace in the other life sciences since roughly the outset of the 20th century. As Barker (1968) pointed out nearly half a century ago, psychology is practically alone among all of the natural sciences in never having had a descriptive phase; and among the life sciences, not to have engaged in ecological inquiry concerning its subject matter.

Such an enterprise of a psychological ecology cannot be a single, one-time effort; it must be on-going as circumstances in local habitats and the wider biosphere change in both small and large ways. Both environments and organisms change over time; and while there are relative stabilities, there are also notable transformations. In this way, among others, how we *now* – post-Darwin, post-Einstein – view the *dynamic* character of the environment and psychological phenomena should sharply differ from the more static views that we have inherited from our Platonic and Newtonian intellectual past.

Still, a psychological ecology will differ from that associated with ecologies in other life sciences owing to the somewhat distinctive character of human habitats.

Although I will not invoke sharp lines of difference with all other species, even those genetically close to us, human habitats appear to have many unique features as compared to those of other species with whom we share the planet.[3] I am not so foolhardy as to attempt to detail the many distinctive features of human habitats except to emphasize here that meaning, values, and symbolism surely underlay most of their distinguishing qualities. For that reason, a psychological ecology must recognize the place of meaning, values, and symbols in how we engage and experience everyday human environments.

Attempting to arrive at a descriptive language that is adequate for delineating the environment from a psychological point of view requires, however, going beyond most of the terms we find in "ordinary language" even though those are starting points. Although we already have at our disposal a vast vocabulary that refers to "things of the world," such as tables, chairs, hammers, pens, and computer keyboards, as well as designated "places" such as homes, schools, stores, and offices where particular types of activities tend to occur, those terms by themselves do not take us very far for the purposes of *psychological inquiry*. This is because they *omit* the users of those things and the participants in those places. An adequate terminology from an ecological point of view must be *relational* in nature; for psychological purposes, it will need to encompass both the environment and the individual from a functional standpoint. Doing so will, for example, open possibilities for understanding how things and places are perceived in the course of action, and sometimes co-constituted by individuals, as well as how individuals come to learn about them over the course of development. In other words, an ecological terminology from a psychological point of view will open up possibilities for scientific inquiry that puts functional considerations at its center. Gibson's concept of *affordances* and Barker's concept of *behavior settings* as bases for a needed terminology seem to do just that. It is for this reason that I find them to be of great value.

Most of the chapters in this volume take up these ideas and concepts as I have explored them in previous work. Other chapters examine related topics and efforts to extend these ideas. Page limitations prevent me from offering extensive remarks on all of the chapters, but that constraint does not reflect the great value I have found in all of them. I must say at the outset that there are fewer higher compliments for an academic than to have one's work examined as carefully and thoughtfully as the authors of these chapters do of mine. In particular, I am pleased to see that so many of the contributors have attempted to develop and refine my work beyond whatever preliminary steps I have taken in the first place, and even to correct earlier missteps.

12.2 Radical empiricism, pragmatism, and realism

I begin with the chapter by Alan Costall because it goes to a core issue in my work: how to conceptualize the historical foundations for Gibson's ecological approach and, arguably, for Barker's approach.[4] The Gibsonian ecological psychology community has benefited for many years from the depth of scholarship and insight that Alan Costall brings to his writings on ecological psychology and to the field of psychology generally. No one has read the literature broadly relating to ecological psychology with greater care and thoroughness, and with a sharper eye for inconsistencies and vagaries. Among my contemporaries, there are few whom I have learned more from than him. Approaching his chapter, I knew that he would not let me off too easily for any miscues.

On that note, Costall invites us to consider "a contrary imagination" than the one I offered about the foundations of Gibson's ecological psychology. What is this "contrary imagination"? Although I previously proposed (Heft, 2001) that Gibson's ecological approach is historically grounded in William James' philosophy of radical empiricism (likely by way of E. B. Holt), Costall claims that historically a more suitable basis for making sense of the origins of Gibson's approach is the pragmatism "which runs from John Dewey, then to William James, and on to figures like George Herbert Mead" (this volume). In my view, what matters here is not so much the relative historical accuracy of each – they both are true – but what their implications are for the continuing development of the ecological approach.

Consistent with Costall's point, I have heard from friendly critics of my book over the years that I failed to give sufficient attention to Dewey in my attempt to trace the recent origins of Gibson's ecological approach. That is a fair criticism if my intentions had been to develop a complete account of the various influences shaping Gibson's thinking (Reed, 1988), but my goal was more limited than that. Even so, if I were writing that book today, I would have brought Dewey and Mead more fully into the book in order to give greater emphasis to the social dimensions of pragmatism (I will return to this point). After all, William James never intended to be a social theorist; and in many ways his thinking was rooted in 19th-century science, philosophy, and religion in America, whereas the American social movements at the end of that century became central to Dewey's developing writings.

What then was the goal of the book – or at least its first half before I turned to examine Barker's ecological psychology? Reflecting back, I suppose that *its starting point was an effort to clarify the concept of an affordance*. I was struck by its potential value for moving away from the dualism that psychology had adopted from its philosophical antecedents, but I was puzzled as to basis for the concept of an affordance in philosophical writings on *ontology*. I understood what an affordance was *not* – "it was neither objective nor subjective" – but I was baffled as to what an affordance was. My puzzlement, at least, stemmed from my prior acquaintance mostly with various philosophies of mind that descended from the dualism of Descartes, which cleaved the world into objective and subjective properties. From that starting point, affordances were initially an utter mystery, and still remain so for many.

I did know that Gibson's thinking had been influenced by the writings of William James, but mostly by way of James' emphasis on the stream of thought, and his distinction between "knowledge of acquaintance" and "knowledge about"

(Gibson, 1966, p. 235). As I learned more about William James, I realized that *The Principles of Psychology* (1890) and *Psychology: A Briefer Course* (1892) – the books that most psychologists knew, if only partially – did not represent in full James' mature thought. After those books appeared, and during the period when E. B. Holt studied with him, William James had some notable breakthroughs in his thinking that were only nascent in the previous work. These later developments appeared most fully in his writings on *pragmatism* and on the philosophy of *radical empiricism*. As Costall points out, however, James indicated that there is "no logical connection" between pragmatism and radical empiricism. To be clear, it is not the case that they are unrelated, but that each could stand on its own. Why then did I emphasize radical empiricism as my starting point for establishing a foundation for ecological psychology? Because it was there that I found the underpinnings for the concept of affordance, and that was my main target. In retrospect, there was a cost in doing so because the active nature of knowing processes is more apparent with pragmatism.

Just to offer a sense of radical empiricism, consider the following sentence that appears in the James' 1895 paper "The knowing of things together": "[T]he paper seen and the seeing of it are only two names for one indivisible fact, which properly named, is *the datum, the phenomenon, or the experience* .... *To know immediately, then, or intuitively, is for mental content and object to be identical*" (pp. 156–157). Likewise, in "Does consciousness exist" (1904), James emphasizes the relational character of immediate experience as follows:

> My thesis is that if we start with the supposition that there is only one primal stuff or material in the world ... then knowing can be easily explained as a particular kind of relation ... one its 'terms' becomes the subject or bearer of the knowledge, the knower, the other becomes the object known. (p. 170)

Affordances, as Gibson employed the term, have this same character. They are known immediately, are relational, and "point both ways" to the thing in the world and the knower.

At the outset of his chapter, Costall demonstrates his historical acumen by identifying earlier contributions that he regards as not having received their due in Gibson's writings. I comment here on only two points Costall raises. First, as to Merleau-Ponty, I have examined Gibson's notes on Merleau-Ponty in the Cornell archives, and judging from those alone, it appears that Gibson limited his reading to a few chapters in *The Phenomenology of Perception* (1963). Further, Gibson shared in a letter to me his admiration for Merleau-Ponty's writings on perception.[5] Second, I agree with Costall that the contributions of Fritz Heider do not seem to have been given the attention they deserve. I have discussed the significance of Heider's brilliant paper "Thing and medium" (1926) for both Gibson and Barker elsewhere (Heft, 2001), and I return to Heider's wider contributions to an ecological approach below. Still, even though the influence of Heider's work on Gibson is most apparent with the latter's development of the ambient optic array,

Heider's approach to perception was lacking the emphasis on action that we find in Gibson.

These observations, however, were only tangentially related to Costall's main point in his chapter, which reprises a theme in many of his writings over several decades. He has argued that the ecological approach is best conceived as a *mutualism* rather than a solely a relational view. That proposal aligns Costall's thinking more with the pragmatism of Dewey and Mead than with William James's radical empiricism. As I understand it, principal differences here are that mutualism recognizes organisms' active contributions to the habitat within which they live, and likewise that there is a greater emphasis on organism-environment reciprocity than one finds with a relational view. I fully concur with Costall here.

Further, the reciprocity of a mutualist perspective necessarily gives greater prominence to the *social* and the *symbolic* character of the psychological domain than sole recognition of a relational focus offers. Although we share the environment with all other organisms, and all organisms alter their econiche to better function in it, the habitat that becomes distinctively salient to humans over the course of our species development is one replete with human artifacts, such as pictures, written texts, and maps, not to mention higher-order social structures. Moreover, even those constructions that have their counterparts in non-human habitats, such as shelters, nests, and places for resource storage, usually take on in human habitats a symbolic significance often tied to a sense of self.

In short, I am in agreement with Costall's mutualist account in most respects, particularly because of the emphasis that is given to the social dimensions of human activities and experience. But still I feel that something is insufficiently emphasized in the mutualist accounts that I have read, and it is the basis for a continuing disagreement over whether or not affordances can be said to exist independently of the perceiving organism. Mutualists are critical of Gibson (and Reed) in making that claim, and I side with the latter.

Focusing only on human habitats at present, what seems to receive insufficient emphasis from the mutualist side – if I am not mistaken – is sociocultural history, and more broadly, cultural evolution. Along with that are technological developments in society and their consequences. Much of the habitat within which an individual begins life, and then develops and lives in, is "already there" independent of his/her actions owing to *prior* human activities and constructions that have already taken place in one's community, and among circumstances and social structures that lay beyond the individual's agentic reach. And if we broaden an exclusive focus from solely human habitats, the ecosystems of all organisms are affected by changes in the global environment beyond the reach of most of them, as is painfully clear today. Even though a mutualist view rightly emphasizes the reciprocity of organisms and environment, that view seems too narrow in scope in an historical vein. While mutualism gives needed prominence to the ways that the agency of life forms changes the environment, those changes reverberate beyond *individual*-environment mutuality. Although affordances and other environmental properties and processes that are relevant to an organism are specified relative to the organism – and there a mutualism prevails – many of them exist independently of perceiving organisms when viewed from a historical perspective.

12.3 Environments of the developing child

Several of the chapters in this volume explore issues relating to my discussions of affordances of children's everyday environments (Heft, 1988, 2013). The motivation behind the initial paper, and anticipated in earlier work (Heft, 1985), was to contribute to a project that is immanent primarily in Gibson's later writings, and that also can be seen in Barker's research. That project, as discussed at the outset, is to offer a terminology for describing the *environment* in ways that are adequate for the study of psychological phenomena.

Gibson's intention to offer such a terminology is most apparent in the third chapter of Gibson (1979), "The meaningful environment" which opens as follows: "The world of physical reality does not consist of meaningful things. The world of ecological reality, as I have been trying to describe it, does" (p. 33). Ecological reality refers to those features of the environment that individuals encounter "naively" (without the mediation of abstract concepts), that are meaningful, and that have immediate, practical consequences for the individual when engaged. While the first two characteristics are consistent with Gestalt thinking, the latter reflects a pragmatist orientation.

Gibson (1979) goes on later in this same chapter to make an initial effort at developing a terminology for describing ecological reality in his discussion of "what the environment affords the animal" (pp. 36–42). He singles out various features that *afford* actions for an individual, and those features are meaningful *in relation* to those actions. Collectively, these features are referred to as affordances, which is an ecological rather than a physical concept precisely because it brackets *relations* between an organism and the environment, in the same vein that the field of ecology, unlike that of physics (traditonally), is primarily the study of the relations among organisms and their habitats.

We have seen above a comparable position adopted by Barker, although with less of a pragmatic emphasis than Gibson's orientation, with his use of the phrase "psychological ecology." Among the ambitious goals of Barker and his research team that were reported in *Midwest and Its Children* (Barker & Wright, 1955/1971; see also Barker, 1968) was to catalogue all of the behavioral opportunities (eco-psychological resources) available to the inhabitants in this small town over the course of a year. Remarkably, they conducted such a year-long inventory (what they called a "behavior setting survey") in that town twice, with roughly a ten-year interval between each, as well as similar inventories over two separate years in a comparable small town in England (Barker & Schoggen, 1973). These behavior setting surveys indicated "what was possible for townspeople to do" in public settings over the time periods studied. Just as one might describe the ecological niche for a particular animal or plant over some time period, they described the ecological niche from a psychological standpoint for inhabitants of these communities. By connecting his work to that of the allied fields of biological ecology, Barker conveyed a deeper sense of the term "ecology" in his writings than Gibson did.

Pertinent to this very point, a reviewer of my book *Ecological Psychology in Context* (Heft, 2001) offered the criticism that in spite of the book's title and its treatment of an "ecological" psychology, that I didn't clearly spell out in what way an "ecological psychology" conveys the meaning of ecological in a biological sense (Drake, 2013). That criticism seems entirely justified to me, and it extends to varying degrees to much of the Gibsonian program, in my view, over the years following Gibson's death. Reed (1996a) is an important exception here. I have attempted to compensate for that shortcoming since then, albeit in limited ways (Heft, 2007, 2013, 2014).

Barker looked toward the potential scientific value to be found in the use of everyday language in his research.[6] It is easy to miss this intentional strategy in the plain-spoken presentation of observations. In the collection of what he called day-long "specimen records" (in contrast to "behavior setting surveys"), he had his individual researcher team members record in writing what they observed a target child was doing "in real time." He deliberately instructed the individuals in his research team "to observe what a person does *together with the situation* of the person and then to *narrate* and set down [in writing] what has been observed in common language" (p. 196, emphases added). Consistent with Heider's (1958) reasoning, Barker judges that "[c]ommon language has much to recommend it for the purpose. *It has been adapted by centuries of daily practice to the variability, the complexity, and the richness of human conduct*" (Barker & Wright, 1955/1971, p. 196, emphasis added). The use of common language in everyday discourse is what

> our social transactions require us to practice on a daily basis … [because it] enables us to deal with our associates on the basis of their goals, obstacles, paths and values, and thereby, to adapt ourselves appropriately to the action of others. (Barker & Wright, 1955/1971, p. 189)

Whereas contemporary researchers may look back at the task of handwriting observations as narratives in common language as being antiquated and only onerous, for Barker (and Heider) the act of recording observations in this way draws upon a shared discourse that has developed *within a cultural tradition* to identify and extract, and in turn be able to communicate, what is salient when observing others' actions. Although video recordings of our day must be subsequently coded, a first "level" of coding already occurs through the act of recording observations narratively in common language. These are complicated methodological issues, however, and require more extensive consideration than is possible here.

12.3.1 An affordance taxonomy for children's environment

The taxonomy offered in the "Affordances of children's environments" (Heft, 1988) brought together the affordance concept from Gibson's writings with primarily the "specimen record" published by Barker and Wright under the title *One*

Boy's Day (1953). The subject of these observations was a seven-year-old boy whose *actions and the situations in which they occurred* over a single day, which were recorded from the time he woke up to the time he went to bed in the evening. Working from these published narratives, I extracted every action directed at or taken in relation to some material feature over the course of his day. Those feature-action pairings were then compiled, and supplemented from a few more limited observational studies, resulting in a taxonomy of affordances that was generated from these records. Rather than using a terminology based on a detached stance that classifies a feature with respect to a "thing-like" category – e.g., trees, fence railings, sidewalks – the focus was on affordance properties that might be shared by different things, such as "climb-on-able" things, "coast-on-able" slopes, and "skate-on-able" surfaces. Based on my graduate school experience of working in the company of individuals trained in design, I referred to the former detached stance as a "form" classification approach, and drew a contrast between that and an affordance approach.

In her chapter for this volume, Justine Hoch insightfully brings out one of the consequences of adopting a "form" approach that was not identified in my original paper. She recognizes that historically such an approach invited a counting up, in some manner, of the number of "things" of various kinds (e.g., toys, books) in some setting. Having done that, one can then designate whether a particular setting is comparatively *enriched* or *impoverished* with respect to some stimulus feature. There is a large research literature that extends over many decades (I have even contributed to it) which considers the effects of the early environment on child development on enriched-impoverished dimensions. In recent decades, there is likewise a spate of research that has assessed the amount of *green space* that is visible for a perceiver,[7] and offers evidence for its effects mostly related to measures of stress and well-being (see chapters in Schutte et al., 2021).

Two implicit assumptions in that approach are noteworthy. First, the environment is typically assessed with respect to these features *independently* of any particular individual rather than relationally. Second, this approach promotes the view that environmental features, attributes, or structures are *imposed* on a passive perceiver, often with the assumption that "the more the better" (Wohlwill, 1973a). The individual is *not* viewed as an agent who selectively engages the environment, and even in some cases, alters it. In contrast, affordances are relational properties, and for that reason, an affordance approach points to *opportunities for action and engagement* that are possible in some setting for a particular individual.[8] This perspective seems much more in keeping with the goal of formulating a psychological ecology for intentional agents.

Of course, this proposed affordance taxonomy was limited in several respects. Based as it was primarily on the observed situated actions of a seven-year-old boy in a small midwestern town of the USA in the mid-20th century on a single day, it could not avoid being so. What available affordances might have been revealed if the boy were younger or older? Or if the subject of observation had been a girl, or children at other ages? Or if the observations had been of a child of a minority group,[9] a child living in an urban area, in a different culture, or during a different historical period? Possibilities for future research are vast. We will return to other limitations below.

12.3.2 Children's environments from a first-person perspective

Investigations of children's early environments over the decades have been carried out from the third-person standpoint of an observer. Hoch's chapter is invaluable for bringing to the attention of readers the various advances made in recent decades in the study of young children's engagement with the environment from a first-person perspective – that is, from the perspective of a particular child. She points out that research conducted from a third-person standpoint can be misleading because it "may give the erroneous impression that the documented features [from a third-person perspective] are simultaneously or equally accessible to all children" (this volume). However, an appreciation for the relational character of perceiving that the concept of affordances highlights brings into focus something that tends to have been neglected in earlier observer-based studies: that objects and properties that are available to be perceived by a child at a particular time depends on person-specific factors, such as first-person observation points, body size, and developmental status. For example, the environment that can be seen from the standpoint of a crawling baby differs from that available to a young walker. Recently developed head-mounted video cameras and eye-trackers reveal the field of view, and even what is being looked at, from a first-person perspective.

Hoch explains that results from this work to date have overturned several previously held claims concerning what aspects of the environment seem to be of greatest interest to young children. Surprisingly, the faces of others are not among them as the child's self-directed mobility improves. Obviously, young infants flat on their backs have a limited field of view, and not surprisingly, faces that loom over them at these ages are a dominating presence that only decreases with greater mobility. Further, this work reveals the kinds of learning opportunities that may be ruled out due to limits on point of view at certain times, with those constraints fewer with changes in body size and mobility. Hoch also points out that challenges in the study of referentiality in language learning become more manageable with information as to where children are looking in relation to accompanying adult speech.

Improved methods for tracking children's mobility open the door to better understanding of *where* they explore in their environment and importantly, *how much* they explore. The sheer amount of exploration and activity that children engage in when they are at home or in other environments has only recently come to light. These data rewrite long held "maturationist" claims that endogenous motor programs merely "switch on" in the absence of prior experience at particular times in development. In fact, nearly countless bouts of practice of all sorts would appear to underlie development and learning across psychological domains.

This body of work so ably reviewed by Hoch concretely confirms, now more than 50 years later, just how significant and far-reaching Barker's plea was to study the developing child in everyday settings. Researchers today may benefit from examining many of Barker's still neglected detailed reports of his data and methods concerning children's engagement with objects and with others (Barker & Wright, 1955/1971, chapters 9–12). Some of these findings might need to be framed with respect to the historical time and geographical place when/where they were collected, but the role of such *contextual* considerations always needs to be taken into account.

12.3.3 Other limitations of the affordance taxonomy

The proposed taxonomy was limited in other ways as well, and the chapter by Bang and Pedersen (this volume) importantly identify some of them. First, it was restricted to actions that involved material features, such as objects, built structures, and surfaces. Omitted in this initial foray into environmental description based on observational data were actions that involved other people, particularly other children. Later work by Kyttä (2002) and by Lerstrup and van den Bosch (2017) clearly showed how commonplace such actions are in a child's everyday habitat. Also, the latter work conducted in a forest elementary school demonstrated that in such settings children not only encounter classmates and teachers, but often encounter other living things (e.g., insects, small animals) that they can observe and even handle (Lerstrup et al., 2021). On this point, see comments later on Chawla's chapter.

Bang and Pedersen also identify another notable limitation of the initial taxonomy. The boy who was the subject of *One Boy's Day*, pseudonymously named Raymond Birch, was not limited by any obvious motor disabilities. However, there is variability within any population of children in this respect; and from the beginning of their work, Barker and his colleagues were sensitive to this fact.[10] To illustrate, throughout Barker and Wright (1955/1971), findings are reported based on observations of a small sample of children with a variety of physical disabilities (Schoggen, 1978). Bang and Pedersen located during their extended visit to the Barker Archives at the University of Kansas the day-long and unpublished behavior record for a physically limited boy referred to as Bobby Bryant. Bobby's congenital heart problem greatly restricted his activities. Their comparisons between the behavior records for Raymond and Bobby revealed striking differences between them with respect to free time spent in public behavior settings; time spent at home on schoolwork; number of objects engaged; and number of persons they interacted with, among other behavioral events. These data plus Bang and Pederson's qualitative assessments of the behavior records clearly show quite different "life worlds" for each boy. The daily experiences of those with various disabilities are unfamiliar to many who do not face such limitations or who do not live with those who do, and comparisons of this nature are enlightening and greatly needed.

Among their many observations, I was especially struck by the conclusion that Bang and Pedersen drew concerning the challenges Bobby faced. Obviously, the state of his health and the limitations it placed on his activity were likely to be a daily source of personal frustration. But Bang and Pedersen also conclude that he rarely faced "the unpredictable challenges and demands from other children his age nor from a schoolteacher in an unpredictable classroom setting" (this volume). To the extent that the development of social resilience and feelings of social self-efficacy can follow from some degree of unpredictability and challenge in daily life, Bobby's daily experiences can be seen as being limited not only terms of access to affordances, but with respect to some benefits that accompany a less constrained and less protected social life.

And yet, while it is the case that some action possibilities may be ruled out for an individual early in life or due to physical challenges, such limitations are not fixed in all cases. Skilled actions can improve over time because of changes in body size and strength (Adolph & Hoch, 2019), and because tools and other supportive implements can be brought to bear on some intended action (e.g., objects once out of reach on a high shelf can be grasped with the aid of a stool; motorized means of locomotion may be available).

In short, the potential affordances available to be engaged in some region vary as a function of the individual in question, along with the changing developmental history of that individual, as well as the availability and skilled use of tools. Shifting affordance possibilities occur throughout the life span and over times of good health and infirmity. That is, the field of possible affordances is historically and developmentally dynamic. New affordance possibilities can also accompany changes in the wider culture as they are manifested in local environments; and they can accompany the development of new action possibilities over ontogeny. As Hoch (this volume) writes: "The environment has a developmental dimension" (Adolph, 2019; Heft, 1985).

The affordance taxonomy that was proposed then is only a snapshot of possibilities for children quite like Raymond, owing to his age, gender, race/ethnicity, and health status, not to mention also the historical period, culture, and geographical location when/where observations occurred. Rather than serving as a template simply to impose on the study of other individuals, in other places, and at different times, the proposed taxonomy represents one formulation of a descriptive account of the environment from an affordance perspective. Thus far, later tests of its generalizability (Kyttä, 2002; Lerstrup and van den Bosch, 2017) have shown both its potential value and its limitations.

12.4 Value properties and affordances

Among Gibson's most radical claims is that "value properties" of everyday objects and events are perceivable. This assertion is one that Gibson surely absorbed from some of the Gestalt literature, and Koffka, Köhler, Tolman, and Lewin in particular. These influences were fundamental in his development of the concept of affordance (Heft, 2001; Withagen, 2022). Apart from the Gestalt literature, reference to perceived values can be found in William James' late writings on affectional properties (Heft, 2001, pp. 126–129), as well as in Dewey's and Mead's pragmatism. It stands in contrast to the standard approach of framing object and event properties in the terminology of classical physics. There, physical properties such as mass, form, location, and velocity are to be found in the mind-independent "external" world and are describable in quantitative and geometrical terms. They are absent of meaning from the stance of everyday human experience, and hence are value-free. The issue of value properties in the world that we perceive comes up most directly in two of the chapters in this volume, but in rather different ways.

Bert Hodges offers an account of his value-realizing approach to ecological psychology that he previously initiated in collaboration with Reuben Baron (Hodges & Baron, 1992). In his chapter for this volume, Hodges draws on Holt's argument of "the recession of the stimulus" to propose that values are present in the circumstances of perceiving – that is, in the "situation" – which is as much a constituent of the act of perceiving as are the actions of the perceiving agent. Holt's (1931) description of perceiving as having the quality of "adience," which means having a directedness or reaching toward the source of sensory stimulation, allows for inclusion into an account of perceiving those higher-order properties of the environment at some distance from the receptors, and even transpiring at some anticipated future time (Heft, 2011). Hodges argues that this conceptualization allows for action to be "located on a much larger stage" than a so-called "proximal stimulus" is, and serving as "constraints guiding action … [while being] deeply recessed from the moment and the place of action …" (in this volume). As a result, values appear to pervade background circumstances, according to Hodges, and in some vein appear – at least in my reading of his chapter – to be transcendent as compared to moment-to-moment activities of everyday life – a "larger ecology of values" in his phrase. In this conceptualization, values function as "the most 'recessed' constraints on acting, perceiving, feeling, and thinking"; and "[i]f values constrain the field of action, then they are constitutive of psychological acts, such as perceiving" (in this volume). Moreover, from this viewpoint, the exploratory nature of perception-action can be considered as a means of uncovering ("realizing") these background values.

I applaud Hodges' efforts in attempting to articulate the value-rich character of perception-action, which most ecological psychologists would accede to; and I am flattered that he sees some of my work as contributing to that effort. However, I would like to raise some questions for consideration that are pertinent to his argument. The discussion of Holt's claim of the "recession of the stimulus" has only been examined in a few other publications, including Reed (1988) and in Heft (2001, 2011). Unfortunately, in his otherwise masterful biography of Gibson, Reed (1988) conflates "recession of the stimulus" with the standard proximal-distal distinction as traditionally used in the perception literature. This is an error, and Hodges makes it as well. "Recession" is taken to mean by Reed and Hodges as being located in some sense "farther away" from the immediate time and place of perceiving – that is, more *distally*. That is an understandable misreading given the proximal-distal distinction often used in the perception literature; but it is a misreading nonetheless. What Holt meant by that phrase is that once we recognize that an organism perceives higher-order structure in the perceptual field, both in a spatial and temporal vein, that the stimulus as such – that which is imposed on receptors, e.g., on the retina – *recedes in significance for a psychological, functional account of perceiving*. Gibson did not fully embrace this claim until he proposed the idea of an ambient optic array of structure by 1966. He still seems to hold on to the proximal-distal distinction in Gibson (1950), and it is only thoroughly abandoned by *The Senses Considered as Perceptual System* (1966). In this light, the values-realizing approach that Hodges proposes at least in this chapter cannot find conceptual support in Holt; and the seemingly transcendent character of values in his account would appear to be "unrealized" here.

What then is the nature of values in relation to environmental properties? To begin to address this question, I suggest that we turn to the pragmatist tendencies in ecological psychology (see the chapter by Costall). Indeed, one of the aims of pragmatism was to find a way to account for values, meaning, and ultimately truth *without appealing to transcendent, foundationalist grounds*. Gibson too appears to resist any appeal to transcendent properties as can be seen in his consistent thrashing of Kantian influences on psychological theory.

Values can arise from engagement with the practical world, as inconsistent as it might seem to pair "values" with "the practical." Affordances, for example, bear on the consequences of engaging properties of the environment for "good or ill." We see this orientation toward values in the chapter by Louise Chawla, who drew some inspiration from Ed Reed and others. Before turning to her chapter, a few prefatory comments are in order.

While it seems apparent that engaging some affordances has extrinsic value, i.e., they may allow me to complete a particular task, sometimes engaging an affordance can also be *intrinsically* satisfying because of the experience that accompanies the action. That is, pragmatic values are not necessarily limited to instrumental outcomes, as when this graspable object affords hammering and cracking the shell of a nut. While such actions have utilitarian, extrinsic value that *go beyond* the action itself – e.g., making the once-shelled nut accessible – they also may have qualities *intrinsic* to the action. The action can be satisfying for its own sake.

We have known for quite some time that organisms will engage in actions directed toward some environmental features even when no extrinsic reward follows (White, 1959). Such evidence contributed to undermining the dominance of reinforcement explanations in learning theory. Actions that are intrinsically motivated toward particular things of the world have, what Koch (1969/1999) has called, "value properties": "I have been drawn to these activities, and not to others, because (among other reasons) they 'contain,' 'afford,' 'generate' specific properties or *relations in my experience* toward which I am adient" (p. 202, emphasis added). Such value properties are realized through acts directed at particular features of environment (Heft, 2001, pp. 389–393).

Affordance-related values can be of this sort. We may use a particular tool not merely because it allows us to complete some task, but also because the experience of using *that particular tool*, rather than some other tool for similar ends, is satisfying. The "feel" of using it is valued, in addition to the extrinsic outcome that results. Quite possibly those intrinsically satisfying actions directed at, or in conjunction with, some object can lead us *to value the object for its own sake*, rather than to judge the object solely for its external value. Actions that are intrinsically satisfying may then lead us to learn *more* about the object that is engaged. At the heart of such experiences is an awareness of change in ourselves and a changed appreciation for the world around us. These possibilities bring me to Chawla's chapter.

Chawla has studied for many years the formative effects on human development of early experience in "natural" environments, that is, those environments that have not been noticeably altered by human activity (Heft, 2021a). In that realm, she proposes that values are imminent in our experience of growth and change in the natural world itself. There is the evident regeneration in the seasonal renewal of biotic life, in the gestation and birth of life forms, and in the human activities of stewardship and cultivation of the land. In relation to these actions, she suggests that we expand our temporal frame of reference when considering affordance possibilities, pointing to "slow-motion affordances" that may only be revealed over extended periods of time corresponding to rates of growth of "flowers, vegetables, grains, and livestock for practical use" (this volume). This proposal not only is compatible with some of Holt's ideas about the experience of temporally extended occurrences[11] but also strikes me as an apt expansion of the conceptualization of affordance possibilities to include instances of niche construction. Organisms not only adapt to environmental circumstances but also alter those circumstances – a process that is characteristic of all life forms. Some intrinsic satisfaction may be necessary in those instances of niche construction, and "slow-motion affordances," when tangible outcomes are not immediately apparent.

Related to these matters, engaging affordances for new purposes promotes the experience of *self-efficacy* and the development of competence (Chawla, 2021; Chawla & Heft, 2002, Heft, 2021). Such outcomes, as well intrinsically satisfying actions as they concern human development, remain understudied.

Chawla, reprising a proposal by Reed (1996b), sees the possibility for *hope* in the prospect of attunement to these earth rhythms and in such engagements with the land; and she presents some preliminary evidence to support this possibility in our time of rapid planetary change. Hope can arise not only from experiencing certain changes (including those of an ameliorative character) but also from an expanded awareness that "I" can affect some of those changes. Hope is rooted in prospects for change in the service of well-being, both at the individual and collective level, and for sustainability of the biosphere.

12.5 Behavior settings: Constraints, normativity, and enculturation

Several of the chapters in this volume discuss the concept of "behavior setting," which is an important outcome of the empirical work by Roger Barker and his research team who studied children's activities in their community. In my opinion, Barker's "discovery" of the role of behavior settings in everyday life, like Gibson's concept of affordance, was a major advance in our understanding of *the structure of the environment from a psychological standpoint*. Both are important contributions to the development of a psychological ecology. Even so, unlike affordances, the concept of behavior settings remains largely unknown to most contemporary psychologists.

What motivated Barker's research program in the first place was his realization after years of laboratory research of children's behavior that he, like nearly all child psychologists, had little awareness of what children's everyday lives were like. When he turned to the study children's actions in their community, Barker "discovered" extra-individual, dynamic structures that he came to call "behavior settings" that constrained action choices while offering new possibilities for action and experience, and that are present throughout everyday human environments. Concrete manifestations of them take countless forms: school class sessions; grocery stores during hours of operation; baseball and basketball games, religious services, club meetings, etc. Their presence was nothing terribly new from the point of view of a "commonsense psychology," by which is meant the "lay" understanding of the everyday realm that individuals (including experimental psychologists) carry around with them in the course of daily life – knowledge that is often (but not invariably) reflected in everyday discourse.[12] But the fact that, from an empirical point of view, behavior settings accounted for so much of the structure of everyday life in the public domain came as a surprise to Barker.

"Behavior settings" are realized through the joint and collective actions of individuals and are supported by available material features. Conceptually, like affordances although of an extra-individual nature than they, behavior settings are relational structures encompassing both the environment and person(s), with their psychologically significant properties residing neither in the environment considering independently of human action possibilities nor sequestered within an individual's mind apart from the environment; but instead, they are *eco-social psychological* structures. In some sense, in their very ordinariness, behavior settings were "hidden in plain sight" to psychologists, like the purloined letter in Poe's short story by that name.

Specifically, what Barker and his colleagues found in their examination of individual children's behavior was that actions over some delimited time duration, such as a day, were best accounted for with reference to "where" a child was in their community. Indeed, knowing "where" a child was, turned out to be a better predictor of what they were doing at a particular time than knowing "who" they were (e.g., knowing about their personality attributes). Recognition of the significance of a place-related explanans followed after finding that antecedent actions by other individuals ("social inputs") were by comparison unreliable predictors of a child's behavior.

But even if we acknowledge the obviousness of place-related explanations, we are still a long way from accounting for *why* we see such regularities in patterns of everyday action.

12.5.1 Accounting for behavior settings

I have previously proposed based on Barker's theoretical background that collective actions among individuals with the support of material features give rise, in a Gestalt-like manner, to these "extra-individual," *higher-order* dynamic structures. In other words, they are emergent phenomena of the sort that Gestalt psychologists have long brought to the attention of psychologists through their work in the domains of perception (Köhler, 1940) and group psychology (Lewin, 1943a). They are *psychologically meaningful* places that are the sites of much everyday activity.

As for the actions and experiences of individuals in the context of behavior settings, because these higher-order dynamic structures are realized mostly by virtue of individuals' actions, the goal-directed activity of individuals must be constrained in ways that are congruent with a setting's collective purposes. That is, the generation and maintenance of a behavior setting necessitates that individuals engage in some limited range of actions while refraining from others.

However, at best, this constraints point of view may only be implicit in Barker's writings, in spite of claims otherwise (see later). Instead, his "theory of behavior settings" – discussed in Barker (1968, chapter 7) – drew on some influential work of the 1950s and 1960s in cybernetics and control systems. He offered a model of complex regulatory circuitry that mechanistically linked behavior settings and its participants. For example, Barker assimilated into his theory of behavior settings Miller et al.'s, 1960) concept of a "TOTE unit" (Barker, 1968, p. 171 and Figure 6.7). The TOTE unit was proffered as a regulatory *cognitive* mechanism operating in the manner of a servo-mechanism that underlies an *individual's* place-specific decision-making and goal-directed actions.

12.5.2 Social normativity and behavior settings

In some of my previous writing on behavior settings, I pointed in a preliminary way to the significance of *socially normative practices* by individuals in the operation of behavior settings (Heft, 2017). This initial treatment called for further development; and I am most pleased to see that the chapters in this volume by Raja and Heras-Escribano as well as by Segundo-Ortin and Kalis attempt to do so. They all found that my prior efforts did not go far enough, and I agree. My own thinking in recent years has been focused on matters of social normativity in large part because doing so may well offer new ways to consider how sociocultural dimensions of everyday life become enfolded into psychological processes from an ecological perspective.

Raja and Heras-Escribano (this volume) propose what seems, on first blush, to be an alternative or at least an expansion of the way in which I conceptualized the constraints operating in behavior settings.[13] They propose that social normativity plays the role of an "enabling constraint" in the functioning of behavior settings. With this proposal they also downplay, if not reject the idea that individual actions are "constituents" of a behavior setting.[14]

Broadly defined, an "enabling constraint" refers to some intrinsic limitation in the way a system or mechanism works such that it is more likely that a particular outcome will come about than would be the case in the absence of that limitation. They offer as example the structure of the human knee which is anatomically configured to bend in only one way. That limitation allows for motor control in bipedal walking to be simpler than it otherwise would need to be if a leg could bend in multiple ways. Here a constraint promotes (enables) a particular functional outcome. Raja and Heras-Escribano propose that the idea of an enabling constraint can also be profitably applied to understanding how behavior settings are generated and operate, with social norms at the individual level functioning as enabling constraints. This seems to be an important idea. How it is developed in this chapter warrants some scrutiny, however.

They state that their ultimate goal is to *develop a model* of behavior setting operations, and they use as a template for that model, the work of Fajen and Warren (2003) on navigation, as well as Warren's (2018) more recent analyses of how individuals in a group follow a leader. The emphasis in this treatment of navigation is on the role that the location of potential obstacles, as they appear in the landscape over time, control action choices. Similarly, modeling the movements of a group of individuals involves monitoring the relative location of other nearby individuals when moving *en masse*. Raja and Heras-Escribano claim that "in the cases of crowds following a leader … we are modeling a behavior setting" (this volume). I disagree with that assertion – for one thing, a behavior setting is located somewhere, while moving crowds, well, move – and more critically, by drawing this parallel they are undercutting an appeal to social norms. After all, we see instances of crowds following a leader in non-human species (e.g., the V formation of a flock of geese) where one would be hard-pressed to find social norms as they are understood among human affairs. Quite possibly, the goal of attempting to model behavior setting dynamics has pushed what is distinctive about human social phenomena to the margins.

Much more promising – and indeed, very exciting – is the discussion of enabling constraints in Raja and Anderson (2021), where they approach the issue of enabling constraints with respect to the relations between different spatiotemporal scales of analysis within a multi-level system. Their concern in that paper is not behavior settings, but rather the relation between behavior and neural processes as self-organized systems operating at multiple and parallel levels of analysis; and that importantly, operate at different temporal rates. They propose, following Van Orden et al. (2012) and others, that on-going behavior operates over a slower temporal rate than does the faster rate of firing of neurons associated with it. In this relation, the "organization at higher spatial scales (usually the slower temporal scales) constrains the activity of lower spatial scales (usually faster temporal ones)" (Raja & Anderson, 2021, p. 224). This constraining relation, or "order parameter," itself "emerge[s] from the collective behavior of different components of a system" (p. 224).

Can we think about the operations of behavior settings along these lines? This is an intriguing idea. It certainly seems justifiable to contrast the temporal rate of behavior settings with that of the temporal rate of individual participant actions, with the former typically operating more slowly and more *stably* than the latter. Viewed in this way, the temporal rate peculiar to a given behavior setting may establish an "enabling constraint" that makes certain actions nested within them more probable than others.

Particularly interesting from the standpoint of sociocultural processes, this approach also suggests how the *histories* of setting types can be introduced into the account. By comparison, slower temporal scales would seem to be more stable than faster ones (Van Orden et al., 2012); and for this reason, by serving as a context for the faster dynamics, they carry hysteretic properties (i.e., patterns of historical continuity) of the *overall* system in ways *not to be found with the faster rates of change at the individual level*. Referring to the relations of behavior and neural activity, Raja and Anderson (2021) state: "In virtue of this relative temporal stability, when changes of neural dynamics occur, the temporal scale of behavior [i.e., higher level units] maintains information about the history of the system …" (p. 226). Extending this idea to behavior settings, the history of the practices within each setting type could be preserved over time among the slower rates of operation at this higher-level of analysis. This conceptualization may offer a way of connecting the functions of behavior settings with a community's social history.

But where do socially normative practices fit in here? The history of these practices can be understood as reflecting socially normative patterns that operate as enabling constraints on individual actions nested within the setting type under consideration. In short, this proposal, if applied to behavior settings and individual action, might nicely capture how the prior history of the operations of behavior settings in a community might sustain the continuity of their effects across *different* individuals by means of social normativity over time. In that respect, behavior settings may be particularly good carriers of prior eco-social psychological history.

12.5.3 Social normativity and human development

The chapter by Segundo-Ortin and Kalis takes as a primary concern the nature of human agency considered in relation to behavior settings.[15] Although they find my prior treatments of *agency* with respect to the selective character of perception-action processes to have been of value, they judge that these accounts fall short in relation to behavior settings. In particular, they found fault with my attempt to account for intentionality with respect to behavior settings by appealing to processes of distributed cognition. They write: "… if agents are required for distributed cognition, it is hard to see how distributed cognition can account for agency in the first place" (this volume). Segundo-Ortin and Kalis suggest instead that we turn our attention back to individual ontogenetic development in social (interpersonal) contexts. This strikes me a good suggestion.

Social normativity is a hallmark of behavior settings. Agency with respect to these higher-order structures entails an awareness of what is "proper" action within them. The proper actions in a classroom differ from those on a playground at recess. However, a child's awareness of socially normative dimensions of action are unlikely to begin with exposure to behavior settings, but instead with the affordances of everyday objects (Gibson & Pick, 2001, pp. 98–101). Young children may learn over time by way of observations and comments from others that, for example, a utensil such as a spoon is properly used for eating and not for pounding on a surface, and that cups are to be used for drinking rather than throwing (Gibson, 1950). Awareness of more rarified social proprieties follow when it is learned that social norms for action can trump affordance possibilities. For example, although a closed door at the entrance to some rooms (e.g., a private bedroom) *can be* opened by turning a doorknob (affords opening), whether it *should be* opened is a matter that goes beyond mere instrumental considerations. Learning which affordance actions are proper rather than possible surely arises from developing in social contexts.

Normative social practices are essential dimensions of any behavior setting. Although Barker doesn't employ the terminology of normativity as far as I have seen, he gives a central place to individuals' awareness of social norms in his account of "maintenance" actions that they may employ in order to preserve a setting's proper functioning (Barker, 1968, chapter 6). Individuals within a community need to be "knowledgeable" about the setting-specific practices characteristic of its behavior settings in order to participate in them. But *how* does intentional action with respect to behavior settings come about? This question is central to Segundo-Ortin and Kalis' chapter.

Before turning to their proposal, we must recognize an even more basic question at work here that they do not consider. Individuals with little experience in some community's settings must come to be aware of *the very presence* of a particular behavior setting in the first place; even aside from its normative "requirements" on action, they must be perceived. What is the challenge here? Behavior settings are not features of the environment that can be perceived "naively," such as some affordances such as graspable objects and sit-on-able surfaces. Unlike such affordances, behavior settings are "socially constructed," arising – "coming into existence" – through joint actions of individuals. These extra-individual structures are present in the environment only by virtue of such actions. Even so, there is evidence that behavior settings may be *perceptually* distinctive, that they have distinctive "physiognomies," as Barker and Wright (1955, p. 55) hypothesized some time ago (Heft et al., 2014). Although more research along these lines is sorely needed, these results point to the role that *perceptual learning* may play as individuals come to be aware of and differentiate among these higher-order structures in their everyday community.

The question remains as to how individuals come to be aware of the socially "proper" actions specific to behavior settings? Drawing on the work of McGreer (2015, 2021), Segundo-Ortin and Kalis make a start here. They point out that human development proceeds within an interpersonal context of normative practices, "[f]rom birth on, humans *shape each other's behavior* and thought by means of folk-psychological regulative practices" (this volume, emphasis added). An important outcome that bears on agency is that through these *regulative practices*, what is taken to be socially normative for others is also, and perhaps more fundamentally, taken to be so for ourselves (Zawidzki, 2013). In the process, one develops propensities for *self-accountability*. And because assessments of others as well as ourselves are *situated*, accountability is tied to the places where one is located. Socially-normative agency, they propose, arises with the development of self-accountability in the context of situated social practices. (Page limitations prevent me from including considerations of the place of language here.)

Their analysis is an important contribution to discussions of agency and social normativity; and I feel that grounding agency in everyday dialogical exchange is particularly noteworthy (Raczaszek-Leonardi et al., 2013). Even so, in an ecological vein, I feel that more consideration of the role that perceiving and perceptual information play here is warranted. Actions within a behavior setting that embody its normative practices are likely to be perceivable (Heft et al., 2014); and attunement to these perceivable patterns of action will support the development of socially normative practices by individuals. This claim invites potential research to assess its merit. In the course of developing these ideas, I urge the authors to continue to be wary of the hazards of a retreat to mentalism (see Leudar and Costall (2009) on "theory of mind"), and encourage an emphasis on perceptual learning processes in relation to dynamic patterns of structure that specify behavior settings and their respective socially normative practices.

12.6 System history, psychological restoration

The chapter by Marsh and Meager (this volume) touches on a variety of topics that have been of much interest to me for quite some time. One of these is the effects of *hysteresis*, which Marsh and colleagues (Richardson et al., 2007) elegantly demonstrated for a perception-action task. Hysteresis refers to the continuing effects of prior history of a dynamic system on its current activities. They showed that when pairs were working on a common sequential task (i.e., moving a series of planks of increasing or decreasing lengths to a new location), the point of transition from solo to joint action (or vice versa) varied depending on whether task required joint action from the start (longer planks) or it began with solo actions (shorter planks). Rather than there being a fixed point where actions switched from one mode to the other, the transition point varied depending on the immediately prior series of actions. Dynamical systems carry their history to the "present" moment.

My interest in the effects of a system's history did not begin with dynamical systems theory, but rather from my formative exposure in graduate school to the developmental writings of Kurt Lewin, which anticipated dynamical systems thinking. Lewin (1943b) recognized that an appreciation for history at various level of analysis (e.g., the individual, the group, the culture) is essential in the study of psychological phenomena. With regard to the individual, he called for a field theoretical approach that includes the person and environment considered "at a given time," recognizing that a given "moment" in time does not exclude prior history but rather incorporates it into what counts as the current "situation." Thus, he advises the adoption of a "time-field" unit of analysis when considering the actions of an individual. The notion of a "time-field" unit of analysis at the level of extra-individual structures was later to be adopted by his student Barker with the development of the behavior setting concept (Heft, 2022).

Another thread in Marsh and Meagher's chapter connects to my early interest in environmental perception and preference. Research on that topic among environmental psychologists mostly, diverged a few decades ago into inquiry about the possible "psychologically restorative" effects of *natural environments*. That shift left questions about the environmental basis for preference in everyday settings unanswered. Because of that, there remains a lack of clarity as to what is even meant by "natural" environments (Heft, 2021).

Also, conceptually research on "psychological restoration" has been burdened by the assumption that individuals are passive recipients of environmental conditions rather than *agents* in a habitat. Emphasis on agency is far more compatible with organismal biology and an ecosystems perspective in the biological sciences and philosophy (Walsh, 2015) than are the information-processing, cognitive-heavy assumptions that underlie most psychological restoration research (Schutte et al., 2021).

Further, in spite of the fact that this latter body of research purports to be based on evolutionary considerations, I find it to be remarkably *ahistorical*. Attention to *the dynamic character of the organism-environment relations over time from an ecosystems perspective* has been short-circuited here by attributing the basis for the natural world's restorative "properties" to genetic predispositions (e.g., biophilia) *fixed* in a distant past due to selection pressures within a single type of ancestral environment. These assumptions are no longer viable among contemporary evolutionary biologists (Planer & Sterelny, 2022; Sterelny, 2013) who recognize the

> variability and dynamics of hominin environments; there is no one environment, physical, social, or biological in which hominins evolved. Indeed, hominin evolution *resulted in the transformation* of hominin social, biological, and physical environments, and *hence of the selective pressures* to which our ancestors were exposed. (Planer & Sterelny, 2022, p. 5, emphases added)

Environments change over time, in part, as a result of the activity of organisms, and selective pressures shift accordingly.

Further, the claim of adaptation to an ancestral habitat as the basis for psychological preference and restoration fails to give weight to cultural processes and the role that social normativity plays in adaptation to human habitats. Here as well this research area appears to operate with outmoded assumptions. Most likely, one of the reasons that cultural considerations have been largely set aside in this research literature is the erroneous view that socio-cultural processes are comparative late-comers in human evolution. Instead, proto-cultural activity (e.g., communication, group processes) was characteristic of the hominin habitat within which our species evolved.

Among other things, this suggests that developing awareness to patterns of social normativity in relation to the environment has been a feature of human development from the first days of life. Indeed, there is considerable evidence for the responsiveness of children to social norms quite early in life (Rakoczy & Schmidt, 2013; Meltzoff, 2007). It is likely that environmental preference patterns are intertwined with our social development (Heft, 2007).

What possible bearing do these sociocultural considerations have on claims concerning the possible restorative value of "natural" environments? Quite likely, a great deal. To offer only a brief comment here, several protypes of environments that in our contemporary US culture are typically offered as candidates for psychological restoration – namely, forest views and mountainscapes – were considered by at least some in earlier times as places to be feared. For example, early European settlers in North America quite realistically assessed the dense, surrounding forests as areas where life-threatening hazards did abound (Richardson, 2007) rather than being psychologically restorative. Restorative "nature" is surely a relatively recent phenomenon traceable to 18th-century Neo-Kantian ideas about "the sublime" and when ventures into "wildernesses" could be supported by appurtenances of "modern living."[16]

Researchers working from the perspective of ecological psychology can bring needed fresh ideas to the study of psychologically restorative environments (e.g., the chapter by Chawla; this volume and 2021 and Heft, 2021a). Although some have proposed that one way to distinguish between natural and built environments is with respect to the sheer number affordances available in each, with natural environments marked by a comparatively greater number, such proposals fail to consider the place of socially normative practices when it comes to the engagement with affordances (see above). For instance, more potential affordances in built (versus "natural") environments are likely to be ruled out as possibilities for action owing to socially normative practices operating in towns and cities.

Finally, future work on restorative possibilities of environments should be informed by the convergence in recent decades of developmental psychology and developmental biology. This convergence embraces an epigenetic approach such that "biology, environment, and culture are seamlessly intertwined" (Narvaez et al., 2021, p. 424) as opposed to the Neo-Darwinian assumptions that have driven much of the prior research. An epigenetic perspective coupled with the recognition of developmental neural plasticity should weaken the unhelpful grip that the biophilia hypothesis has exerted on this research area for decades.

12.7 Brief remarks on other chapters

The chapter by Withagen and Van Dijk provides a much-needed historical overview of ecological psychology in The Netherlands. Important research from the perspective of Gibsonian psychology has been on-going there for decades; and The Netherlands is now among the research centers in ecological psychology.

I am gratified that Withagen and Van Dijk's discussion of my work highlighted so clearly two long-standing concerns of mine. First, and as discussed earlier, early in my studies I became frustrated by the limited attention that experimental psychologists had paid to the nature of the environment relative to psychological functioning beyond the laboratory. Worse, on the heels of the cognitive turn in psychology, *environmental* psychologists seemed more concerned with how individuals conceptualized the environment than they did with the environment of everyday life itself (Wohlwill, 1973b). But where to find a psychologically adequate account of the environment that rejected constructivist approaches to perception and eschewed talk of "meaningless" environmental stimuli? Discovering Gibson (1966), thanks to the Jack Wohlwill, was a revelation, and it prompted a year-long, post-PhD visit to Cornell. So was my growing familiarity with Barker's work during my graduate studies.[17]

Second, my study and teaching of the history of psychology over many years shaped much of my thinking about the place of ecological psychology in the wider discipline. A formative comment for me appeared in Heidbreder's *Seven Psychologies* (1933), in which she drew a contrast between William James' vision for psychology as compared to that Wilhelm Wundt's disciple in the USA, E. B. Titchener. Wundt is aptly considered to be the founder of experimental psychology. Heidbreder wrote: "Whereas Titchener was intent chiefly on making the new psychology a *science*, James was more concerned that the new science be *psychology*" (p. 152, emphasis added). That pithy and insightful assessment struck a chord with me; and it did much to shape how I thought about the development of ecological psychology over the decades. I set my scholarly compass to James' insistence that psychology maintain human experience at the center of its inquiry.

The chapter by Baggs and Steffensen takes up an issue that might seem to some to lay outside of the orbit of Gibsonian ecological psychology: problem solving. It is often claimed that Gibson limited his attention to perceiving, while mostly setting aside considerations of what is traditionally referred to as cognition. I agree, however, with Reed (1987) that "[a]s it turns out, this sentiment – however widely promulgated – is simply and utterly false" (p. 142). Apart from the fact that Gibson took perceiving to be a cognitive function – after all, it is a process of *knowing* by means of staying in touch with the environment – he did sporadically discuss non-perceptual cognitive processes (e.g., remembering, imagining, use of language) from an ecological perspective, particularly in later writings (Gibson, 1966, 1979). He also wrote a great deal about the nature of human artifacts of a visual nature, such as pictures.

Gibson's reconceptualization of perceiving as functioning of "perceptual systems" was also intended to lay the foundations for a reconsideration of non-perceptual cognitive processes. In doing so, he rejected the view that perceiving and non-perceptual cognitive functions are separate, encapsulated "faculties," while instead recognizing the continuity and synergy operating among these functions. In this respect, Gibson shared the position adopted by Gestalt psychologists who worked on problem-solving, such as Wertheimer (1945), Duncker, 1945), and Arnheim (1990).

Consistent with this orientation, Baggs and Steffensen describe several compelling experiments showing that when a problem of an *abstract* (non-perceptual) nature is presented in a material form, and hence is perceivable, that its solution might become more readily apparent than otherwise. A similar claim can be found in Gibson's (1966) discussion of Köhler's famous case of *insight learning* among apes. It will be remembered that the apes in Köhler's experimental enclosure "discovered" that a stick could be used as a rake as they handled it in order to reach food just outside of the enclosure. Whereas Köhler attributed this discovery to a reorganization of the "field" of experience, Gibson saw it as a case of discovering an affordance. He comments that the "information for its useability [as a rake] was available in the ambient light … The acts of picking up and reaching with *reveal* certain facts about objects …" (pp. 273–274).

Baggs and Steffensen propose that the effectiveness of transforming conceptual problems into material form when solving problems illustrates how Gibsonian perceptual theory and distributed cognition (Hutchins, 1995) can be linked to extend the ecological approach into the domain of non-perceptual cognition (Heft, 2021b). However, there remains much conceptual work to be done here because some of the assumptions that recur in the distributed cognition literature and those in Gibsonian ecological psychology seemingly differ. Such an assessment may also extend to the manner in which *material representations* (e.g., pictures, diagrams) function as tools for thinking (Reed, 1987).

Finally, Erik Rietveld and Julien Kiverstein prepared very thoughtful and probing questions for their interview with me. As always, talking with them pushed me to think more carefully and deeply about ecological psychology and its possibilities. I appreciate their insights as interlocutors.

12.8 Concluding thoughts

I am very thankful to the authors of these chapters for their efforts, and especially to the editors of this volume for initiating and organizing this project and bringing it to conclusion. To be candid, this project was completely unexpected by me, and I am humbled and honored by everyone's contribution to it.

Notes

1 The phrase "psychological ecology" originates in the writings of Kurt Lewin (1943a).
2 Most of the phenomenological psychology literature was of little use either because it seemed too ungrounded in the natural sciences and too individually insular.
3 Perhaps our habitats are so distinctive as compared to other species because we are the sole remaining species of the lineage of Homo that remains.
4 Gibson's and Barker's frameworks developed independently, although they had common roots (Heft, 2001). Barker initially drew on the perceptual writings of

5 Brunswik in constructing his theoretical framework. I have attempted to show how Gibson's work is a more suitable foundation. Others may disagree.
5 I have seen no evidence to support a recent rumor that Gibson taught a seminar on Merleau-Ponty. Perhaps others may find evidence for this claim.
6 Fritz Heider, who was a friend and colleague of Gibson's at Smith College, and later a colleague of Barker's at the University of Kansas, surely was influential here. He wrote that "fruitful concepts and hunches for hypotheses *lie dormant in what we know intuitively*" and are to be found in everyday discourse (Heider, 1958, pp. 5–6, emphasis added).
7 I say "visible" because most of this research only involves presenting photographic displays of settings or tallying what is visible from some location rather than observing behavior in those settings.
8 These alternative approaches have been discussed recently in Heft (2021a).
9 There are also limitations in the composition of the population of children in the small midwestern town they studied due to its history and social practices. For example, there were 27 African American residents in the town of approximately 700 at the time of the observations in *One Boy's Day*, and only six children were between preschool age to adolescence.
10 Barker himself struggled with motor impairments throughout his life due to a childhood illness.
11 See Holt (1915, pp. 186–187).
12 Heider (1958) attempted to develop a commonsense psychology based on the character of everyday discourse in his book on interpersonal interaction (Malle & Ickes, 2000).
13 Raja and Heras-Escribano (this volume) attribute to Barker a constraints account of individual action within behavior settings. This is not the case. By adopting the TOTE unit as a model, Barker's formulation of the circuitry underlying behavior setting participant interrelations was more along the lines of what Raja and Anderson (2021) describe as a "realizer-outcome" approach, whereby internal mechanisms of a system are proposed as generating particular behavioral outcomes. I am unaware of Barker utilizing the terminology of constraints, which is more characteristic of multi-scale biological models that came to prominence after his primary writings.
14 The notion of "enabling constraints" was developed more fully in other work (Anderson, 2015; Raja & Anderson, 2021) than it is here, and I will incorporate some parts of those writings in what follows.
15 It was gratifying to see that Segundo-Ortin and Kalis recognized Barker's exposition of behavior settings to be "a precursor of what we nowadays refer to as 'situated cognition.'"
16 To offer one anecdote, a cultural anthropologist colleague who conducts field work in West Africa shared with me that her remarks to a villager about the beauty of the local landscape were met with puzzlement as to the very nature of the observation.
17 My fellow graduate student, the late Robert Daubert, deserves much credit here.

References

Adolph, K. (2019). An ecological approach to learning in (not and) development. *Human Development, 63*, 180–201.

Adolph, K., & Hoch, J. (2019). Motor development: Embodied, embedded, encultured, and enabling. *Annual Review of Psychology, 70*, 26.1–26.24.

Anderson, M. L. (2015). Beyond componential constitution in the brain: Starburst amacrine cells and enabling constraints. In T. Metzinger & J. M. Windt (Eds.), *Open MIND*: 1(T). Frankfurt am Main: MIND Group. doi:10.15502/9783958570429

Arnheim, R. (1990). *Visual thinking*. Berkeley, CA: University of California Press.

Barker, R. G. (1968). *Ecological psychology: Concepts and methods for studying the environment of human behavior*. Stanford, CA: Stanford University Press.

Barker, R. G., & Schoggen, P. (1973). *Qualities of community life: Methods of measuring environments and behavior applied to an American and an English town.* San Francisco: Jossey-Bass

Barker, R. G., & Wright, H. F. (1953). *One boy's day. A specimen record of behavior.* New York: Harper.

Barker, R. G., & Wright, H. F. (1955/1971). *Midwest and its children: The psychological ecology of an American town.* Hamden, CT: Archon Books.

Chawla, L., & Heft, H. (2002). Children's competence and the ecology of communities: A functional approach to the evaluation of participation. *Journal of Environmental Psychology, 22,* 201–216.

Chawla, L. T. (2021). Knowing nature in childhood: Learning and well-being through engagement with the natural world. In A. Schutte, J. Torquati, & J. Stevens (Eds.), *Nature and psychology: Biological, cognitive, developmental, and social pathways to well-being* (pp. 153–194). Nebraska Symposium on Motivation, Vol. 67. Cham, Switzerland: Springer.

Drake, J. M. (2013). What has ecology to do with psychology? *Theory & Psychology, 13,* 573–576.

Duncker, K. (1945). On problem solving. *Psychological Monographs, 58,* 1–113 (whole No. 270).

Fajen, B. R., & Warren, W. H. (2003). Behavioral dynamics of steering, obstacle avoidance, and route selection. *Journal of Experimental Psychology: Human Perception and Performance, 29,* 343–362.

Gibson, E., & Pick, A. D. (2001). *An ecological approach to perceptual learning and development.* New York: Oxford University Press.

Gibson, J. J. (1950). The implications of learning theory for social psychology. In J. G. Miller (Ed.), *Experiments in social process: A symposium on social psychology.* New York, NY: McGraw-Hill.

Gibson, J. J. (1966). *The senses considered as perceptual systems.* Boston: Houghton-Mifflin.

Gibson, J. J. (1979). *The ecological approach to visual perception.* Boston: Houghton-Mifflin.

Heft, H. (1985). High residential density and perceptual-cognitive development: An examination of the effects of crowding and noise in the home. In J. F. Wohlwill & W. van Vliet (Eds.), *Habitats for children: The impact of density* (pp. 39–75). Hillsdale, NJ: Erlbaum.

Heft, H. (1988). Affordances of children's environments: A functional approach to environmental description. *Children's Environments Quarterly, 5,* 29–37. [Reprinted with a new afterword in J. Nasar & W. Preiser (Eds.), *Directions in Person-Environment Research and Practice* (pp. 43–69). Aldershot, UK: Ashgate Publishing.]

Heft, H. (2001). *Ecological psychology in context: James Gibson, Roger Barker, and the legacy of William James's radical empiricism.* Mahwah, NJ: Lawrence Erlbaum Associates, Publishers.

Heft, H. (2007). The social constitution of perceiver-environment reciprocity. *Ecological Psychology, 19,* 85–105.

Heft, H. (2011). E.B. Holt's concept of the recession of the stimulus and the emergence of the "situation" in psychology. In E. P. Charles (Ed.), *A new look at new realism: E. B. Holt reconsidered* (pp. 191–219). Piscataway, NJ: Transactions Publishing.

Heft, H. (2013). An ecological approach to psychology. *Review of General Psychology.* Special issue: Unifying approaches to psychology, *17,* 162–167. doi:10.1037/a0032928

Heft, H. (2014). What makes ecological psychology ecological? *Man-Environment Research Journal* (Japan), *16,* 11–16.

Heft, H. (2017). Perceptual information of "an entirely different order": The "cultural environment" in the senses considered as perceptual systems. *Ecological Psychology, 29,* 122–145. 10.1080/10407413.2017.1297187

Heft, H. (2021a). Perceiving 'natural' environments: An ecological perspective with reflections on the chapters. In A. Schutte, J. Torquati, & J. Stevens (Eds.), *Nature and psychology: Biological, cognitive, developmental, and social pathways to well-being* (pp. 252–273). Nebraska Symposium on Motivation, Vol. 67. Cham, Switzerland: Springer.

Heft, H. (2021b). Grasping what?: Ecological anchors for abstract thought. *Human Development*. doi:10.1159/000515868.

Heft, H. (2022). Lewin's 'psychological ecology' and the boundary of the psychological domain. *Philosophia Scientiae*, 26, 189–210.

Heft, H., Hoch, J., Edmunds, T., & Weeks, J. (2014). Can the identity of a behavior setting be perceived through patterns of joint action? An investigation of place perception. *Behavioral Sciences*, 4, 371–393. doi:10.3390/bs4040371

Heidbreder, E. (1933). *Seven psychologies*. New York: Century.

Heider, F. (1926). Thing and medium. Reprinted in F. Heider (1959), *On perception and event structure, and the psychological environment. Psychological Issues*, 1, Monograph 3, 1–34.

Heider, F. (1958). *The psychology of interpersonal relations*. New York: Wiley.

Hodges, B., & Baron, R. (1992). Values as constraints on affordances: Perceiving and acting properly. *Journal for the Theory of Social Behaviour*, 22(3), 263–294.

Holt, E. B. (1915). *The Freudian wish and its place in ethics*. New York: Henry Holt.

Holt, E. B. (1931). *Animal drive and the learning process: An essay toward radical empiricism*, Vol. 1. New York: Henry Holt.

Hutchins, E. (1995). *Cognition in the wild*. Cambridge, MA: MIT Press.

James, W. (1890). *The principles of psychology*. New York: Holt.

James, W. (1892). *Psychology: The briefer course*. New York: Holt.

James, W. (1895). The knowing of things together. *Psychological Review*, 2, 105–124.

James, W. (1904). Does consciousness exist? *Journal of Philosophy, Psychology, and Scientific Method*, 1, 477–491. [Reprinted in W. James (1912). *Essays in radical empiricism*. New York: Longmans, Green, & Co.]

Koch, S. (1969/1999). The concept of 'value properties' in relation to motivation, perception, and the axiological disciplines. In D. Finkelman & F. Kessel (Eds.), *Psychology in human context: Essays in dissidence and reconstruction* (pp. 192–230). Chicago: University of Chicago Press. (Original essay published in 1969.)

Köhler, W. (1940). *Dynamics in psychology*. New York: Liveright.

Kytta, M. (2002). Affordances of children's environments in the context of cities, small towns, suburbs, and villages in Finland and Belarus. *Journal of Environmental Psychology*, 22, 109–123.

Lerstrup, I., Chawla, L., & Heft, H. (2021). Affordances of small animals for young children: A path of environmental values of care. *International Journal of Early Childhood Education*, 9, 58–76

Lerstrup, I., & van den Bosch, C. (2017). Affordances of outdoor settings for children in preschool: Revisiting Heft's functional taxonomy. *Landscape Research*, 42(1), 47–62.

Leudar, I., & Costall, A. (2009). Introduction: Against 'theory of mind.' In I. Leudar & A. Costall (Eds.), *Against theory of mind* (pp. 1–18). London: Palgrave Macmillan.

Lewin, K. (1943a). Psychological ecology. Reprinted in D. Cartwright, (Ed.), *Field theory in social science: Selected theoretical papers* (pp. 43–59). New York: Harper Torchbooks.

Lewin, K. (1943b). Defining the "field at a given time." Reprinted in D. Cartwright (Ed.), *Field theory in social science: Selected theoretical papers* (pp. 170–187). New York: Harper Torchbooks.

Malle, & Ickes (2000). Fritz Heider: Philosopher & psychologist. In G. A. Kimble & M. Wertheimer (Eds.), *Portraits of pioneers in psychology*, Vol. 4, (pp. 195–214). Washington, DC: American Psychological Association.

McGreer (2015). Mind-making practices: The social infrastructure of self-knowing agency and responsibility. *Philosophical Explorations*, *18*, 259–281.
McGreer (2021). Enculturating folk psychologists. *Synthese*, *199*, 1039–1063. doi:10.1007/s11229-020-02760-7.
Meltzoff, A. (2007). 'Like me': A foundation for social cognition. *Developmental Science*, *10*, 126–134.
Merleau-Ponty, M. (1963). *The phenomenology of perception* (C. Smith, trans.) London: Routledge & Kegan Paul. (Original work published in 1942.)
Miller, G., Galanter, E., & Pribram, K. (1960). *Plans and the structure of behavior*. New York: Holt, Rhinehart, & Winston.
Narvaez, D., Moore, D. S., Witherington, D. C., Vandiver, T. I., & Lickliter, R. (2021). Evolving evolutionary psychology. *American psychologist*, *77*, 424–438.
Planer, R. J., & Sterelny, K. (2022). *From signal to symbol: The evolution of language*. Cambridge, MA: MIT Press.
Raczaszek-Leonardi, J., Nomikou, I., & Rohlfing, K. J. (2013). Young children's dialogical actions: The beginnings of purposeful intersubjectivity. *IEEE Transactions on Autonomous Mental Development*, *5*, 210–221. doi:10.1109/TAMD.2013.2273258
Raja, V., & Anderson, M. (2021). Behavior considered as an enabling constraint. In F. Calzavarini & M. Viola (Eds.), *Neural mechanisms: New challenges in the philosophy of neuroscience* (pp. 209–232). New York: Springer.
Rakoczy, H. & Schmidt, M. F. H. (2013). The early ontogeny of social norms. *Child Development Perspectives*, *7*, 17–21.
Reed, E. S. (1987). James Gibson's ecological approach to cognition. In A. Costall & A. Still (Eds.), *Cognitive psychology in question* (pp. 142–173). New York: St. Martin's Press.
Reed, E. S. (1988). *James J. Gibson and the psychology of perception*. New Haven, CT: Yale University Press.
Reed, E. S. (1996a). *Encountering the world: Toward an ecological psychology*. New York: Oxford University Press.
Reed, E. S. (1996b). *The necessity of experience*. Yale University Press.
Richardson, M., Marsh, K. L., & Baron, R. (2007). Judging and actualizing intrapersonal and interpersonal affordances. *Journal of Experimental Psychology: Human Perception and Performance*, *33*(4), 845–859. doi:10.1037/0096-1523.33.4.845
Schoggen, P. (1978). Environmental forces on physically disabled children. In R. G. Barker (Ed.), *Habitats, environments, and human behavior* (pp. 125–145). San Francisco: Jossey-Bass.
Schutte, A., Torquati, J., & Stevens, J. (2021). *Nature and psychology: Biological, cognitive, developmental, and social pathways to well-being*. Symposium on Motivation, Vol. 67. Cham, Switzerland: Springer.
Sterelny, K. (2013). *The evolved apprentice*. Cambridge, MA: MIT Press.
Van Orden, Hollis, G., & Wallot, S. (2012). The blue-collar brain. *Frontiers in Physiology*, *3*, article 207. doi:10.3389/fphys.2012.00207.
Walsh, D. (2015). *Organisms, agency, and evolution*. Cambridge, UK: Cambridge University Press.
Warren, W. H. (2018). Collective motion in human crowds. *Current Directions in Psychological Science*, *27*, 232–240.
Wertheimer, M. (1945). *Productive thinking*. New York: Harper.
White, R. W. (1959). Motivation reconsidered: The concept of competence. *Psychological Review*, *66*(5), 297–333. doi:10.1037/h0040934
Withager, R. (2022). *Affective Gibsonian psychology*. New York: Routledge.

Wohlwill, J. F. (1973a). The concept of experience: S or R? *Human Development, 16,* 90–107.

Wohlwill, J. F. (1973b). The environment is not in the head! In W. F. E. Peiser (Eds.), *Environmental design research*, Vol. 1 (pp. 166–181). Stroudsburg, PA: Dowden, Hutchinson, & Ross.

Zawidzki, T. W. (2013). *Mindshaping: A new framework for understanding human social cognition.* Cambridge, MA: MIT Press.

INDEX

Note: *Italicized* and **bold** page numbers refer to figures and tables. Page numbers followed by "n" refer to notes.

Action Club 24
Adolph, K. E. 140–145, 160
affordances 2–6, 13, 30, 80, 89, 99–108, 151, 152, 155; animate agents 101; boundaries 126; canonical 94; of children's environments 4–5, 11; as constraints on action 14–15; definition of 112; field of soliciting 32; and goal-directed action 14; within higher order structures, embedding 127–132; of indoor spaces 125, 129–130; intentional analysis of 31; language 100–101; mutuality of 6; of natural processes 112–113; place-affordances 31; postal system 100, 101; relational 100; slow-motion 6, 112, 113, 163; social 2, 6, 100, 122, 126, 127, 134, 137; socializing 125; in social world 126–127; sociocultural approach to 23; systemic 100; taxonomy, for children's environment 156–158, 159–160; theory of 39, 61; values and 101, 150–163; young people's responses to earth's affordances of regeneration 112–123
agency 5, 40, 101, 102, 106–108, 132, 154, 167–170; agency-indicative information 79; in behavior settings 72–84; cultural 106
Alexander, S. 37
Alley, T. R. 126

Anderson, M. L. 5, 87, 89, 90, 96, 96n4, 166, 167, 174n13, 174n14
animate agents 101
Araujo, D. 31
Arnheim, R. 173

Baggs, E. 46, 88, 89, 96n2
Baker, R. 2
Ball, L. J. 57
Bang, J. 62
Barker, J. S. 60
Barker, R. G. 4, 5, 26, 31, 33, 72–74, 81, 83n1, 83n2, 83n4, 99, 102, 130, 131, 144, 150–153, 155, 156, 158, 159, 163–165, 168, 170, 172, 173–174n4, 174n6, 174n10, 174n13, 174n15; behavior settings *see* behavior settings 72; Bryant and Birch, comparison of 59–71; ecological psychology 38; *Midwest and Its Children: The Psychological Ecology of an American Town* 149, 155; *Midwest Psychological Field Station, The* 59; *One Boy's Day* 28–29, 30, 59, 128, 156–157, 159
Baron, R. M. 23, 30, 100, 101, 103, 126, 161
Barrett, L. 57
Batson, C. D. 133
Bechtel, W. 90
Beek, P. J. 24–26, 104

180 Index

Beer, R. 76
behavioral analysis 7, 138, 139; morning activities after breakfast 64; schoolwork activities 64–66
behaviorism 100
behavior objects, analysis of 66–67
behavior settings 2, 4–5, 15–16, 30, 31, 86–97, 102, 130–131; accounting for 165; agency in 72–84; analysis of 62–66; constraints 163–169; enabling constraints and 90–92; enculturation 163–169; modelling 92–96, *94*; norms and 87–89, 92–96; social normativity and 165–169; survey 155, 156
Berger, S. E. 140
biodiverse habitat on community lands, restoring 116–121, **117**; engaging with the land 118; meaning and value 120; perceiving landscape changes 118–119; restoration work, social aspects of 120–121
bipolar cells and SACs, relationship between 90, 96n4
Birch, R. 59–71
Blau, J. 18
Bongers, R. 27, 28
Bootsma, R. 24–26
Bourdieu, P. 17
Bradley, R. H. 144
Brancazio, N. 79, 82
Breeze, K. W. 144
Brown, N. A. 130
Bruineberg, J. 27, 29, 31, 32
Brunswik, E. 39, 174n4
Bryant, B. 59–71
Brymer, E. 132
Burns, C. M. 48
Burtt, E. E. 37
Byrne, D. 24

Caljouw, S. R. 29
campus navigation maps 54–56, *55*
canonical affordance 94
Carello, C. 54
Carr, H. A. 38–39
Chawla, L. 3, 6, 19–20, 114, 121, 159, 162, 163, 171
Chemero, A. 76, 96n2
child's environment 138–148; affordance taxonomy for 156–158, 159–160; first-person point of view 141–144, 158–159; formal description 139; functional description 139–141; functional description for behavioral analyses, benefits of 140–141; lab *versus* life 144–145
Clark, A. 45
climate change: impact of 19
climate crisis 19–20
cognition 172; distributed 4, 46, 47, 56, 57, 75–77, 167, 173; ecological theory of 3; embodied 4; situated 74, 174n15; symbolic 56
"cognitive" behavior 26
cognitive maps 3, 16
cognitive psychology 16
cognitivism 16, 43n4
Cohn, J. 143
common-sense psychology 150
conceptual knowledge in perceiving and acting in social places, role of 133–134
Costall, A. 14–15, 17, 23, 27, 30, 32, 38, 40, 42, 43n4, 94, 100, 125, 130, 151–154, 162, 169
Cox, R. 27
Craver, C. F. 90
cultural-historical psychology 71
cultural relativism 104
culture 102–106
Custode, S. A. 143

Dadvand, P. 138, 139
Darden, L. 90
Darwin, C. 144
Darwinian revolution 150
Davids, K. 31
Deacon, T. W. 99
de Barbaro, K. 141, 144, 145
De Boer, B. 23
De Bruin, L. C. 77
De Haan, S. 32
De Jaegher, H. 77
De Pinedo García, M. D. 88, 89, 91, 96n2
De Poel, H. 27
developing child, environments of 155–160
developmental psychology 3
Dewey, J. 37, 38, 42n3, 130, 152, 154; pragmatism 41, 42, 161
dialogical arrays 108
Dings, R. 23, 32
Di Paolo, E. A. 107
direct perception, based on structure in energy 47–48
discriminanda 40
distributed cognition 4, 46, 47, 56, 57, 75–77, 167, 173

Dobson, J. 29
Donald, M. 17; *Origins of the Modern Mind, The* 16
Drake, J. M. 156
Dreyfus, H. L. 27; phenomenology 32
DST *see* dynamical systems theory (DST)
Duncker, K. 14, 173
dynamical systems theory (DST) 76, 77, 92

eco-behavioral science 4, 5, 72–74, 81
ecological community 23, 27, 31
ecological crisis 19
ecological psychology (EP) 1, 10–21; background condition for 17; challenges to 20; development of 11; experimental mainstream of 17–18; historical and intellectual foundations of 12; humanizing 125–135; mindshaping perspective on 5, 72–84; as "non-dualist psychology." 12; scope of 16; social constitution of, in the Netherlands 23–34
ecological reality 155
ecological restoration 113
ecological theory 2, 28, 30, 32, 107; of cognition 3; of perception 6
ecological values-realizing theory 6, 101–106
ecosystems 102–106
Effken, J. A. 100
embodied cognition 4
enabling constraints 5, 165–167, 174n14; and behavior settings 87, 89–96, 96n3–5; definition of 90
enactivism 28
environment: approaches to description 138–141; children's 138–145; of the developing child 155–160; developmental perspective of 59–71; functional analysis of 59; functional taxonomy of 60–62, 132; higher order dynamic units of 128; historized functional concept of 62–68; sociocultural 2, 87, 89; variability profiles 69–70
environmental design community 19
environmentalism 6
environmental psychology 19, 125, 129, 132, 134, 138
EP *see* ecological psychology (EP)
equality 106
ethnography 18
European Workshop on Ecological Psychology 27
Evans, G. W. 138

Fagard, J. 139
Fajen, B. R. 93–95, **94**, 166
Fausey, C. M. 138, 141, 142, 144, 145
figure-ground inversion 49–50
Fogel, A. 143
folk-psychology 78–81
Fowler, C. A. 103, 107
fractality 131
Franchak, J. M. 139, 141–144
Fridriksson, K. E. **117**, 118, 120, 122
Froese, T. 77
Frykholm, G. 126
functional taxonomy of the environment 60–62, 129
Funder, D. C. 99

Gabbard, C. 138, 139, 144
Gallagher, S. 74
Gesell, A. 144
Gestalt psychology 28, 38
Geyer, A. 103, 105
Gibson, E. J. 1, 3, 11, 140, 168
Gibson, J. J. 1–3, 10–11, 13, 14, 19, 23, 26, 30, 33, 37–39, 42n2, 61, 71, 72, 75, 76, 82, 96n1, 99–102, 104–108, 112, 119, 130, 134, 139, 140, 142, 150–156, 160–162, 164, 168, 172, 173–174n4, 174n5, 174n6; contrary imagination 152; distributed 56–57; and legacy of pragmatism 40–42; optic flow 39; perception 45–57; *Senses Considered as Perceptual Systems, The* 10, 162; theory of direct perception 48
Gibsonian psychology 4, 10, 26, 32, 45, 75, 172
Gilmore, R. O. 145
Glotzbach, P. 26
goal-directed action 14, 165
Good, J. 100
Grace, G. W. 101
Graeber, D. 101, 105, 106
green spaces 132
Grese, R. E. 113, 114
Grindley, G. C. 39
Guillaume, E. 130

Hamlyn, D. 11
Hawken, P. 114, 123; *Regeneration: Ending the Climate Crisis in One Generation* 114
Heft, H. 1–7, 10–21, 23, 30–31, 42, 112; "Affordances of children's environments: A functional approach to environmental description" 59; on agency in behavior settings 72–84; approaches to

182 Index

environmental description 138–139; on behavior settings 87–97; on child's environment 138–141, 144, 145; *Ecological Psychology in Context* 2, 4, 28, 38, 45, 156; functional taxonomy of the environment 60–62; and Kiverstein, interaction between 12–20; on perception 45–57; psychological ecology 149–174; and Rietveld, interaction between 10–11, 13, 14, 16, 18–21; sociohistorical into perceiving and acting, incorporation of 125–135
Heidbreder, E.: *Seven Psychologies* 172
Heider, F. 39, 150, 153–154, 156, 174n6, 174n12
Helmholtz, H. von 48
Heras-Escribano, M. 88, 89, 91
Herzberg, O 144
Hickman, C. 114
higher order structures, embedding affordances within 127–132
historized functional concept of the environment: behavior objects, analysis of 66–67; behavior settings, analysis of 62–66; social world, analysis of 67–68; variability analysis 62–68
Hoch, J. E. 143, 144, 157, 158, 160
Hodges, B. H. 23, 30, 100, 101, 103, 105, 107, 108, 161, 162
Holekamp, K. E. 91
Hollan, J. 46, 57
Holt, E. B. 2, 26, 33, 37–39, 45, 102, 103, 152, 153, 161–163, 174n11
Howard, M. 116, **117**, 122
human agency 77–81
human development, social normativity and 167–169
Hummels, C. 25
Hutchins, E. 57, 75, 76, 173; *Cognition in the Wild* 47
hysteresis 14, 127, 169

Ickes, W. 174n12
implicit psychological hypotheses 57
Ingold, T. 107
intentionality 13–14, 79, 101, 167
Iverson, J. M. 143

James, W. 2, 26, 32, 33, 45, 152–154, 160–161, 172; "knowing of things together, The" 153; mutualism 40; pragmatism 41, 42; *Principles of Psychology, The* 12, 153; *Psychology: A Briefer Course* 153; radical empiricism 38, 39
Järvilehto, T. 130, 134
Jayaraman, W. 142, 143
Jensen, J. 113
Jiang, S. 132
Johansson, G. 24
Jongeneel, D. 20
Juarrero, A. 96n3

Kadar, E. E. 100
Kalis, A. 79
Kant, I. 48
Kaplan, R. 133
Kaplan, S. 132, 133
Katz, S. 42
Kaye, K. 143
Kelley, H. H. 130
Kern, A. 116, **117**, 122
Kiverstein, J. 3, 12–20, 23, 27, 29–32, 125; "rich landscape of affordances, A" 30
Koch, S. 162
Koffka, K. 39, 160
Köhler, W. 160, 165, 173
Kretch, K. S. 142, 143
Krueger, J. I. 99
Kugler, P. 24, 25, 27, 33
Kyttä, M. 29, 159, 160

language 100–101, 106–108, 150, 151, 156
laws of locomotion 26
Lee, D. I. 17, 26, 130
Leontjev, A. N. 62
Lerstrup, I. 20, 159, 160
Leudar, I. 169
Lewin, K. 13, 69, 150, 160, 165, 169–170, 173n1
Linden, S. J. **117**, 118–121
Lindhiem, O. 103
Lobo, L. 97n7
Lovejoy, A. O.: "revolt against dualism" 37

MacLeod, R. 13
MacWhinney, B. 145
Maiese, M. 77
Malle, B. F. 174n12
manipulanda 40
Marsh, K. L. 14, 31, 126, 129, 132
Masland, R. H. 90
McArthur, L. Z. 126
McGann, M. 31, 74, 83n6
McGeer, V. 5, 72, 77–83, 83n8
McGraw, M. B. 144

McGreer, V. 168
Mead, G. H. 37, 38, 152, 154; pragmatism 161
Meagher, B. R. 129, 130, 132–133
medical anthropology 23
Meijer, C. G. 24, 25
Meltzoff, A. 171
Mendoza, J. K. 138
Merleau-Ponty, M. 14, 26, 27, 39, 174n5; phenomenology 13, 23, 24, 32, 97n6; *Phenomenology of Perception, The* 153
Messinger, D. S. 144, 145
Michaels, C. F. 26, 54
Michotte, A. 24
Midgley, M. 104
Miles, I. 114
Miller, G 165
mind, theory of 169
mindshaping perspective, on ecological psychology 5, 72–84
mission, definition of 113
Mollon, J. 39
Moore, R. 19
Moras, P. S. **117**, 118–121
motor problem 24
Mulder, T. 24, 26–27
Murphy, A. E. 37
mutuality/mutualism 40, 154–155
Myin, E. 28

Narvaez, D. 171
natural history 18–19
natural processes, affordances of 112–113
nature of the environment 28–29
navigation studies 3
Netherlands, the: ecological movement in 23–28; ecological psychology, social constitution of 23–34; nature of the environment 28–29; psychology's job 28–29; social in changing world, primacy of 29–31
Neuberg, S. L. 130
Noble, B. 42
non-social individual 42n3
norm-abiding behavior 82
Norman, D. A. 53, 54
normativity 5, 14, 31, 32, 80, 87–89, 96, 132, 135; naturalization of 89, 96; social 89, 165–171

obsessive compulsive disorder 32
occluding edge 2, 48, 52, 134
Ojala, M. 114
Olmsted, F. L. 113

optic flow 39
Ormerod, T. C. 57
Overbeeke, K. 25

Payne, A. C. 138, 139
Pedersen, S. 62
Pepping, G.-J. 27
perceiver-environment reciprocity, social constitution of 2
perceiving 16, 17, 30, 45, 48, 75, 77, 99–102, 104; conceptual knowledge in, role of 133–134; landscape changes 118–119
perception 45–57; classical theory of 48; direct, based on structure in energy 47–48; in problem solving 48–56; theory of 4, 6, 48; visual 21, 25, 47, 48, 52
perception-action 77, 79, 87, 126, 127, 161, 169; cultural dimension of 135; skills 103; sociohistorical dimension of 135; system 108, 138
perceptual mystery 133
phenomenology 13, 23, 24, 32, 97n6
physical reality 155
Pick, A. D. 168
Pick, C. M. 130
Pick, H. 10
Planer, R. J. 170
Polanyi, M. 100
postal systems 100, 101, 134
pragmatism 4, 38–39, 151–155, 161, 162; legacy of 40–42
Prieske, B. 23, 29
problem solver, as perceiver 46–47
problem solving 45–57; definition of 46; perception in 48–56
Project HAWK 118
psychological ecology 149–174; definition of 149
psychological inquiry 151
psychology's job 28–29
Pythagorean theorem, visual proof of 51–52, *52*, 56

Quine, W. 143

RAAAF 27; *End of Sitting* 28
Rączaszek-Leonardi, J. 103, 125, 169
radical empiricism 4, 12, 32, 38–39, 151–155
Raja, V. 5, 87, 89, 90, 96n2, 99, 165–167, 174n13, 174n14
Rakoczy, H. 171
realism 151–155

Reddy, V. 106
Reed, E. S. 3, 16, 24, 25, 27–29, 43n6, 57, 75, 82, 99–101, 152, 154, 156, 161–163, 172, 173; *Encountering the World* 18; *Necessity of Experience, The* 123
Reis, H. T. 130
relativism 104
responsibility 106–108
restorative environments 6, 125, 132, 171
restorative spaces 132–133
"revolt against dualism" 37
Richardson, M. J. 14, 127, 169, 171
Rietveld, E. 3, 10–11, 13, 14, 16, 18–21, 23, 27, 29–32, 83, 125; "rich landscape of affordances, A" 30
Rietveld, R. 27
righteousness 5, 99
Riley, M. A. 126
Rio, K. W. 95
Rogoff, B. 57
Ross, W. 49
Roth, K. 25
route learning 3
Roy, B. C. 144
Runeson, S. 126
Russell, B. 37
Ryan, R. L. 113
Ryan, T. A. 39

Saccani, R. 138, 139, 144
Saldaña, J. 116
Salo, V. C. 144
Salthe, S. N. 96n3
Sanches de Oliveira, G. 82
Sanders, J. T. 100
Sandseter, E. B. H. 29
Savelsbergh, G. J. P. 24, 26
Schmidt, M. F. H. 171
Schoggen, P. 87, 131, 155, 159
Schraube, E. 62
Schroeder, H. W. 114
Schutte, A. 157, 170
Sedawi, W. 116, **117**, 122
Segundo-Ortin, M. 79, 82
selective control 75, 77
self-accountability 169
self-efficacy 163
17 animals problem 49–51, *50*, *51*, 56
Shotter, J. 32
Simon, H. A. 46–47
situated cognition 74, 174n15
slow-motion affordances 6, 112, 113, 163
Smets, G. 25
Smith, J. 27

Smith, L. B. 141–143
Smitsman, A. 25, 27
social affordances 2, 6, 122, 126, 127, 134, 137; synergistic approach to 126
social normativity: and behavior settings 165–167; and human development 167–169
social psychology 5, 62, 70, 86, 89, 95, 125, 128, 130, 134, 135, 164
social world, analysis of: affordances 126–127; play activities 67–68; social interactions 67–68
Society for Ecological Restoration 113
socio-cultural environment 2, 87, 89
socio-cultural norms 88
socio-cultural psychology 2, 7
Sommer, B. 18
Soska, K. C. 145
Sporrel, K. 129
Stappers, P. J. 25
Starburst Amacrine Cells (SACs)
Stebbing, S. 37, 42n2
Steffensen, S. V. 49
Sterelny, K. 170
Still, A. 100
stimulus: information 48; proximal 161; recession of 102, 161
stove knobs 52–54, *53*
Stuart-Smith, S. 113
subjectivism 104, 105
Sullivan, J. 141, 145
symbolic cognition 56
Szokolszky, A. 17

Tamboer, J. W. I. 24
Tamis-LeMonda, C. S. 143, 144
Tauchi, M. 90
Taylor, C. 12
technology studies 23
time-field-units 102
Tolman, E. 39, 40, 43n5, 160
Tomasello, M. 101
Tronick, E. 143
Turvey, M. T. 25–28, 33

Ulrich, R. S. 132

Valadi, S. 138, 139, 144
Vallée-Tourangeau, F. 49
values 101–106; properties 160–163
van den Bosch, C. 159, 160
van Der Kamp, J. 26, 126, 127
Van Der Niet, A. G. 23
Van Der Schaaf, A. L. 23, 29

van Dijk, L. 23, 27, 29, 32, 105, 125
Van Dijk-Wesselius, J. 29
Van Orden, H., G. 166, 167
van Wermeskerken, M. 23
van Wieringen, P. 24
Varga, S. 74
Vicente, K. J. 48
visual perception 21, 25, 47, 48, 52
visual system, neurophysiology of 90
Vygotsky, S. L. 5, 63, 70, 71

Wagman, J. 18
Wallot, S. 166, 167
Walsh, D. 170
Wann, J. 93
war landscape 13
Warren, W. H. 25, 93–95, *94*, 126, 139, 166
Watson, J. 43n4
Wells, N. M. 19–20
Wengrow, D. 101, 105, 106
Wertheimer, M. 173
West, K. L. 142, 143
White, R. W. 162
Whitehead, A. N. 37
Whiting, J. 24
Whyte, W. 18

Wicker, A. W. 83n3
Wilkie, R. 93
Withagen, R. 23, 26, 29, 32, 160, 171, 172
Wohlwill, J. F. 11, 113, 132, 138–140, 157, 172
Wray, A. 101
Wright, H. F. 5, 72–73, 144, 155, 156, 159, 168; *Midwest and Its Children: The Psychological Ecology of an American Town* 149, 155; *One Boy's Day* 28–29, 30, 59, 128, 156–157, 159

young people's responses to earth's affordances of regeneration 112–123; biodiverse habitat on community lands, restoring 116–121, **117**; restoration work 114–116, *115*
Yu, C. 143
Yurkovic-Harding, J. 143
Yurovsky, D. 143

Zaal, F. 27, 28
Zawidzki, T. W. 169
Zebrowitz, L. A. 126
Zhang, M. 103
Zimmerman, F. J. 144

Printed in the United States
by Baker & Taylor Publisher Services